THE INTERPRETATION OF THE MUSIC OF THE SEVENTEENTH AND EIGHTEENTH CENTURIES

The Interpretation of the Music of the Seventeenth and Eighteenth Centuries

Revealed by Contemporary Evidence

By ARNOLD DOLMETSCH

With an Introduction by R. Alec Harman

UNIVERSITY OF WASHINGTON PRESS

SEATTLE AND LONDON

Original hardcover edition published 1915
by Novello & Co., Ltd., London
Washington Paperback edition, 1969, reprinted from the corrected edition of 1946 by arrangement with Novello & Co., Ltd.
Second printing, 1972
Third printing, 1974
Fourth printing, 1977

Library of Congress Catalog Card Number 76-75611
ISBN 0-295-78578-0
Printed in the United States of America

Appendix containing twenty-two illustrative pieces is published separately and is available from Novello & Co., Ltd., London

A two-record Stereo LP album, with illustrated notes, has been prepared to accompany this book, in order to enable the reader to hear many of the musical examples performed on authentic instruments of the period. Included are a spoken commentary by Dr. Carl Dolmetsch and complete performances by Dr. Dolmetsch and Joseph Saxby of several representative compositions. The album is entitled *Ornaments and Graces in the Music of the Seventeenth and Eighteenth Centuries* and is available from the University of Washington Press. $12.50

INTRODUCTION TO THE 1969 EDITION

Published in 1915, this book was the first in any language to deal in a comprehensive and scholarly manner with the problems of performing Baroque music. It remains, moreover, a classic, for although there have been a number of later books, monographs, and articles on the same subject, none of them, with one exception, has attempted to deal with the performance practice of the entire Baroque era in every major European country. The exception is *The Interpretation of Early Music* (1963) by Robert Donington, an outstanding work, and dedicated to Arnold Dolmetsch, of whom the author writes in acknowledgment: "No help has been so great as the advantage of serving my apprenticeship under [him], whose pioneering genius gave him the surest touch with baroque music I have ever known."

Pioneering genius Arnold Dolmetsch certainly was, and while it is impossible adequately to explain genius, we can go a long way to understanding how remarkable this particular man was when we recognize that he was not only a fine musician, teacher, and researcher, but also an extremely gifted performer on and skilled maker of many of the instruments common in the Baroque, a combination of talents unmatched by any European in this or, I dare say, any other century.

This may seem an exaggerated claim, but a brief sketch of Dolmetsch's life will, I think, substantiate it. Born in Belgium in 1858, and later studying the violin with the internationally famous virtuoso Vieuxtemps, he subsequently went to England, where he spent the rest of his life, apart from a few years in France, dying at Haslemere in 1940. In 1885 he was appointed violin master at an English school, where he evolved a new and successful system of teaching the instrument which replaced, in the early stages, the traditional scales and exercises with simple tunes in parts, and with the keyboard fretted to help intonation. In 1890 he began playing early music on authentic instruments or replicas of them, and was widely acclaimed for the quality of his tone, no matter what the instrument, and the musicality of his interpretations. In 1894 and 1895 he made his first clavichord and harpsichord, respectively, following these with viols, lutes, and recorders, some of these being made for the firm of Chickering in Boston, some for Gaveau in Paris, but the majority coming from his own workshops in Haslemere. His workshops soon achieved fame, and the name of Dolmetsch became synonymous, then as now, with a high excellence of craftsmanship and beauty of tone.

But Dolmetsch was not content merely to produce the kind of instruments on which early music was performed, he was also deeply concerned that the music itself should be understood, correctly interpreted, and appreciated as a living art; hence the present work. In 1915, music composed before Haydn and Mozart was rarely heard and little enjoyed, except for a largely unrepresentative selection from Bach and Handel. Dolmetsch attempted to rectify this situation, both in practice and in print, and in his Introduction to this book he advises us to "put aside intolerant modernity" and to "take warning from the 18th century connoisseurs, who declared Gothic architecture barbarous. . . ." To him music of any age was something that was alive and expressive, something that we should try and respond to emotionally, and it was his especial concern that we should understand, as nearly as possible, just how the music of a particular earlier age, the Baroque, was performed, so that its expressive intent and emotional impact could be more truly felt.

During the fifty-odd years since the book was written the general interest in Baroque and earlier music has increased greatly, but performances of it are, unfortunately, all too often unauthentic. We still hear Bach's keyboard works played with incorrect ornamentation, Handel's *da capo* arias sung with no ornamentation whatsoever, Corelli's violin sonatas rendered exactly as they appear in print, and realizations of figured basses that are inartistic, unstylistic, and played on the anachronistic piano! There is absolutely no excuse for such performances, and this book is one of the reasons why, for although it is not, and never pretended to be, the last word on its subject, the breadth and scholarly depth of its treatment, couched in an eminently readable style, make it an indispensable source of reference for all who are concerned in any way with Baroque music, whether as performers, conductors, or editors.

For this paperback edition I have provided a new

Index, and have corrected a number of minor errors and inconsistencies in the text. I have also appended a short Bibliography of those works that are available in modern editions or reprints, or in unpublished doctoral theses, and which are in English.

R. Alec Harman

University of Washington, 1969

PREFACE TO THE 1946 EDITION

This book embodies the results of many years of practical study and research on the part of my father, Arnold Dolmetsch. Although it was originally published in 1915, it has lost nothing by the passage of years, but has, on the contrary, gained in significance. At the time of its first appearance, it aroused the interest of a comparatively small number of musical enthusiasts; now its appeal is world-wide. Thanks to the labours of Arnold Dolmetsch and his followers, the value and interest of the music of past centuries performed on the instruments for which it was written, with the correct interpretation, is today generally recognized.

None of the rules for the correct performance and interpretation of 17th and 18th century music laid down in this volume can be regarded as a matter of personal opinion, since all are supported by documentary evidence drawn from the writings of musicians of the period.

Through the courtesy of Mr. R. Alec Harman, who has made an exhaustive study of this work, various misprints and minor errors concerning music-type, names and dates have been called to our attention. His letter caused us to refer to Arnold Dolmetsch's private copy of the book, wherein we found recorded a number of corrections, some of which coincided with certain of those of Mr. Harman, while others were in addition to these. It was evidently Arnold Dolmetsch's intention to transmit these corrections to the publisher when a new edition should be contemplated, and they are now, therefore, incorporated in the 1946 edition.

We wish to express our grateful thanks to Mr. Harman for his contribution to these amendments. While the substance of the book is in no way affected, there is cause for satisfaction in having every detail correct.

CARL F. DOLMETSCH

INTRODUCTION TO THE ORIGINAL EDITION

When our musical notation began, in the early part of the 11th century, the pitch of the notes was indicated by square dots upon a stave. There were no signs to denote the different lengths of sounds. The rhythm of the song had to be taught orally, as well as its *tempo*, phrasing, and ornamentation. Gradually, special shapes were given to the notes, to indicate their relative duration. Time-signatures, ligatures, signs for the various ornaments, and all the other necessary devices came gradually to complete the system.

For nine hundred years notation has progressed, and still it is far from perfect. We are not often conscious of this with regard to modern music, for most of what we wish to play is already known to us from previous hearing; and when it is not, the style of the music is familiar enough to enable us to interpret the written text correctly without having to think much about it. But future generations will find difficulties and doubtful interpretations where all seems clear to us. A hundred years ago people wrote their music still less accurately than we do now, so that if we want to play in the original style a composition of Beethoven, for example, we find the text incomplete and imitative interpretation perplexing, for the leading players of our time do not agree in their readings.

There might indeed be an unquestionable tradition for a period comparatively so recent, since people are now living who could have learned to play Beethoven's music from someone who had heard the composer himself play it. Time, however, has already obscured these memories.

If we go back half-a-century further, the difficulties become greater. We come to the time when what is now called "Old Music" was merely old-fashioned. From that time to the revival which is now in progress, the attention of musicians was so completely withdrawn from this "Old Music" that no tradition of it survived. The tradition now claimed by some players only goes back to the early pioneers of the present revival, who knew much less about it than we do now. Reliable information is to be found only in those books of instruction which the old musicians wrote about their own art. Happily there are many such, well filled with precepts, examples, and philosophical considerations.

In order to get a comprehensive view of the subject, we must analyse and compare all available documents. No single author gives full light on every point, even concerning his own works. The thing we most want to know is frequently exactly what has been left out or passed over lightly. The author, perhaps, considered it too simple or too well known to require any explanation. In such cases we must look elsewhere for the desired knowledge; and if no single document gives it, we must attempt to deduce it from a combination of sources. There is no lack of material for our studies, and it is well it should be so, for we have much to learn. Until far into the 18th century several important problems were left to the player. Thus, before we can play properly a piece of old music we must find out:—

Firstly, the *Tempo*, which frequently is not indicated in any way;

Secondly, the real Rhythm, which very often differs in practice from the written text;

Thirdly, the Ornaments and Graces necessary for the adornment of the music; and

Fourthly, how to fill up the Thorough Bass in accompaniments.

These various problems will be considered here, in turn. But the student should first try and prepare his mind by thoroughly understanding what the Old Masters *felt* about their own music, what impressions they wished to convey, and, generally, what was the *Spirit of their Art*, for on these points the ideas of modern musicians are by no means clear.

A number of quotations from old books whose authority is not open to question are gathered together in the first chapter. They are most interesting and helpful, and will show how erroneous is the idea, still entertained by some, that expression is a modern thing, and that the old music requires nothing beyond mechanical precision.

It is advisable, however, before beginning this study, to clear our mind of prejudice and preconceived ideas, and put aside intolerant modernity; or else we may, as others have done, corrupt and twist about the meaning of even the clearest statement. We should take warning from the 18th century connoisseurs, who declared Gothic architecture barbarous, or the early 19th century art critics, who could see no beauty in pre-Raphaelite art.

CONTENTS

THE INTERPRETATION OF THE MUSIC OF THE SEVENTEENTH AND EIGHTEENTH CENTURIES

CHAPTER I.

EXPRESSION.

A BOOK which from its title could hardly be suspected of containing matter of interest for our subject, but does nevertheless contain most valuable information, is " L'Art du Facteur d'Orgues," by Dom Bedos de Celles, a Benedictine monk, who published it in 1766.

An important part of this book treats of " La Tonotechnie," which is the art of pricking music upon the cylinder of self-playing instruments. This art was brought to a very high degree of perfection in the 18th century. Its aim was to reproduce with absolute precision the execution of the music as intended by its composer. It thus gives us indications of almost mathematical accuracy on *tempo*, rhythm, and ornaments. The following phrase, taken from this book at page 596, could well serve as motto to the present work:—

" There is a manner of conceiving Music entirely different from the one taught in all the Treatises upon this Art; it is founded upon the execution itself."

In a footnote on the same page, speaking of previous writers on his subject, the author says:—

"They have not said a word about the ornaments, nor of the combination of *silences*, *held* and *touched* notes to form the articulations of the music, &c.; of the distinction between *first* and *second* quavers, and of the *crotchets*, &c.; of their *inequality*, &c.; all these observations are, however, essential, and form the essence of beautiful execution as practised by the most famous organists, and as I have had the occasion to remark in several pieces which Mr. Balbastre, a very skilful organist, has been so kind as to play for me. . . ."

The imperfections of musical notation could not be pointed out more clearly. The explanations with which musicians have endeavoured from time to time to palliate these imperfections are precious documents for us now; they are the foundation of the present work.

Giulio Caccini, in the Introduction to "Le Nuove Musiche" (Florence, 1601, with an enlarged second edition in 1607), gives valuable directions upon various points of interpretation from which we shall gather together here some extracts concerning the expression and spirit of the music. We shall quote from an English translation and adaptation given, without acknowledging its source, in Playford's "Introduction to the Skill of Music" (London, 1st edition, 1654). Playford introduces the subject, which fills some thirty pages of the book, in the following quaint manner:—

"Courteous Reader,

"This Manuscript fortunately came to my hand, which having diligently perused, and perceiving the Author's intent to have published it, I thought it would be useful to add some part thereof to this my Discourse of the Theorie of Musick; but being cautious of publishing anything of this kind on my own weak judgment, I communicated my intended purpose to some of the most Eminent Masters of this Kingdome, who (after their perusal) gave a good approbation thereof; so that if thou dost reap any benefit thereby, thou art beholden to them, and not to me, any more than for Publishing the same.

"The Proem to the said Discourse is to this effect.

"Hitherto I have not put forth to the view of the world those fruits of my Musick Studies employed about that noble manner of *Singing* which I learnt of my Master the famous *Scipione del Palla* in *Italy*; . . .

"I have endeavoured in those my late Compositions to bring in a kind of Musick by which men might as it were Talk in Harmony, using in that kind of singing a certain noble neglect of the song, as I have often heard at *Florence* by the Actors in their Singing *Opperas*, in which I endevoured the Imitation of the Conceit of the Words. . . . In Encreasing and Abating the Voyce, and in Exclamations is the foundation of Passion. . . . *Art* admitteth no Mediocrity, and how much the more curiosities are in it, by reason of the excellence thereof, with so much the more labour and love ought we, the Proffessors thereof, to find them out. . . . There are some that in the *Tuning* of the first Note, Tune it a *Third* under: Others Tune the said first *Note* in his proper Tune, always increasing it in Lowdness, saying that this is the good way of putting forth the *Voyce* gracefully. . . . I have found it a more affectuous way to *Tune* the *Voyce* by a contrary effect to the other, that is, to Tune the first *Note*, Diminishing it: Because Exclamation is the principal means to move the Affections; and Exclamation properly is no other thing, but in the slacking of the Voyce to reinforce it somewhat . . .

"*Exclamations* may be used in all Passionate Musicks . . . Yet by consequence understand ye, that in *Airy* Musicks or *Corants* to dance instead of these Passions, there is to be used only a lively, cheerful kind of Singing, which is carried and ruled by the *Air* itself. . . .

"Whereupon we see how necessary a certain judgment is for a Musician, which sometimes useth to prevail above Art. . . . I call that the noble manner of singing, which is used without tying a mans self to the ordinary measure of time, making many times the value of the notes less by half, and sometimes more, according to the conceit of the words; whence proceeds that excellent kinde of singing with a graceful neglect, whereof I have spoken before."

A very important document is the Preface to the first volume of Toccatas of Girolamo Frescobaldi, published at Rome in 1615. It is reproduced here *in extenso* :—

"TO THE READER.

"Knowing by experience how well appreciated is that manner of playing with expressive passages and varied divisions, I have thought it right to show my aptitude and my zeal to succeed in it by publishing these small results of my labour, with the explanations hereunder: but I declare that I bow before the merits of others, and that I respect the value of every one. And now, let the devoted care with which I have presented these principles to the amiable and studious reader be accepted.

"1°. Firstly, that kind of style must not be subject to time. We see the same thing done in modern madrigals, which, notwithstanding their difficulties, are rendered easier to sing, thanks to the variations of the time, which is beaten now slowly, now quickly, and even held in the air, according to the expression of the music, or the sense of the words.

"2°. In the *Toccate*, I have endeavoured not only to give a profusion of divisions and expressive passages, but, moreover, to arrange the various sections so that they may be played separately from one another, in such a way that the player, without being obliged to play them all, can stop wherever he pleases.

"3°. The beginnings of the *Toccate* should be played *adagio* and *arpeggiando;* the same applies to the syncopations and discords even in the middle of the pieces. The chords should be broken with both hands so that the instrument may not be left empty; this battery can be repeated at pleasure.

"4°. On the last note of the shakes, or passages by skips or degrees, you must pause, even if this note is a quaver or semiquaver, or unlike the following note, for such a stop avoids confusion between one phrase and another.

"5°. The cadences, though written rapid, should be played very sustained; and as you get nearer the end of the passage or cadence, you should retard the time more and more. The separations and conclusions of the passages are indicated by concords for both hands. written in minims.

"6°. When you find a shake for the right hand, or the left, and that at the same time the other hand plays a passage, you must not divide the shake exactly note for note, but only try to have it rapid, and let the passage flow less quickly and with expression, otherwise there will be confusion.

"7°. When you find any passage of quavers and semiquavers to be played together for both hands, you must not play it too fast; and the hand which has semiquavers should make them somewhat dotted; dotting not the first but the second, and so on for the others, one without dot, the other dotted.

"8°. Before playing double passages in semiquavers with both hands, you must pause on the preceding note, even if it be a short one; then resolutely play the passage, which will better show off the agility of your hand.

"9°. In the *Partite*, when you find rapid divisions and expressive passages, it will be advisable to play slowly; the same observation applies to the *Toccate*. Those without divisions may be played a little more quickly, and it is left to the good taste and fine judgment of the player to regulate the *Tempo*, in which consist the spirit and perfection of this style and manner of playing. The various sections of the *Passacailles* may be played separately at pleasure, if you take care to fit the various movements to one another; the same applies to the *Chacones*."

There are many points worthy of notice in this Preface, and a few comments upon some of them may prove useful.

According to par. 1, it is clear that madrigals, about 1600, were sung very freely as regards *Tempo:* now slowly, now quickly, the beat even stopping awhile if the sense of the phrase required it. This is not in accordance with modern methods, but as the point is not open to doubt, modern conductors might try to apply this principle, and let us hear some madrigals of that time as they were intended to sound. It should prove quite a revelation. We are also told that the same principle applies to instrumental music. This ought not to be difficult to realise, for modern music is played in no other way. As soon as it is recognised that not only is it not "wrong" to give the old music its natural expression, but, on the contrary, that the so-called traditional way of playing it is an insult to its beauty, the players will not be afraid to follow their own instinct, and the music will come to life again.

In par. 2 we learn that one is not obliged to play the whole of a long piece, and that "cuts" were not only tolerated, but actually prepared for. It is useful to know this, for many a player who hesitates to give a long piece may be pleased to play some parts of it, when supported by good authority.

The breaking of the chords mentioned in par. 3 will be considered later in its proper place. Pars. 4 and 5 are very clear; they merely enforce the necessity of good phrasing and thoughtful expression.

Par. 6 will be exemplified with the other ornaments. We may remark here, however, that as Frescobaldi *apparently* wrote his shakes in full, it is difficult for a modern musician, trained to play what is before his eyes, to realise that the author did not intend his text to be followed. But thus it is, and similar cases are frequent in the old notation.

Par. 7 will be discussed in the third chapter, with the other conventional alterations of rhythm.

Par. 8 requires no elucidation; it recommends a device which is frequently resorted to in modern music.

Par. 9. The *Partite* of Frescobaldi are sets of variations upon a theme. As many as twelve or more upon a fairly long subject are found. They differ in character; some should be played slowly, others fast. Their *tempo* is left to the *good taste and fine judgment of the player*—which qualities, if to some extent inborn, need nevertheless to be perfected by study.

As to his remarks upon the selection of some of the sections of the *Passacailles* or *Partite* these are still more to the point, perhaps, than his similar advice about the *Toccate*, for some of them are very long. One *Passacaille* in his second book contains *one hundred Partite*. It would require a good deal of enthusiasm to listen to them all. I have, perhaps, insisted too much upon this Preface, sufficiently clear in itself. Its great importance should be my excuse, an importance recognised by Edward Dannreuther, who gave a version of it in his work on Ornamentation, with the Italian text side by side. Unfortunately, his text and translation are obscured by misreadings, excusable enough, perhaps, for the original text is written in an obsolete and confusing lettering, and in an idiom far from easy to understand at times. I have been so fortunate as to be helped in the present translation by an eminent specialist in old Italian, M. Paul Marie Masson, the worthy President of the French Institute at Florence, whose authority has been very valuable to me. Let him accept my heartfelt thanks. It is not my intention in this book either to contradict or approve of received opinions; but I feel I must warn the reader that the works on this subject written within the last fifty years need constant verification and comparison with the originals from which their statements purport to be drawn. In many cases their reliance on second-hand quotations has led to statements founded only on gratuitous suppositions.

Thomas Mace, one of the clerks of Trinity College in the University of Cambridge, published in 1676 a book entitled: "Musick's Monument; or a Remembrancer of the Best Practical Musick, both Divine and Civil, that has ever been known to have been in the World." It is divided into three Parts: the First is devoted to Church singing, the Second "Treats of the Noble Lute (the Best of Instruments) now made Easie; and all Its Occult-Lock'd-up-Secrets Plainly laid Open . . ."; in the Third Part, "The Generous Viol, in Its Rightest Use, is Treated Upon; with some Curious Observations, never before Handled, concerning It, and Musick in General."

The book is written in a quaint style, often much involved, full of parentheses, and parentheses inside parentheses. Its appearance is strange, for every third word or so is printed in italics, and half the words begin with a capital. But its 272 pages are filled with interesting and valuable information, much of which could not be found elsewhere. The author's engraved portrait gives his age as sixty-three when the book was published; he was therefore born about 1613. The date of his death is not known. We shall have to return to this book several times; indeed the whole work could be studied with much pleasure and profit.

For the present the following extracts must suffice.

In chap. xi., which is devoted to Time, we find this :—

" . . you must Know, That, although in our First Undertakings, we ought to *strive*, for the most Exact Habit of *Time-keeping* that possibly we can attain unto, (and for severall good Reasons) yet, when we come to be *Masters*, so that we can *command all manner* of Time, at our own Pleasures; we Then *take Liberty*, (and very often, for Humour, and good Adornment-sake, in certain Places) to *Break Time;* sometimes Faster, and sometimes Slower, as we perceive the *Nature of the Thing* Requires, which often adds, much *Grace*, and *Luster*, to the Performance."

In chap. xxiii., which is devoted to the Explanation of Graces, we find this (page 109) :—

"The next is to play some part of the Lesson Loud, and some part Soft; which gives much more Grace, and Lustre to Play, than any other Grace, whatsoever: Therefore I commend It, as a Principal and Chief-Ornamental-Grace (in its Proper Place).

"The last of all, is the *Pause;* which although it be not a *Grace*, of any performance, nor likewise numbered amongst the Graces, by others, yet the performance of It, (in proper Places) adds much Grace: and the thing to be done, is but only to make a kind of *Cessation, or standing still*, sometimes *Longer*, and sometimes *Shorter*, according to the Nature or Requiring of the Humour of the Musick; which if in Its *due Place* be made, is a very Excellent Grace."

The conclusion of all this is:

1°. That *Tempo Rubato* and alterations in the time of a piece for the sake of expression were in common use in England in the 17th century.

2°. That although no indications of *p* and *f* were given in the music, such were expected to be made. The performer had to find the proper places for them.

3°. That the several phrases of a composition had to be punctuated: divided from one another so as to make the sense clear, although the music showed no indication of it. But modern music is in no way different from the old on that point, and Mace says the same thing as Frescobaldi.

At page 118, after some direction for the Invention of Preludes and the composition of "Lessons," Mace gives the following "Digression," which vividly pictures the effect of music as felt by him:—

"But thus much I do affirm, and shall be ready to Prove, by Demonstration, (to any Person Intelligible) That Musick is as a Language, and has Its Significations, as Words have, (if not more strongly) only most people do not understand that Language, (perfectly).

"And as an Orator (when he goes about to make a Speech, Sermon, or Oration) takes to Himself some Subject Matter, to Exercise himself upon, as a Theam, Text, or the Like; and in that Exercise, can order His Discourse, or Form, various and sundry ways, at his Pleasure, and yet not stray from, or loose His intended Matter. Even so may a Learned Master, in This Art, do the like; and with as much Ease, Scope, and Freedom (significantly).

"And as in Language, various Humours, Conceits, and Passions (of all sorts) may be exprest; so likewise in Musick, may any Humour, Conceit, or Passion (never so various) be exprest; and so significantly, as any Rhetorical Words or Expressions are able to do; only (if I may not be thought too Extravagant in my Expressions) if any Difference be; It is, In that Musick speaks so transcendently, and Communicates Its Notions so Intelligibly to the Internal, Intellectual, and Incomprehensible Faculties of the Soul; so far beyond all Language of Words, that I confess, and most solemnly affirm, I have been more Sensibly, Fervently, and Zealously Captivated, and drawn into Divine Raptures, and Contemplations, by Those Unexpressible, Rhetorical, Uncontrolable Persuasions, and Instructions of Musick's Divine Language, than ever yet I have been, by the best Verbal Rhetorick, that came from any Man's Mouth, either in Pulpit or elsewhere.

"Those Influences, which come along with It, may aptly be compar'd, to Emanations, Communications, or Distillations, of some Sweet, and Heavenly Genius, or Spirit; Mystically, and Unapprehensibly (yet Effectually) Disposessing the Soul, and Mind, of All Irregular, Disturbing, and Unquiet Motions; and Stills, and Fills It, with Quietness, Joy, and Peace; Absolute Tranquility, and Unexpressible Satisfaction."

Even allowing that our author is occasionally rather "Extravagant in his Expressions," as he himself puts it, it is evident that music had some meaning for him, and that he did not consider "Sound-patterns" and experiments in Counterpoint as the goal of the Art!

Here follow some practical directions as to style :—

Page 130: "And as to the General Humour of any Lesson, take This as a Constant Observation: viz., observe It, in its Form, or Shape; and if you find it Uniform, and Retortive, either in its Barrs, or Strains, and that It expresseth Short Sentences, ... Then you will find it very Easie, to Humour a Lesson, by Playing some Sentences Loud, and others again Soft, according as they best please your own Fancy, some very Briskly, and Couragiously, and some again Gently, Lovingly, Tenderly, and Smoothly. And forget not especially, in such Humours, to make your Pauses, at Proper Places, which are commonly at the End of such Sentences, where there is a Long Note, as easily you will know how to do, if you give your mind to regard such Things, which give the Greatest Lustre in Play, as I have already told you."

At page 132, after some directions similar to those quoted above, he says :—

"Such Observations, as These, will prove several ways Beneficial unto you; both as to your Delight, in your undertaking; and also, a Help to Increase your Knowledge, and Judgment; far beyond that Common way of Poaring, and Drudging at the Practice of Lessons, only to Play them Readily, and Quick, which seldom, or never Produceth Judgment, but leaves This Knowledge ever behind it; which is much more than the one Half of the Work."

Is not this strikingly true, as well as regards modern as old music, and ought not every teacher to steep himself in it and impart it to his pupils?

What a relief it would be to the world if some of the stupid, mechanical practice of the present time could be done away with!

At page 133, after another Lesson, he says:—

"Its Humour is Toyish, Joccond, Harmless, and Pleasant; and, as if it were, one Playing with, or Tossing a Ball, up and down; yet it seems to have a very Solemn Countenance, and like unto one of a Sober, and Innocent Condition, or Disposition; not Antick, Apish, or Wild, &c. As to the Performance of It, you will do well to Remember, (as in all the rest, so in This) to Play Loud and Soft; sometimes Briskly, and sometimes Gently and Smoothly, here and there, as your Fancy will (no doubt) Prompt you unto, if you make a Right Observation of what I have already told you."

A running commentary in this style follows every piece in the book. The same thing is repeated over and over again. But he was a good teacher, and knew how pupils should be treated. One more quotation, from page 147, and we must leave Mace:—

"Many Drudge, and take much Pains to Play their Lessons very Perfectly as they call it (that is, Fast) which, when they can do, you will perceive Little Life, or Spirit in Them, merely for want of the knowledge of this last Thing, I now mention, viz.: They do not labour to find out the Humour, Life, or Spirit of their Lessons: Therefore I am more Earnest about It, than many (It may be) think needful: But experience will confirm what I say."

French books on Music are very rich in material for our study.

Jean Rousseau, "Maître de Musique et de Viole," published at Paris in 1687 a "Traité de la Viole," from which the following extracts are taken. Speaking of Hottman, one of the foremost viola da gamba players of the 17th century, he says (page 23): "One admired him often more when he played tenderly some simple little song than in the most learned and complicated pieces. The tenderness of his playing came from these beautiful bowings which he animated, and softened so cleverly and properly that he charmed all those who heard him."

Page 56: "The playing of Melodious Pieces should be simple, and in consequence requires much delicacy and tenderness, and it is in that playing that one should most particularly imitate all the agreeable and charming effects the Voice can produce. It is specially proper to the Treble Viol."

Page 57: "The playing of Melodious Pieces is very agreeable, and even most touching, when it is well done."

Page 60: "But Genius and fine taste are natural gifts, which cannot be learned by Rules, and it is with their help that the Rules should be applied, and that one takes liberties so *à propos* as always to please, for to please is to have genius and fine taste."

Speaking of playing accompaniments upon the viol, he says:—

Page 66: "This kind of playing also requires much cleverness and application, because you must know instantly how to take the various movements, and what passions to express, and that is what is commonly called entering into the spirit of the piece. At this word 'movement' there are people who imagine that to give the movement is to follow and keep time; but there is much difference between the one and the other, for one may keep time without entering into the movement, because Time depends upon the Music, but the Movement depends upon genius and fine taste. . . .

"He who accompanies must have no affectation in playing, for nothing is more opposed to the spirit of accompaniment or concerted playing than to hear a person who is only anxious to show off; this manner is only good when one plays alone. . . .

"The spirit and science of accompaniment goes still further, if one is obliged to accompany a Voice who cannot sing in Time; for then, if one only follows the ordinary Value of Notes it is only rarely and by chance that the chords will fit the tune. . . ."

Page 72, speaking of the Treble Viol:—

"The playing of Melodious Pieces is its proper character; that is why those who wish to play well on this instrument must attach themselves to delicate singing, to imitate all that a beautiful Voice can make. . . .

"You must employ all the Graces, to their full extent, especially the shake with appoggiatura and the plain appoggiatura, which are the foundation of singing; and one must omit nothing, in one's playing, of what can give pleasure to the ear by tender and well-filled ornaments.

"You must, however, avoid a profusion of divisions, which only disturb the tune, and obscure its beauty; neither must you ever play these runs up and down the instrument with rebounding bow which are called 'Ricochets,' and which are hardly bearable on the Violin; but all the Graces and Divisions must be natural and appropriate and practised with discretion. . . .

"And you must take care, in lively movements, not to mark the beat too much, so as not to depart from the Spirit of the Instrument, which will not be treated in the manner of the Violin, of which the purpose is to animate, whilst that of the Treble Viol is to flatter."

Another French master from whom there is much to be learned is François Couperin, "The Great," who published in 1716 a book entitled: "L'Art de toucher le Clavecin," dedicated to the King.

It is a deep-minded work, full of subtle remarks useful to teacher and pupil alike. It is, unfortunately, a very rare book; as, indeed, are most of those I have quoted. Here is the Preface:—

"The method I give here is unique, and has nothing to do with Musical Theory, which is only a science of numbers; but in it I treat above all things (by demonstrated principles) of Fine Harpsichord playing. I even believe I give in it clear enough notions of the taste suitable to that instrument to be approved of by the accomplished player and to help those who hope to become such. As there is a great difference between Grammar and Declamation, so there is one infinitely greater between Musical Theory and the art of fine playing. I need not fear, therefore, that enlightened people will misunderstand me; I must only exhort the others to be docile, and to get rid of such prejudices as they may have. I must at least assure them that these principles are absolutely necessary to succeed in playing my pieces well."

Page 6: "One should only use at first a spinet, or one single keyboard of a Harpsichord for young pupils; and either the one or the other should be quilled very weakly. This point is of infinite consequence, a fine execution depending much more upon Suppleness, and great freedom of fingers, than on strength; so that if in the beginnings a child is allowed to play upon two keyboards (coupled), he must of necessity force his little hands to make the notes sound; and from this come ill-placed hands and hardness of touch.

"Softness of Touch depends also upon keeping one's fingers as near as possible to the keys. It is reasonable to believe (experience apart) that if a finger falls on the key from high, it gives a drier blow than if it had been kept near it, and that the quill draws a harsher tone from the string.

"It is better during the first lessons one gives to children not to advise them to practise in the absence of their teacher. Young people are too thoughtless to bind themselves to hold their hands in the position one has prescribed for them. As to myself, in beginning with children, I take away, as a precaution, the key of the instrument upon which I teach them, so that they may not spoil in an instant what I have been most carefully teaching for three-quarters of an hour."

Couperin's remark upon the necessity of beginning upon a very light instrument is most true. Many pianoforte players have a hard, unsympathetic touch, and are unable to play lightly and rapidly merely on account of having practised at first upon a heavy keyboard. And what Couperin says as to keeping the fingers close to the keys is as true about the pianoforte of to-day as it was then about the harpsichord.

Page 10: "The manner of fingering is a great help to good playing; but as it would take an entire volume of remarks and varied examples to demonstrate what I think, and what I teach to my pupils, I shall only give here a general notion of it. It is proved that a certain melody, a certain passage, being fingered in a certain way, produces quite a distinct effect upon the ear of a person of taste."

The system of fingering used by Couperin was very nearly the same as that of Bach and other players of that period. We shall discuss it later, for it is a most important point. In modern editions of Bach and other old masters, the fingering given is frequently arranged so as to render proper phrasing very difficult, if not impossible. It is based upon a system which, however efficient for the rendering of modern music, is not adapted to compositions based upon a technique wholly different from that of the present time. This bad fingering is often responsible for the dryness and general ineffectiveness of modern performances of old music.

To return to Couperin's book, we find at page 12 the following excellent precept:—

"One should not begin to teach children to read music until they are able to play a certain number of pieces. It is almost impossible that, whilst looking at their book, their fingers should not get disarranged, and twisted about; that the very Graces be not altered. Besides, memory develops much better if one is used to play by heart."

At the bottom of page 13 he further explains :—

"I hope no one has doubted so far, that I have supposed that the children had been taught, first of all, the names of the notes on the keyboard."

At page 38 there is a most important passage to which we shall have occasion to return later. When he speaks of "les étrangers" and "les Italiens" his opinion is not worth much, for he knew little about them. But about his own music and the French music of his time one must listen to him :—

" . . . I thought it would not be useless to say a word about French movements, and how they differ from the Italian.

"There are, according to me, in our way of writing music, faults similar to the manner of writing our language. We write differently from what we play, which is the cause that foreigners play our music less well than we play theirs. On the contrary, the Italians write their music as they imagined it. For example, we play as dotted several quavers following one another by degrees ; and yet we write them even. We are bound by use, and we continue. Let us examine whence comes this discrepancy. I find that we confuse Time, or Measure, with what is called Cadence or Movement. Measure defines the quantity and equality of beats ; Cadence is properly the spirit, the soul that must be added to it.

"The Sonatas of the Italians are hardly adapted to this Cadence. But all our Airs for Violins, our Pieces for Harpsichord, Viols, &c., point to, and seem to want to express, some sentiment. So that, not having imagined any signs, or characters to communicate our particular ideas, we try to palliate this defect by indicating at the beginning of our pieces, with such words as *Tendrement*, *Vivement*, &c., the idea we desire to convey. I wish someone would take the trouble to translate this for the use of foreigners, and thus give them the means to judge of the excellency of our Instrumental Music . . ."

Page 45: " . . . You must above all be very particular as to Keyboards, and have your instrument always quilled with care. I understand, however, that there are people to whom this may be indifferent, for they play equally badly upon any instrument whatever."

Here are the concluding "Observations" in the book. No doubt they will prove interesting. They occur in the middle of a collection of eight Preludes. There is one in each of the eight keys used by Couperin, so that the performer may always find one to play before any piece,—as the author says, "to untie his fingers, or test the touch of an unfamiliar instrument."

Page 60: " . . . Although these Preludes are written in measured time, there is however a customary style which should be followed. A Prelude is a free composition, in which the imagination follows all that comes to it. But as it is rare to find geniuses capable of production on the spur of the moment, those who will use these set Preludes must play them in an easy manner, without binding themselves to strict time, unless I should have expressly marked it by the word '*mesuré*.' Thus one may make bold to say that in many things music, by comparison with poetry, has its prose and its verse.

"One of the reasons why I have measured these Preludes is the facility one will find to teach them or to learn them." (He is quite right in this, for the unmeasured preludes of D'Anglebert and others are very troublesome to learn.)

"To conclude, on harpsichord playing in general, my feeling is not to depart from the style which suits it. Passages, broken chords well under the hand, things in Lute style and syncopations should be preferred to long-sustained or very low notes. You must bind perfectly all you play. All the graces must be precise; the shakes should be even and get quicker by imperceptible gradations.

"Take great care not to alter the time of set pieces, and not to hold notes longer than their proper value. Finally, form your playing on the good taste of to-day, which is without comparison purer than formerly."

This last remark is amusing, in view of the fact that at all times people have been convinced of the superiority of their own taste over that of their predecessors.

Now we shall study a most valuable German book entitled: "Johann Joachim Quantzens, Königl. Preussischen Kammermusikus, Versuch einer Anweisung die Flöte traversiere zu Spielen; mit verschiedenen, zur Beförderung des guten Geschmackes in der praktischen music dienlichen Anmerkungen begleitet, und mit Exempeln erläutert. Nebst xxiv. Kupfertafeln. Berlin. Johann Friedrich Voss. 1752."

This book was also published, at the same time and place, in French, under the title of: "Essai d'une Méthode pour apprendre à jouer de la Flute Traversière, avec plusieurs remarques pour servir au bon goût dans la musique. . . . par Jean Joachim Quantz."

The French of this translation is poor and incorrect. Still it is clear enough when the reader has become accustomed to its peculiarities. Both the German and the French versions are in my library, as well as most of the other works quoted in these pages. And indeed if I had not been the owner of these precious books I could not have accomplished my work, for it is only by studying them again and again, at leisure, for years, that the light has come to me. The reading possible at a public library is necessarily too superficial to assimilate the details of such an intricate subject.

Quantz was a philosopher, a deep thinker, and an admirable teacher. He had obviously completely mastered the musical art of his time. His opinions are rendered all the more valuable by the fact that he was a friend and devoted admirer of J. S. Bach. His book should be republished and translated, for the whole of it is worthy of study.

Chap. xi. is entitled: "Of good Expression in General in Singing or Playing." Here are some extracts from it:—

Page 102: "Expression in Music may be compared to that of an Orator. The Orator and the Musician have both the same intention, in the composition as well as the rendering. They want to touch the heart, to excite or appease the movements of the soul, and to carry the auditor from one passion to another. . . .

"The good effect of Music depends almost as much upon the player as the composer. The best composition can be spoiled by a bad rendering, and a mediocre composition is improved by good expression. . . .

"Almost every musician has a different expression from that of others. . . .

"A good rendering must be first clear and distinct. Not only must every note be heard, but each one must be given in its proper value, so that all become intelligible to the auditor. None should be omitted, and each sound must be made as beautiful as it is possible to produce it. . . .

"You must avoid slurring such notes as should be detached, and not detach those which should be slurred. The notes must not sound as if they were stuck together. You must use the tongue for wind instruments and accented bowing for string instruments to obtain proper articulation. . . .

"You must not separate ideas which belong to each other, and, on the contrary, you must divide them when the musical sense is finished, whether there be a pause or not. You must, in your execution, know how to make a difference between capital- and passing-notes. Capital-notes must always, if possible, be more emphasised than passing ones. According to this rule, in pieces of moderate movement, or even in the Adagio, the shorter notes should be played somewhat unequally, although to the sight they appear to be of the same value; so that you must in each figure dwell on such notes as come on the beats, namely the first, third, fifth and seventh, more than on the passing ones, which are the second, fourth, sixth and eighth. You should not however hold them as long as if they were dotted."

Page 108: "The execution should be easy and flowing. However difficult may be the passage, you must carefully avoid all stiffness or uneasiness in playing it. A good execution should also be full of variety. You must continually oppose light and shade; for you will certainly fail to be touching, if you play always either loud or soft—if you use, so to speak, always the same colour, and do not know how to increase or abate the tone when required. You must therefore use frequent changes from *forte* to *piano*."

Page 109: "The player must try to feel in himself not only the principal passion but all the others as they come. And as in most pieces there is a perpetual change of passions, the player must be able to judge which feeling is in each thought, and to regulate his execution upon that. It is in this way that he can do justice to the intention of the composer and to the ideas the latter had in composing his pieces."

Page 110: "Another indication of the dominant passion in a piece is the word to be found at the beginning. It may be: *Allegro*, *Allegro non tanto*, *Allegro assai*, *Allegro molto*, *Moderato*, *Presto*, *Allegretto*, *Andante*, *Andantino*, *Arioso*, *Cantabile*, *Spiritoso*, *Affettuoso*, *Grave*, *Adagio*, *Adagio assai*, *Lento*, *Mesto*, &c. All these words, unless they be used thoughtlessly, severally demand a particular expression. And besides, as was said before, each piece of the character described above being capable of possessing a mixture of thoughts—pathetic, caressing, gay, sublime,—or light, you must at each bar, so to speak, adopt another passion, and be sad, gay, serious, &c., as these changes are absolutely necessary in music. Whoever can acquire this perfection will not fail to gain the applause of his auditors, and his expression will always prove touching. But it must not be thought that these fine distinctions can be acquired in a short time. We cannot even hope to find them in young people, who are usually too quick and impatient for that. We grow into them gradually as feeling and judgment ripen."

All this is so clear and logical that comments would be superfluous. We cannot help feeling somewhat discouraged, however, for if it was so difficult to find the proper expression of music when its style was familiar to all, and good models were available, what studies and meditations shall we have to go through to achieve even a measure of success, we who not only have no examples to follow, but are hampered by modern training and the prejudices of our time!

CHAPTER II.

TEMPO.

THE proper *tempo* of a piece of music can usually be discovered by an intelligent musician, if he is in sympathy with its style, and possesses sufficient knowledge of the instrument for which it was written. But here again we must guard against prejudice and so-called tradition, for many a musician who would be sensitive enough to the *tempo* of modern music, will not hesitate at committing the most glaring absurdity when "old music" is concerned.

Moreover, the influence of the "eye" has to be considered, especially in the case of the earlier music. Breves, semibreves, and minims suggest long notes to a modern. In reality they may represent moderately short or even very short notes. At one time minims were employed as quavers or semiquavers are nowadays. The common opinion that the old music was slow may well come from that fact, although there must also be some other cause for it, for we find it expressed at almost all times. Perhaps the younger players of every generation are naturally fond of showing off the nimbleness of their fingers, even at the expense of clearness and beauty, whilst mature artists, or at least some of them, understand that there is a limit of speed beyond which the ear and the eye can no longer follow and enjoy the music.

Be that as it may, it is unquestionable that the old music, as such, was neither slower nor quicker than the modern. It comprises all sorts of movements: slow, moderate, or fast, according to the idea to be expressed; and even the most gifted performer will be helped in finding the true movement of a piece by such knowledge as can be derived from contemporary writers.

For convenience' sake, we shall consider separately arbitrary movements and dance measures, and begin with the former.

SECTION I.

The treatises of Music of the 16th and early part of the 17th centuries give, as a rule, very complete information as to the relative value of notes, an intricate question in those days of "moods" and "prolations"; but they do not say much about *tempo*. Mersenne, in his "Harmonie Universelle," published 1636, first gives the time-value of a *Minim* as that of a beat of the heart. There is more thorough information in Christopher Simpson's "Compendium of Music," published in London in 1667. It is a valuable book of instruction, and being, like most works of that kind, fifty years or so behind its time in nearly all its teaching, may be considered as an authority upon the music of the early part of the 17th century.

At page 13 it gives the relative value of notes in two schemes; one goes from the "Large" to the Semibreve, the other from the Semibreve to the Demisemiquaver. They are followed by these explanations:—

"Where note, that the *Large* and *Long* are now of little use, being too long for any Voice or Instrument (the Organ excepted) to hold out to their full length. But their *Rests* are still in frequent use, especially in grave Musick, and Songs of many Parts.

"You will say, If those Notes you named be too long for the Voice to hold out, to what purpose were they used formerly? To which I answer: they were used in *Tripla Time*, and in a quick measure; quicker (perhaps) than we now make our *Semibreve* and *Minim*. For, as After-times added new Notes, so they (still) put back the former into something of a slower Measure."

Note the "perhaps" in brackets, which shows that Simpson was not quite sure of the exact relation between the earlier long notes and the shorter notes of his time, but he knew that the music itself was not any the slower for having been written in "long" notes. The remark about "Tripla Time" will find itself explained later. Simpson continues thus:—

"§7. Of Keeping Time.

"Our next business is, to consider how (in such a diversity of long and short Notes) we come to give every particular Note its due Measure, without making it either longer or shorter than it ought to be. To effect this, we use a constant motion of the Hand. Or, if the Hand be otherwise employed, we use the Foot. If that be also ingaged, the Imagination (to which these are but assistant) is able of itself to perform that office. But in this place we must have recourse to the motion of the Hand.

"The motion of the Hand is *Down* and *Up*, successively and equally divided. Every *Down* and *Up* being called a *Time* or *Measure*. And by this we measure the length of a *Semibreve;* which is therefore called the *Measure-Note*, or *Time-Note*. And therefore, look how many of the shorter Notes go to a *Semibreve*, (*as you did see in the Scheme*). So many do also go to every *Time* or *Measure*. Upon which accompt, two *Minims* make a *Time*, one down, the other up ; Four *Crotchets* a *Time*, two down, and two up.

"Again, Eight *Quavers* a *Time*, four down, and four up. And so you may compute the rest.

"But you may say, I have told you that a *Semibreve* is the length of a *Time*, and a *Time* the length of a *Semibreve*, and still you are ignorant what that length is.

"To which I answer, (in case you have none to guide your Hand at the first measuring of Notes) I would have you pronounce these words [*One, Two, Three, Four*] in an equal length, as you would (leisurely) read them : Then fancy those four words to be four *Crotchets*, which make up the quantity or length of a Semibreve, and consequently of a *Time* or *Measure:* In which, let those two words [*One, Two*] be pronounced with the Hand Down ; and [*Three, Four*] with it Up. In the continuation of this motion you will be able to Measure and compute all your other Notes.

"Some speak of having recourse to the motion of a lively pulse for the measure of *Crotchets;* or to the little Minutes of a steddy going Watch for Quavers, by which to compute the length of other Notes; but this which I have delivered, will (I think) be most useful to you."

The beat of the pulse is the same as that of the heart; of course, it is variable in speed. Some consider it to average 72 beats per minute. We shall see later that Quantz estimates it at 80. But 75 corresponds exactly with Simpson's other direction, which makes the quavers agree with the "little minutes" or strokes of a watch, which usually beat five times a second or 300 times a minute. This gives 75 for minims; a variation of eight or ten strokes per minute is hardly perceptible. Anyway, the time of a piece of music continually does and must vary if the music has any meaning. Such indications as these can, therefore, only be taken in a general way.

𝅗𝅥=75 agrees well with the average Madrigal, Fancy, Ricercare, In Nomine, &c., of the period 1550-1650.

This is from Simpson again:—

"§ 10. Of Tripla Time.

"When you see this figure [3] set at the beginning of a Song or Lesson, it signifies that the Time or Measure must be computed by *Threes*, as we formerly did it by *Fours*.

"Sometimes the *Tripla* consists of three *Semibreves* to a Measure, each *Semibreve* being shorter than a *Minim* in Common Time.

"The more *common Tripla*, is three Minims to a Measure, each *Minim* about the length of a *Crochet* in Common Time . . .

"In those two sorts of *Tripla* we compt or imagine these two words [One, Two] with the Hand *down*, and this word [*Three*] with it *up*."

The information given here is very important, since by it we are warned of a diminution of over half the value of notes when the time of a piece changes from Common to Triple Time. This agrees admirably with the sections in Triple Time often to be met with in pieces starting in Common Time, and also with the *Galliards* following *Pavans*, which will be considered later among the Dance movements.

The many editions of Playford's "Introduction to the Skill of Music" between 1654 and 1730 agree with Simpson's directions. So does Mace in his "Musick's Monument," only in a more strenuous though less correct way, thanks to his own picturesque style. His advice as to keeping time is worth quoting.

Page 78: " . . . And thus must your Foot constantly be in Motion, during your Play, and equally dividing your Down from your Up, so exactly that not the least Difference may be perceived; which if you carefully practice at the first, you will ever continue It; but if you be remiss in the beginning, you will always after be uncertain, not only to your *own hindrance*, but also to all others, who shall play in Consort with you. . ."

In the first edition of Purcell's "Lessons for the Spinet," 1696, the following directions are given. There is no proof that they are Purcell's; the book was published by his widow, one year after his death. Here they are :—

"There being nothing more difficult in Musick then playing of true time, tis therefore nessesary to be observ'd by all practitioners, of which there are two sorts, Common time and Triple time, & is distinguish'd by this C, this ₵ or this ɸ mark, ye first is a very slow movement, ye next a little faster, and ye last a brisk & airy time, & each of them has allways to ye length of one Semibreif in a barr, which is to be held in playing as long as you can moderately tell four, by saying one, two, three, four; two Minums as long as one Semibreif, four Crotchets as long as two Minums, eight Quavers as long as four Crotchets, sixteen Semiquavers as long as eight Quavers.

"Triple time consists of either three or six Crotchets in a barr, and is to be known by this $\frac{3}{2}$, this 3-1, this 3 or this $\frac{6}{4}$ marke, to the first there is three Minums in a barr, and is commonly play'd very slow, the second has three Crotchets in a barr, and they are to be play'd slow, the third has y^{e} same as y^{e} former but is play'd faster, y^{e} last has six Crotchets in a barr & is Commonly to brisk tunes as Jiggs and Paspys. . . ."

It must be said, however, that although the majority of Purcell's pieces agree with the above explanations, the exceptions are frequent. For example, he uses the sign 2 sometimes for "brisk," sometimes for slow movements. He uses $\frac{3}{2}$ for Hornpipes, which are *very fast*, and not very slow, as they should be according to the explanations. He uses 3-1 sometimes for three crotchets in a bar, at other times for three quavers in a bar. He also uses $\frac{3}{4}$, $\frac{3}{8}$, $\frac{12}{8}$, about which nothing is said; at times he gives no indications whatever. It follows that there was much difference between theory and practice in those days as now, and one has to know more than the explanations tell us to decide upon the right *tempo* of a piece by Purcell.

"The Compleat Flute Master, or the whole Art of playing on y[e] Rechorder" (Anonymous, London, *c.* 1700), gives the following Table of Time-signatures :—

> " C Very slow motion.
> " ¢ Somewhat faster.
> " Ↄ̸ Brisk and light Ayres.
> " $\frac{3}{2}$ Grave movement.
> " 3 Slow.
> " $\frac{6}{4}$ Fast, for Jiggs, Paspies, &c."

"Paspies," of course, means "Passepieds." Note that ¢ is not double the speed of C, but only "somewhat faster."

"The Compleat Tutor for the Violin," by "Mr. Dean," London, 1707, has the following :—

> " C Very solid or slow movement.
> " ¢ Quicker.
> " Ↄ̸ or ƻ as quick again as the first, and are call'd Retorted Time.
> " $\frac{3}{C}$ Very slow.
> " $\frac{3}{2}\frac{3}{4}$ Much quicker."

This does not agree with the preceding. We may note that Ↄ̸ or ƻ is "as quick again" as C. ƻ is not often to be met with, and neither is $\frac{3}{C}$. Then $\frac{3}{2}$ is now said to be "much quicker" instead of "Grave Movement." These contradictions are hard to understand; but the practice of Purcell, as shown before, is sufficient warning of the necessity of carefully analysing a piece before deciding its *tempo*.

Of all the authors who have given indications for the *tempi* of old music, Quantz, the 18th century writer already quoted, is the clearest, most thorough, and most precise. His system is also based upon the beat of the pulse, but with additional directions. Chronometers had been proposed in earlier times; but these, he rightly observes, you cannot always carry about, whilst your pulse is ever there.

Chap. xvii., Sect. vii., §55. "I must answer in advance some objections which might perhaps be made against my method of finding the movement. One might say that the beats of the pulse are not equally fast at each hour of the day and in each person, which would be necessary, if one would regulate upon it the movement in music. It will be said that the pulse beats in the morning before dinner more slowly than it does after dinner; item that it beats more slowly in a man inclined to sadness than in another who is quick and merry. This may be true; however it may be possible on this point to determine something precise. You need only take the beat of the pulse, as it is after dinner until the evening, and in a bright man, in good humour, who is besides of a quick and warm disposition and you will be sure to be right. A man in low spirits, sad, cold and heavy, could give the time of each piece a little quicker than the beat of his pulse. In case this is not yet sufficient, I shall determine it still further. *You take for measure the pulse which beats about eighty times in a minute.*

Eighty beats of the pulse make forty bars of the quickest Common time. A few beats more or less make no difference here; for example, five beats more or less in a minute make forty bars each a semiquaver longer or shorter; but this is so little that one could not notice it. He whose pulse makes in a minute much more or less than eighty beats will know what he has to do with regard to the augmentation or diminution of the speed of the movement.

"Supposing even that notwithstanding all this the means I have just proposed could not be given as general and universal, although I could prove it not only by the beat of my own pulse but by other and various experiments which I have made, not only about my own works but about those of others and with different persons, the pulse could at least be useful to the one who, by this method, will have made for himself a clear idea of the four principal kinds of movement, so that he will not wander too far from the movement of each piece. One can see every day how the movement is ill-treated, and that the same piece is played now moderately, then quickly, or again still more quickly. One knows that in some places music is played anyhow; a *Presto* is often turned into an *Allegretto* and an *Andante* into an *Adagio*, which could not help being to the greatest disadvantage of the composer, who cannot always be present.

"It is pretty well known that when a piece is repeated directly one or more times, specially if it is a quick piece, for example the *Allegro* of a Concerto or a Symphony, one always plays it the second time a little quicker than the first, so as not to make the auditors fall asleep. If one did not do this, the auditors would not know that the piece has already been finished.

"If, on the contrary, it is repeated in a slightly quicker *tempo*, it will get by it a livelier air, new and strange, so to speak; and this calls fresh attention from the auditor. This practice is not disadvantageous to the pieces, and it is used by good and mediocre players who all find the effect equally good.

"But, there would be no harm, anyway, if a man in low spirits played, according to his disposition, the pieces a little slower, and a quick man a little quicker, so long as they render the spirit of the music.

"To conclude, if anybody knows of a means more easy, more precise or commodious to learn to know and not miss the movement, he would do well not to delay to communicate it to the Public."

We will now study in detail the teachings of Quantz as to *Tempo*.

Chap. xvii., Sect. vii., § 49:—

"Before going any further, I must examine more exactly the different sorts of movement. There are so many in Music that it would be impossible to determine them all. However, there are some principal kinds, from which one can deduct the others; and taking them as they are found in Concertos, Trios, and Solos, I shall make four classes of them, which will be our foundations. They are taken in Common time, with four beats in a bar, and are as follows: 1°. *Allegro assai.* 2°. *Allegretto.* 3°. *Adagio cantabile.* 4°. *Adagio assai.* In the first class I include the *Allegro molto*, the *Presto*, &c. In the second: the *Allegro ma non tanto*, *non troppo*, *non presto*, *moderato*, &c. In the third: the *Cantabile*, *Arioso*, *Larghetto*, *Soave*, *Dolce*, *Poco andante*, *Affettuoso*, *Pomposo*, *Maestoso*, *alla Siciliana*, *Adagio spiritoso*, &c.; lastly, in the fourth class: *Adagio pesante*, *Lento*, *Largo assai*, *Mesto*, *Grave*, &c. These appellations indicate differences proper to each kind; however, they concern as much the expression of feelings which predominate in each piece as the *tempo* itself. Provided you understand well the four typical kinds of movement, the others will be learned easily, for their difference is not great.

"§ 50. It is therefore the *Allegro assai* which is the fastest of these four types. The *Allegretto* goes half the speed of the *Allegro assai*. The *Adagio cantabile* half the speed of the *Allegretto*. The *Adagio assai* half the speed of the *Adagio cantabile*. In the *Allegro assai* the runs are in semiquavers or triplets of quavers, and in the *Allegretto* in demisemiquavers or triplets of semiquavers. But, as these runs should be played mostly at the same speed, be they semiquavers or demisemiquavers, it follows that notes of the same value are played in the one double the speed they are in the other. It is the same thing in the *Alla breve*, called by the Italians *Tempo maggiore*, and which is always marked by a capital C crossed (¢), be the movement slow or quick, except that the notes are here played twice as quickly as in the full Common time of four in a bar. In consequence, in that sort of movement, the runs of the *Allegro* are written in quavers, but are played like the semiquavers of the Common time.

"It is the same thing with regard to Triple time, for example, $\frac{3}{4}$, $\frac{3}{8}$, $\frac{6}{8}$ or $\frac{12}{8}$, &c. When in a $\frac{3}{4}$ there are only quavers, in a $\frac{3}{8}$ semiquavers, and in a $\frac{6}{8}$ or $\frac{12}{8}$ quavers, it is a proof that the quickest *tempo* is intended. But if there are semiquavers in a $\frac{3}{4}$ or demisemiquavers in a $\frac{3}{8}$ or triplets of semiquavers in $\frac{6}{8}$ or $\frac{12}{8}$, then a moderate movement should be taken, and the speed half of that mentioned before. It is just the same thing with the *Adagio*, provided you pay attention to the degree of slowness I have mentioned at the beginning of this paragraph, and to the kind of *tempo*, that is, whether full time or *Alla breve*.

"§ 51. To explain more clearly how it is possible by means of the pulse to find the right speed of each movement, one must note that it is necessary, before everything to consider the word written at the beginning of the piece, and which indicates the *tempo*, as well as the quickest notes which form the runs. And, as it is hardly possible to execute, during one beat of the pulse, more than eight very quick notes, either with double-tongueing or with the bow, it follows that:—

"In Common time:

"In the *Allegro assai* each half-bar lasts one beat of the pulse.
"In the *Allegretto* each crotchet one beat of pulse.
"In the *Adagio cantabile* each quaver the same.
"In the *Adagio assai* each quaver two beats of the pulse.

"In *Alla breve* time:

"In the *Allegro* each bar one beat of the pulse.
"In the *Allegretto* each half-bar one beat of the pulse.
"In the *Adagio cantabile* for each crotchet one beat.
"In the *Adagio assai* for each crotchet two beats.

"There is, especially in ordinary Common time, a kind of moderate *Allegro*, which is half-way between *Allegro assai* and *Allegretto*. It is often found in pieces for the Voice or such instruments as are unable to play very quick runs. It is indicated by the words *Poco allegro*, *Vivace*, or more commonly, *Allegro*. You should count in this sort of movement one beat of the pulse for every three quavers, the second beat falling upon the fourth quaver.

"In $\frac{2}{4}$ or $\frac{6}{8}$ time, *Allegro*, each bar lasts one beat of the pulse. In $\frac{12}{8}$ time when there are no semiquavers each bar takes two pulse-beats.

"In a $\frac{3}{4}$ *Allegro*, when there are runs of semiquavers or triplets of quavers, it would not be possible to determine the speed accurately by the pulse, for one single bar. But, it is possible by combining two bars, for then one counts the beat of the pulse upon the first and last crotchets of the first bar, and on the second crotchet of the second bar, and consequently three pulse-beats for six crotchets.

"It is the same in $\frac{9}{8}$ time.

"In $\frac{3}{4}$ or $\frac{3}{8}$ time, in quick time, when there are not more than six notes in a bar, one must only count one pulse-beat in a bar. In a *Presto*, however, this would be too slow. To know the speed of these three crotchets or quavers in a *Presto*, one should take the speed of the Common time when it is very fast and four quavers come in one pulse-beat, and play the three crotchets or quavers as fast as the quavers in the Common time aforesaid.

"In an *Adagio cantabile* in $\frac{3}{4}$ time, when the bass moves in quavers (as in many Sarabandes of Corelli, Bach, &c) each quaver takes one pulse-beat. But, if the bass moves in crotchets, and that the tune be rather *Arioso* than sad, one counts for each crotchet one pulse-beat. However, one should also consider the style, and the word written at the beginning; for if there is *Adagio assai*, *Mesto* or *Lento*, then each crotchet should take two pulse-beats.

"In an *Arioso* in $\frac{3}{8}$, each quaver has one pulse-beat.

"A *Siciliana* in $\frac{12}{8}$ would be too slow if one gave one pulse-beat to each quaver. But if you divide *two* pulse-beats into three parts, there comes upon both the first and third quavers one pulse-beat. And after you have divided these three notes, you must pay no more attention to the pulse, otherwise the third quaver would be too long.

"When in a quick piece the runs are composed of triplets only, without admixture of ordinary semi- or demisemiquavers, the piece might be played, if agreeable, a little faster than the pulse beats."

Here an interpolation might be allowed; it is useful, and, moreover, its mention of a "musical machine" is interesting in its curious anticipation of a modern invention.

Chap. xii., § 11: "Whatever quickness the *Allegro* may require, one must never go beyond a regulated and reasonable movement. Art might well invent a musical machine which could play certain pieces with a speed and accuracy so singular that nobody could equal it, either with finger or tongue. One would admire it, but one could never be touched by it; and after hearing such a thing once or twice, and knowing how it is done, one would cease to admire it. If one wishes to touch and please the ear in an *Allegro*, one must indeed play each piece with its proper fire; but the movement must never be precipitated, otherwise the piece would lose all its attraction."

The above directions can be condensed into the following table:—

Allegro assai or *Presto* in Common time, with semiquavers	♩= 160
Allegro moderato or *Poco allegro*, or *Vivace* or plain *Allegro*	♩= 120
Allegretto	♩= 80
Adagio cantabile	♪= 80
Adagio assai	♪= 40

The speed of the *Allegro assai* or *Presto* is very great; few players would care to exceed it. That of the *Allegro moderato* plenty fast enough. Obviously, the "Old Music" was not devoid of speed.

Now let us return to Quantz:—

"§ 52. What I have explained above applies most exactly and most often to Instrumental music. As to vocal music, especially Airs in the Italian style, it is true that almost every one demands its particular movement.

"But these divers movements are nearly all derived from the four principal types I have described. One should consider the sense of the words, the movement of the notes, especially the quickest, and in quick airs the ability and the voice of the singer. A singer who uses the chest voice for runs is hardly able to execute them as quickly as one who uses his head-voice, although the former will always be the more valuable of the two, especially in a large hall. With a little experience and the knowledge that Vocal music does not as a rule require so fast a *tempo* as music for instruments, one should find out the right one without particular difficulties.

"§ 53. It is the same with Church music as with the Airs; except that the expression as well as the *Tempo* should be more moderate than in Opera, to show due regard to the Holiness of the place."

The speed of the *Allegro*, as given above, is confirmed in a book entitled: "La Tonotechnie, ou l'Art de Noter les cylindres et tout ce qui est susceptible de Notage dans les Instruments de Concerts Méchaniques, par le Père Engramelle, Religieux Augustin de la Reine Marguerite. Paris, 1775."

It treats of the same matter as the last part of "L'Art du Facteur d'Orgues," of Dom Bedos, already mentioned at page 1, and appeared about the same time. We shall have occasion to return to "La Tonotechnie," for its statements as a rule possess that *absolute* scientific precision which is but too rarely observed in our subject.

"La Tonotechnie," page 9:—

"In all carefully noted Pieces of Music, one expresses with a few Italian or French words the approximate degree of speed of the piece; but these words being only general do not indicate precisely the quantity of minutes or seconds which must be employed in their execution. Taste only decides it; so that if the player is naturally gay, or sad, his genius being affected by his disposition, he will play either too fast or too slow, and consequently spoil the piece.

"Let us give, I suppose, to a Musician naturally slow or sad, an *Allegro* in $\frac{2}{4}$ of 20 bars; instead of the 20 seconds its execution should take in the speed necessary to its proper expression, he may take 40 or 50, and this *Allegro*, which would be a charming air if played within 20 seconds, becomes a pitiful thing, and capable of sending one to sleep in the hands of such a player: and it is the same with other movements. If they are too slow, they become wearisome; if they are too hurried, they irritate, for they depart from their proper character."

SECTION II.

The Tempo of Dance Movements.

With regard to the earlier dances, we have no precise indications of *Tempo*, only relative values and descriptions. It would be possible to approach very near to the truth by a conscientious study of the dancing steps. There are plenty of treatises on dancing containing all the needful information. Their study, and the consequent authentic revival of the old dances, would be most interesting and delightful; unfortunately it is still in a rudimentary stage. Practical musicians, it is true, are little inclined towards historical research, but dancers are even worse on that point. The revivals of old dances now in fashion do not as a rule go much deeper than invented steps upon a more or less correct tune. *(See Note on page 52.)*

One of the difficulties of our subject is that owing to the variations of speed and character which affect dances through their career, the name of a dance does not in itself carry a sufficiently precise meaning, for most dances have become deeply altered by changes of country and the influence of fashion. A familiar instance is the Waltz, which has undergone so many transformations within living memory.

As a rule, dances are rapid and lively when first introduced. They become slow and sentimental as they grow old. This would make an interesting subject for research. It is beyond the scope of the present work, but some general indications will be found useful in explaining the contradictions contained in some of the statements which follow.

The *Galliard* in the 16th century was true to its name, being lively and stirring. It had become "Grave and Sober" about 1650.

The *Courante*, or *Coranto*, as its name implies was very rapid about 1600. It had become much slower about 1700.

The *Saraband*, about 1650, in England was the quickest of the dances; very nearly at the same time, in France, the "Sarabande Grave" was slow and pathetic. The *Sarabands* of Handel and Bach are all more or less slow movements.

The *Menuet* had a chequered career. Its name nowadays evokes a moderately slow, graceful movement, of the type of Mozart's *Menuet* in "Don Giovanni." Fifty years ago it was played fast.

If we look into Brossard's Dictionary of Music, published at Paris in 1703, we find:—"*Menuet:* Very merry Dance, which came from Poitou. One ought, in imitation of the Italians, to use the signature $\frac{3}{8}$ or $\frac{6}{8}$ to mark its movement, which is always *very gay* and *very fast.* But the custom of marking it by a simple 3 or $\frac{3}{4}$ has prevailed."

Now let us see the "Encyclopédie" of Diderot and d'Alembert, compiled about 1750:—"*Menuet*, kind of dance which, the Abbé Brossard tells us, came originally from Poitou. He says that this dance is very gay and its movement very fast. This is not quite right. The character of the *Menuet* is a noble and elegant simplicity; the movement is moderate rather than quick. It may be said that the *least gay* of all the kinds of dances used in our balls is the *menuet*."

The contradiction is as flat as can be. Yet both authors are right; the writer in the "Encyclopédie," like most musicians of our epoch, only knew the music in common use at his time! A little English Dictionary of Music, published in 1724, says: "*Minuetto*, a Minuet, a French Dance so-called, or the Tune or Air belonging thereunto. This Dance and Air being so well known that it needs no Explanation." This is scant information.

These few facts must warn the student that before deciding on the *tempo* of a dance he must consider its period and country.

The following extracts are from Thomas Morley's "Plaine and Easie Introduction to Practicall Musicke," first edition, London, 1597, page 181: ". . . *Pavane*, a kind of staide musicke, ordained for grave dauncing, and most commonlie made of three straines, whereof everie straine is plaid or sung twice . . . in this you must cast your musicke by foure, so that if you keep that rule it is no matter how many foures you put in your straine, for it will fall out well enough in the ende, *the arte of dauncing being come to that perfection that everie reasonable dauncer will make measure of no measure*, so that it is no great matter of what number you make your strayne." (The italics are added; the passage applies so well to some of the characteristics of our latest school of dancing that it seems as if it had just been written, instead of 300 years ago.)

"After every *pavan* we usually set a *Galliard* (that is a kind of musicke made out of the other) causing it to go by a measure . . . consisting of a long and short stroke successivelie . . . the first being in time of a semibrefe, and the latter of a minime. This is a lighter and more stirring kinde of dauncing than the *pavane* . . . The Italians make their *Galliardes*, (which they tearme *Saltarelli*) plaine, and frame ditties to them, which in their *mascaradoes* they sing and daunce, and many times without any instruments at all, but in steed of instrumentes they have Curtisans disguised in men's apparell, who sing and daunce to their owne songes.

"The *Alman* is a more heavie daunce than this, (fitlie representing the nature of the people, whose name it carrieth), so that no extraordinarie motions are used in dauncing of it.

"Like unto this is the French *bransle* (which they call *bransle simple*) which goes somewhat rounder in time than this, otherwise the measure is all one.

"The *bransle de Poictou* or *bransle double* is more quick in time . . . Like unto this (but more light) be the *voltes* and *courantes* which being both of a measure, are notwithstanding daunced after sundrie fashions, the *volte* rising and leaping, the *courante* travising and running, in which measure also our countrey daunce is made, though it be daunced after another forme then any of the former. . . . There bee also many other kindes of daunces (as *hornepypes*, *jygges*, and infinite more) which I cannot nominate unto you, but knowing these, the rest can not but be understood, as being one with some of these which I have alreadie told you."

Here is Thomas Mace's (*c.* 1676) list of Dances :—

Page 129 :—

"*Pavines*, are Lessons of 2, 3, or 4 Strains, very *Grave* and *Sober;* full of Art, and Profundity, but seldom us'd, in These our Light Days.

"*Allmaines*, are Lessons very Ayrey, and Lively; and generally of Two Strains, of the Common or Plain-Time.

"*Ayres*, are, or should be, of the same Time, (yet many make Tripla's, and call them so ;) only they differ from Allmaines by being commonly Shorter, and of a more Quick, and Nimble Performance.

"*Galliards*, are Lessons of 2 or 3 Strains, but are perform'd in a Slow, and Large Triple-Time; and (commonly) Grave and Sober.

"*Corantoes*, are Lessons of a Shorter Cut, and of a quicker Triple-Time; commonly of 2 Strains, and full of Sprightfulness, and Vigour, Lively, Brisk and Cheerful.

"*Serabands*, are of the Shortest Triple-Time; but are more Toyish, and Light, than Corantoes; and commonly of Two Strains.

"*A Tattle de Moy*, is a New Fashion'd Thing, much like a Seraband; only It has more of Conceit in It, as (in a manner) speaking the word, (*Tatle de Moy*) and of Humour; That Conceit being never before Publish'd, but Broached together with this

Work. It may supply the Place of a Seraband, at the End of a Suit of Lessons, at any Time.

"*Chichona's*, are only a few Conceited Humorous Notes, at the end of a Suit of Lessons, very Short, (viz.) not many in Number; yet sometimes consists of Two Strains, although but of Two Semibreves in a Strain, and commonly, of a Grave kind of Humour.

"*Toys*, or *Jiggs*, are Light-Squibbish Things, only fit for Fantastical, and Easie-Light-Headed People; and are of any sort of Time.

"*Common Tunes* (so called) are Commonly known by the Boys, and Common People, Singing them in the Streets, and are of either sort of Time, of which there are many, very Excellent, and well Contriv'd Pieces, Neat and Spruce Ayres.

"*The Ground*, is a set Number of Slow Notes, very Grave, and Stately; which, (after it is express'd once, or Twice, very Plainly) then He that hath Good Brains, and a Good Hand, undertakes to Play several *Divisions* upon it, Time after Time, till he has show'd his Bravery, both of Invention, and Hand."

In the above, notice: the *Galliard*, *slow*; the *Coranto*, *lively*, *brisk*, &c. The *Saraband*, more *toyish* and *light* than the *Coranto*.

The *Tattle de Moy* is an invention of Mace, and has but slight importance.

The *Chichona* I have never met with, not even amongst Mace's works. (*See Note* 2 *on page* 52.)

His appreciation of popular tunes is interesting, and very true. His description of *Grounds* is excellent. These two last are out of place amongst the dances, but they are in Mace's list and worth quoting.

We shall now proceed with Quantz, where priceless information concerning the Bach-Handel period is obtainable.

"Chap. xvii., Sect. vii., § 58. The *Entrée*, the *Loure* and the *Courante* are played with majesty, and the bow is detached at each crotchet, whether there be a dot or not. One counts for each crotchet one beat of the pulse.

"The *Sarabande* has the same *Tempo*, but it is played with an expression a little more agreeable.

"A *Chacone* is also played with majesty. One beat of the Pulse makes two crotchets.

"A *Passecaille* is equal to it, but is played a little faster. A *Musette* is expressed very flatteringly. One counts one beat of the pulse for each crotchet in a $\frac{3}{4}$ or for each quaver in a $\frac{3}{8}$. Sometimes a fancy comes to certain dancers to have it played so fast that there is only one beat of the pulse for a whole bar.

"A *Fury* is played with much fire. One counts one beat of the pulse on two crotchets, whether in Common or Triple Time.

"A *Bourrée* and a *Rigaudon* are played merrily and with a short and light bowing. Each bar has one beat of the pulse.

"A *Gavotte* is almost equal to the *Rigaudon;* it has, however, a more moderate movement. A *Rondeau* is played with a certain tranquillity, and one beat of the pulse comprises almost two crotchets, either in the *Allabreve* or in the $\frac{3}{4}$.

"The *Gigue* and the *Canarie* have the same movement. If they are composed in $\frac{6}{8}$ time, each bar has one pulse beat. The *Gigue* is played with a short and light bow, but in the *Canarie*, which consists always of dotted notes, the bowing is short and sharp.

"The *Menuet* is played in a manner which nearly bears or lifts the Dancer up, and one marks the crotchets with a rather heavy bowing, though short. One counts for two crotchets one pulse beat.

"A *Passepied* is played a little more lightly and quickly than a Menuet.

"A *Tambourin* is played like a Bourrée or Rigaudon, only a little faster.

"A *Marche* is played seriously. When it is written in Alla Breve or Bourrée time, two pulse-beats are given to each bar."

These explanations may be resumed thus :—

Entrée, Loure, Courante	♩=80.
Sarabande	♩=80.
Chaconne	♩=160.
Passacaille	♩=180.
Musette	♪ or ♩=80.
Furie	♩=160.
Bourrée, Rigaudon	♩=160.
Gavotte	♩=120.
Rondeau	♩=140.
Gigue, Canarie	♩.=160.
Menuet	♩=160.
Passepied	♪=180.
Tambourin	♩=180.
Marche ₵	𝅗𝅥=80.

It should be remembered that these are actually for *dancing*. Some of the expressive *Chaconnes* or

Sarabandes of Bach might well be played a little slower, and some of the *Courantes* quicker; in fact, one must use one's judgment in applying the time of a real dance to a piece composed indeed on the same rhythm, but intended only to please the ear.

In "Dom Bedos" (1766), already mentioned at page 1, we find the following indications:—

Page 606: "Marches of 24 bars, in lively movement commonly last only 20 seconds, which makes a second a bar, half a second per minim, one quarter of a second per crotchet, &c. Menuets of 24 bars, of lively character, also last 20 seconds; movements in $\frac{6}{4}$ and $\frac{6}{8}$ of the same character last also 20 seconds; pieces in $\frac{2}{4}$ or quick *Allemandes* of 32 bars, 20 seconds: all these airs would fill up each their turn of the cylinder."

It may be that they would not be all so even, had not the "cylinder" to be filled. Still they cannot have been much out, and they indicate a standard of speed which effectually disposes of the notion that the old music was played slower than that of the present time.

NOTE TO PAGE 44.

Since these lines were written, many old dances have been revived by Mrs. Arnold Dolmetsch, and important discoveries made. See her books, *Dances of England and France from 1450 to 1600* (London: Routledge & Kegan Paul [1949]), and *Dances of Spain and Italy from 1400 to 1600* (London: Routledge & Kegan Paul [1954]).

NOTE TO PAGE 49.

The "Chichona" mentioned by Thomas Mace was a corruption of "Chacona."

CHAPTER III.

CONVENTIONAL ALTERATIONS OF RHYTHM.

Section I.

In modern notation the rhythm of the music is indicated with almost perfect accuracy. It was not the same in the old music. As Couperin says, "We write differently from what we play." Alterations of time were frequent and important. We must therefore know the rules and conventions by which they were governed, or else the foundation of our playing will be lacking.

In instruction books, be they old or new, we learn that "a dot after a note makes it half as long again." In spite of the intended modern precision there are still exceptions to that rule. In military marches, for example, figures like

♩. ♪ and ♪. ♬ are played ♩.. 𝅘𝅥𝅯 and ♪.. 𝅘𝅥𝅯,

but such instances are rare. In the old music, on the contrary, the exceptions were extremely frequent and important. Quantz, in the book already quoted (1752), will help us to find out the real value of the dot in his time.

Chap. v., § 21: "Quavers, semiquavers, and demisemiquavers with dots do not follow the general rule on account of the vivacity which they must express. You must remark, above all, that the note which follows the dot in examples (*c*) and (*d*) must be played as quick as the one at (*e*), let the movement be slow or quick:—

From this it follows that the dotted note at (*c*) takes nearly all the time of a crotchet, the one at (*d*) that of a quaver. To get a more distinct idea of this, play slowly the notes of the lower part at (*f*) and at (*g*), each example according to its proportion of time; that is, the one at (*d*) double the speed of that at (*c*), and the one at (*e*) double the speed of that at (*d*), and imagine at the same time the notes of the upper part (at (*f*)) with the dots:—

Then, doing the reverse, play the notes of the upper part, and make the dotted notes last until the dotted notes of the lower part are finished; the semiquavers will last only as long as the hemidemisemiquavers of the lower part. In this way you will see that the dotted quavers in the upper part at (*f*) must have the length of three semiquavers plus a dotted demisemiquaver, and those at (*g*) of a semiquaver and a dotted demisemiquaver. But those at (*h*) will have only the length of a demisemiquaver with a dot and a half, because the notes in the lower part have two dots."

§ 22 : "This rule must also be observed, when one of the parts has triplets, whilst the other has dotted notes :—

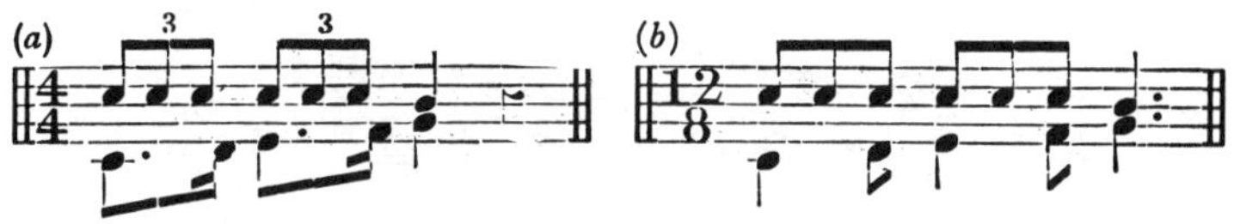

"Ex. (*a*) : The small note which follows the dot should only be played after the third note of the triplet, and not with it, or else it would bring confusion with $\frac{6}{8}$ or $\frac{12}{8}$ time, Ex. (*b*). These two kinds of notes require quite a different treatment. . . . If one did play the dotted notes under triplets according to their ordinary value, their expression would be blurred and insipid, instead of brilliant."

§ 23 : "The notes in the example below have some resemblance with the dotted notes mentioned above. With regard to the duration of the dot and of the first note, the order is merely reversed :—

The notes (D) and (C) in Ex. (*a*) must last no longer than those at Ex. (*c*), either in slow or in quick time. One does the same thing with the two short notes at (*b*) and (*d*); here the two only take the time of one. You must also play the notes after the dots at Exx. (*e*) and (*f*) (below) as quickly, and with the same precipitation as those before the dots at (*b*) and (*d*):—

"The quicker you make the first notes at (*a*), (*b*), (*c*), (*d*), the more vivacious and bold the expression. On the contrary, the longer you hold the dots at (*e*) and (*f*), the more caressing and agreeable will the expression be."

In Chap. xvii., Sect. vii., § 58, after some remarks about the *tempo* of the measure of two beats in a bar, the ₵, he says: "In that measure, as well as in the time of three crotchets in a bar ($\frac{3}{4}$), which is used for the *Loure*, the *Saraband*, the *Courante*, and the *Chacone*, the quavers which follow the dotted crotchets are not to be played according to their exact value, but very shortly and sharply. The dotted note must be emphasised and the bow stopped during the dot. All dotted notes should be played in the same way whenever the time allows it; and when there are three or more semiquavers after a dot, or a rest, they should not be given their exact value, especially in slow pieces; but waiting until the very end of the time allotted to them, one plays them with the utmost speed, as is often the case in *Overtures*, *Entrées*, and *Furies*. One must, however, give every one of these quick notes a separate bowing, and one can hardly slur anything."

This is written for violin players, but the reader will understand that it applies to music in general, and not to a particular instrument. The author, advising the violoncellist, also says in Chap. xvii., Sect. iv., § 10: "He should play his dotted notes more seriously and heavily than the violins; but as to the semiquavers which follow, he must make them short and sharp either in slow or quick time."

Attention should here be called to a point upon which Quantz does not insist quite enough. When he says, in the above quoted paragraph, that "the bow should be stopped during the dot," he obviously means that the dot becomes a rest. There being no example given, this very important fact might be overlooked. We find it clearly demonstrated in Rellstab's "Anleitung für Clavierspieler, den Gebrauch der Bach'schen Fingersetzung, die Manieren und den Vortrag betreffend" (Berlin, 1789):—

But to return to Quantz.

Chap. xvii., Sect. ii., § 16: "When after a long note and a short rest come some demisemiquavers, the latter should always be played very quickly, either in *Adagio* or *Allegro*.

"You must, then, before playing them, wait until the very end of the time which belongs to them, thus avoiding faulty time:—

"If in a slow *Allabreve*, or ordinary Common time, there is a semiquaver rest on the accented beat followed by dotted notes:—

you must play the rest as if there were a dot to it or another rest of half its value, and that the following note were a demisemiquaver."

The last example, according to this rule and the explanations of Chap. xvii., Sect. vii. above, would be played thus:—

In Chapter XII, § 24, Quantz again mentions the lengthened dots. Explaining the various styles of *Allegro* movements, he says:—

" . . . The majestic is expressed by long notes, during which the other parts have rapid passages, and by dotted notes. The latter must be marked with strength and accent. One holds the dot and disposes quickly of the following note." (See Chap. v., §§ 21 and 22, already quoted at pp. 54, 55.)

Carl Philipp Emanuel Bach, in his treatise on harpsichord playing entitled "Versuch über die wahre Art das Clavier zu spielen," first published in 1753, also gives rules about the irregular value of dots: Chapter III, par. 24: "The short notes which follow dots are always made shorter than the written text indicates, so that it would be superfluous to write them with dots to the long ones or additional strokes to the stems of the short ones.

"The short notes at Exx. (*a*), (*b*), (*c*) would all be played at the same rate :—

"The short notes of the two parts at Ex. (*d*) would be played together :—

"It may sometimes happen, principally in quick time, that the note following the dot had better be given its written value, to facilitate the movements of other parts" :—

Nothing could better prove how general was this habit of lengthening dots than this one exception (*e*) given by the author against the mass of directions enjoining the other way of playing them.

But let us return to our author and continue the same paragraph :—

"The point, after long notes as well as short notes, in slow time generally indicates that the sound should be sustained. But it happens that in quick movements, when there are many dotted notes in succession, this rule is not followed. It is desirable that in such cases the composers would give all requisite precision to their text. If they have not done so, one may derive much light from the inner meaning of the Piece."

Here another digression is necessary. It will be remembered that according to Quantz's directions (Chap. xvii., Sect. vii., par. 58, given before at page 56) to violin players, the bow should be stopped during the dot, a rest taking the place of the dot or part of the dot. This is so natural that Quantz does not give any further explanations about it. But C. Ph. E. Bach belongs to a newer generation. Not only does he favour new methods of expression, but he endeavours in every way to introduce more precision in the notation.

The rest of the paragraph says :—

"The dots after short notes, followed by notes still shorter, should be sustained :—

"§ 24. The first note of such figures as given below, because they are slurred, will not be so shortly dismissed, when the *Tempo* is moderate or slow, or else too much time would be left to the next note. These first notes require a gentle pressure, not a quick jerk":—

This does not agree with Quantz's rule, given before at page 56. But if we turn to the "Klavierschule" of Daniel Gottlob Türk, published at Leipzig in 1789, and one of the last of these philosophical methods of music, we find the difference greater still. Here are his precepts:—

Page 363, end of § 48: "The figures of which the first note is short and the second dotted are without exception gently slurred and flattered The first certainly takes the accent, but the emphasis should be very gentle (*a*):—

"One must not hurry the first note, particularly in slow movements, so that the melody may not be corrupted in a careless way, or lose its roundness, when the first sound is played so short and the dot moreover transformed into a rest as at (*b*).

"Note: Formerly, one gave the first note of such figures a very short duration, so much so that

Agricola writes: 'When the short note is first, and the dot is after the second, then the first note should be as short as possible, which will render the dotted note more pleasant.' Bach on the contrary says at page 113: 'The first note will not be so shortly dismissed, when the *Tempo* is moderate or slow,' &c."

All this points to a gradual change of style. Quantz, although twelve years younger than J. S. Bach, belonged to his school. Agricola, although very much younger, was a direct pupil of Bach, and followed his master's ideas for a long time. But C. Ph. E. Bach was the leader of the new school; it is he that Türk calls "Bach." At the time of Türk's writing J. S. Bach's music was out of fashion. Therefore Türk's interpretation applies to the C. Ph. E. Bach-Haydn-Mozart period. Quantz and Agricola should be followed for the works of the preceding generation, which includes Danglebert, Couperin, Rameau, Handel, J. S. Bach.

This conventional lengthening of dots and rests does not seem to have been mentioned in books anterior to Quantz. If, however, we remember that double dots or combined rests were not used till the end of the 18th century, that their rhythm is quite natural, and that the music of the 16th and 17th centuries abounds in passages which demand it, we can but feel justified in treating all the old music alike in this respect. Moreover, Quantz does not speak of it as of an innovation. Were modern players less bound by the written text, they never would have played any other way; their instinct would have guided them to the proper interpretation, which is much more natural and beautiful.

We can hardly over-estimate the importance of this knowledge of the meaning of dots and rests in old music, which transforms an apparently ponderous movement into one of majestic beauty or thrilling energy. See, for example, the "Sinfonia" in Handel's "Messiah," as given below:—

The works of Handel abound with similar passages. See, for example, in the "Messiah," "Comfort ye, My people," "Ev'ry valley," "Thus saith the Lord of Hosts," "Behold the Lamb of God," "The Trumpet shall sound," &c., &c. In Bach's "St. Matthew" Passion: "Ach nun ist mein Jesus hin?"; the bass part of "Geduld, wenn mich falsche Zungen," "Erbarme dich," "Komm, süsses Kreuz," &c., &c. And try the following examples from his clavier-music: Prelude in E♭ minor from Book I. of the "Forty-eight Preludes and Fugues":—

or the Fugue in D major from the same work :—

And further, in the same Fugue :—

See also in the chapter on Ornaments the example at page 111.

SECTION II.

The alterations of rhythm to be considered here are not made for the sake of expression ; they are the consequence of imperfect notation, and their interpretation is hardly ever doubtful. One finds whole movements in ternary rhythms written in binary measures: $\frac{4}{4}$ or C doing duty for $\frac{12}{8}$, $\frac{3}{4}$ for $\frac{9}{8}$, and $\frac{2}{4}$ for $\frac{6}{8}$. The figure ♩ ♪ ♩ ♪ is either written ♩. ♬ ♩. ♬, in which case the dot is robbed of part of its value, or ♫ ♫, when the first quaver has to be double the length of the second. The figure ♪♪♪ is then written as a triplet.

Many movements in Corelli's sonatas give the melody correctly, but the bass imperfectly. Here are some examples:—

should be written thus:—

and later:—

should be written thus:—

Sonata VIII. Giga. CORELLI.

should be written thus :—

and later :—

should be written thus :—

Sonata X. Giga. CORELLI.

and later :—

should be written thus :—

Couperin shows an instance of this incorrect writing in the "Fanfare" of the "X Ordre" in his second book of "Pièces de Clavecin." The note is his :—

"Although the values of the Treble do not seem to fit with those of the Bass, it is customary to write thus."

In the following Sonata of Handel, we find that the crotchet unit of time in that movement is divided in turn by *two*, *three*, and *four*, each of the parts being actually of the same length in performance :—

Original :—

should be written thus :—

Instances of this kind of writing are very frequent in Bach. Here are two examples :—

should be played thus :—

Concerto in D major, for Flute, Violin and Harpsichord. J. S. BACH.

should be played thus:—

An amusing case is that of C. Ph. E. Bach, who, in his "Wahre Art das Clavier zu spielen" explains this rule, and gives the following example:—

Tab. VI., Fig. XII.

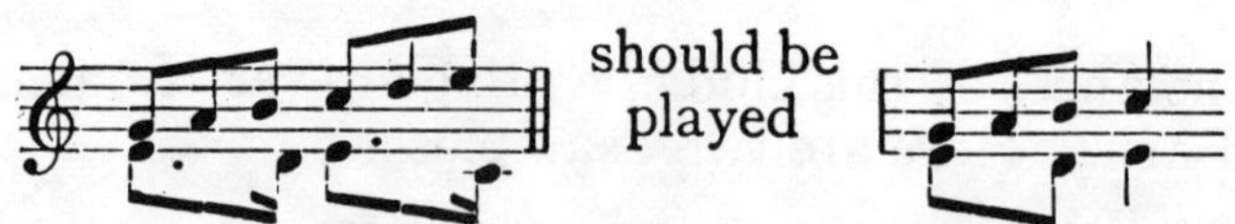

He is apparently unconscious of the fact that his explanation needs explaining, for he makes the first quaver double the length of the second!

This method of writing survived until the beginning of the 19th century. Jean Louis Adam, in his "Méthode de Piano," Paris, An. XII. (1804), gives the following:—

J. L. ADAM.

SECTION III.

§ 1. It frequently happens, in old music, that notes of apparently equal value are to be performed unevenly. Giulio Caccini, in the preface to his "Nuove Musiche" (Venice, 1601) gives the following examples:—

The seventh paragraph of Frescobaldi's "Avertimenti" (see page 6) is another instance of this practice; and the fact that he insists upon the *second* note and not the *first* being dotted in such passages, implies that the reverse way—that is, to dot the *first*—was in common use at the time.

According to Frescobaldi's rule, the following passage, which occurs near the end of the *Toccata secunda* of his second book:—

should be played thus:—

Jean Rousseau, "Traité de la Viole," 1687, speaking of the *Mordent*, which he calls *Martellement*, says:—

"In Common Time, when one plays *even quavers*, the *martellement* should be made on the first half of a beat. . . .

"In *Alla Breve* Time (₵) on *even* crotchets, you must make the *martellement* on the first half of a beat. . . ."

This does not in itself prove that notes of apparently even value were generally played unevenly. But it would not be natural to give another interpretation of the passage; and taken in conjunction with the following statements it becomes very weighty.

Couperin, in the Table of Graces prefacing his first book of Pieces, 1713, mentions a similar practice when he describes the following example thus:—

"Slurs, in which the dots indicate that the second note of each beat must be emphasised." It should therefore be played:—

This is precisely the reverse of what a modern player would do, for to him the slur indicates an accent on the first note, whilst the dot on the second, which lightens it, further confirms this reading. But Couperin's precept is not open to doubt. And *a dot over a note at that time did not mean a staccato.* A dash was used for that purpose.

§ 2. It was more frequent to make the first quaver, the accented one, the longest.

In the "Principes de la Flute Traversière," &c., by Hotteterre-le-Romain (Paris, 1707), we find this at page 24:—

"It will be observed that quavers must not always be played evenly, and that in certain measures there must be a long and a short one; this is regulated by the number. When it is even, the first is to be made long, the second short, and so forth. When it is an odd number, the contrary plan is to be followed. This is called 'to dot' (*i.e., pointer*). The measures in which this is most commonly done are those of two in a bar, the $\frac{3}{4}$ and the $\frac{6}{4}$."

Couperin alludes to the same thing when he says in the passage already quoted: "We write differently from what we play. . . . We play as dotted several quavers following one another by degrees, and yet we write them even."

In two pieces of Couperin's first book the two ways of playing unevenly are contrasted with good effect. They are: "La Badine" and "Les Vendangeuses." The beginning of the first one, given below, will illustrate this point. In such cases not only must one take care not to exaggerate the length of the dots, but on the contrary to make them rather short. Their rhythm should not be hard or too precise. If the long note were double the length of the short, as in a triplet ♩ 3 ♪ or ♪ 3 ♩, the unevenness should be sufficient :—

should be played:—

This uneven playing of passing-notes was so universally understood that when even playing was required the composer gave special directions to that effect.

In the "Avertissement" prefacing the "Second Livre de Pièces de Violes," by Marin Marais, the "privilege" of which is dated 1692, we find the following:—

"EXAMPLE.

"12th Variation on *La Follia*:—

"The dots which are above the notes not slurred indicate that you must make all the notes equal, instead of dwelling on the first and shortening the second, in the usual way. And when there are no dots, in that kind of movement, you may still play as if there were, for the style of the piece sometimes demands it naturally, as, for example, the *Allemandes*, which have no need of this observation. I have only marked these dots in such places as are at all doubtful, and even in the figured basses."

The phrase "above the notes *not slurred*" refers to a preceding explanation about "the dots marked over or under slurred notes," which, he tells us, indicate that "you must articulate all these notes, in one bow, as if they were played with different bowings."

One should note also what he says about the *Allemandes*, which are not subject to the general rule of uneven playing.

This is confirmed by Couperin, who heads the *Allemande* opening the "Second Ordre" of his first book of Pieces by this direction: "Not too slow; and the semiquavers *a very little dotted*." He obviously takes it for granted that in his other *Allemandes*, in which there are no such directions, the semiquavers will be played evenly.

In the third book of "Cantates Françoises," by Clérambault, published at Paris, 1716, we find this interesting direction:—

"All the quavers with dots over them must be even, the others uneven":—

In this piece we have uneven quavers in the usual way, and even quavers specially marked. They occur combined together in the 8th bar. The last quaver in the bass, B, would be played after the last quaver in the treble, which is also B.

Below will be found a list of directions from the works of various composers, which now will be readily understood by the reader:—

Couperin.—"Second Book of Pieces," 1717. 10ème Ordre, first movement: *Rondeau, Bruit de Guerre*, "*Vivement, et les Croches égales.*" In English, "Quickly, and the quavers even."

Couperin.—"Fourth Book of Pieces," 1730. 20ème Ordre. *Air dans le goût Polonais*, "*Vivement, Les notes égales et marquées.*" "Quickly. The notes even and accented." The notes in this piece have dots over them. In the same book: *Les Satires*, "*Gravement, ferme, et pointé*," which means: "Gravely, firm, and dotted," *i.e.*, the quavers uneven.

Marin Marais.—"Pièces de Violes," Third Book, 1717. *Saillie du Caffé*, "*Petits coups d'archet égaux.*" "Bowing short and equal." The notes have dots over them. In the "Fourth Book of Pieces," *Le Labyrinthe*, "*Gayement, Coups Egaux.*" "Merrily, even strokes." The notes also have dots.

De Caix d'Hervelois.—"Pièces de Violes," First Book, *c.* 1725. First Prelude, second part: "*Vivement, nottes égales.*" In the "Second Book of Pieces," *Fantaisie*, "*pointé*": *i.e.*, "dotted," uneven quavers. This direction is very useful, for the style of the piece might induce one to play evenly. In the third book, 1736: *Sarabande*, page 5, "*Croches égales.*"

Rameau.—"Pièces de Clavecin avec une Table pour les Agrémens." Paris, 1731, page 16: *Les Niais de Sologne*, "*nottes égales.*"

Mondonville, Op. 5.—"Pièces de Clavecin avec Voix ou Violon," 1748, page 8: "*nottes égales,*" &c., &c.

The instructions given by Quantz on this subject are most precise and complete. They should be carefully studied. The following paragraph has already been partly quoted. It is worth while to repeat it and complete it here:—

Chap. xi., § 12: "You must, in your execution, know how to make a difference between capital and passing-notes. Capital notes must always, if possible, be more emphasized than passing ones. According to this rule, in pieces of moderate movement, or even in the *Adagio*, the shorter notes should be played somewhat unequally, although to the sight thev appear to be of the same value;

so that you must, in each figure, dwell on such notes as come on the beats, namely the first, third, fifth, and seventh, more than on the passing ones, which are the second, fourth, sixth and eighth; you should not however hold them as long as if they were dotted. By these shorter notes I understand the crotchets in a $\frac{3}{2}$, the quavers in a $\frac{3}{4}$, the semiquavers in a $\frac{3}{8}$, the quavers in a ₵, the semiquavers in a $\frac{4}{8}$. This however does not take place when these notes are mixed with figures of notes quicker still, or half their value, for then it is these quicker notes which should be played unevenly. If, for instance, one played the semiquavers in the following example slowly in the same value, their expression would not be as agreeable as if one stayed a little longer on the first and third of the groups of four, and gave them a slightly louder tone than the second and fourth:—

"But one must except from this rule, rapid passages, in a quick measure, where the time does not allow to play them unevenly, and one can only accent the first of every four. One also excepts all passages which singers must execute quickly and not slurred; for, as each note in such passages for the voice must be made distinct, and marked by a movement of the throat, there is no room for unevenness. Finally, one must except all notes marked with dots or dashes. You should also make the same exception when several notes follow one another upon the same sound, or when there is a tie over notes the number of which exceeds two—namely four, six or eight and lastly all quavers in Jiggs (Gigues). All these must be equal, the one no longer than the other."

Chap. xvii., ii, § 12: " . . . To render with elegance, in a slow movement, such semiquavers as are found in the example below, one must always give more importance, as well for duration as for strength, to the first of the two than to the one following, and here the note B, in the third part of the bar, should be played *almost* as if there were a dot behind it":—

Thus (*a*) should come out approximately as given at (*b*).

There is one more passage in Quantz relating to this subject; it is in Chap. xii., § 12.

The author, explaining how the *Allegro* should be played, says:—

"As to the short rests which are found in the place of the principal notes on the accented beat, you must take care not to play the notes which follow before their time; for example, when out of four semiquavers the first is a rest, you should wait further half as long again as the written value of the rest, because the following note should be shorter than the first. The same should be done with regard to demisemiquavers."

The above brings forward no new fact, but makes it plain that in cases where the first note, in passages requiring uneven playing, is replaced by a rest, the duration of that rest must be augmented, as should be that of the note of which it takes the place.

Dom Bedos, in the book already mentioned at page 1, treats most clearly of this matter, and moreover explains how some notes are "held" and others only "touched." Here is the passage (page 601, § iv.) :—

"*Of the Distinction in First and Second for the Quavers and sometimes for the Crotchets.*

"1422. In the movements in 2, 3 and 4 beats, the quavers are accented in twos, and distinguished in *first* and *second:* this distinction also takes place sometimes for the crotchets. It is as essential to the pricking upon the cylinder as to the execution. The two quavers together make the total value of a crotchet; the one which is supposed to hold the first half of the crotchet is called *first quaver*, and the one which takes the second half *second quaver:* the first is generally *held*, and the second is always *touched;* there is only one case when the *first* ceases to be *held*, it is when it happens to be the same note as the *second*, as they can then be more clearly detached.

"This distinction in *first* and *second* can also take place with the semiquavers of a $\frac{2}{4}$ in a moderate *tempo*, for the reason I gave in § 3. The crotchets also are sometimes liable to this distinction. . . ."

§ v.

"*Of the Inequality of Quavers.*

"1423. After the distinction we have just made of the quavers in *first* and *second*, it is essential to remark upon their *inequality* in most movements.

"Almost always the *first* are longer, and the *second* shorter. I except however the movements where they are marked from 3 to 3, as in the $\frac{6}{4}$ and $\frac{6}{8}$: but in the movements where they are marked from 2 to 2, it is rare that they be equal.

"This *inequality* must vary according to the kind of expression of the air; in a merry tune, it must be more marked than in a graceful and tender air, in a march than in a minuet; there is however many a minuet in which the inequality is as much marked as in a march.

"Taste, or rather the practice of 'pricking,' will make this difference felt. In general, whatever may be this difference between the *first* and the *second*, the *first* are the longest, and the *second* the shortest, in such a way that the two together do not exceed the value of the crotchet they represent.

"There are also many cases where the crotchets are *unequal*, as well as the quavers; the *first* then becoming longer and the *second* shorter; but as this degree of *inequality* varies according to the kind of expression suitable to the pieces of music, the 'pricker' will make a special study of it, especially when it is a case of catching the manner of a composer: one will see later several detailed examples of this in 'La Romance de Mr. Balbastre.'" This Romance is given in the Appendix to the present book.

The Père Engramelle, in the "Tonotechnie," mentioned on page 43, also treats of the inequality of notes in a manner so thorough and scientific as to leave no doubt upon any aspect of it.

Page 32: "There are cases where this difference is one-half, so that you must play the *first* as if they were dotted quavers, and the *second* semiquavers; others where the difference is one-third, as if the *first* were worth two-thirds of a crotchet, and the *second* the other third; others again, where this difference, less noticeable, must be as 3 to 2, so that the *first* will be worth three-fifths of a crotchet and the second two-fifths."

Page 33: ". . . I have observed in pricking cylinders that there are many Marches, among others that of 'Le Roi de Prusse,' where the difference between the *first* and the *second* is as 3 to 1. In certain Menuets, among others the *petit menuet de la Trompette*, the difference is 2 to 1; lastly, in many menuets, the difference is less marked, as 3 to 2, or 7 to 5."

Page 230: "You must observe that all I say upon the inequality of quavers, is only to make you appreciate those inequalities; for there are many places where they vary in the same air; it is left to fine taste to appreciate this variety in these inequalities. A few experiments will make you find the good, and the best, either for the equality or the inequalities; you will see that a little more or less inequality in the quavers *alters considerably the expression of an air*."

The practical application of these principles has far-reaching consequences upon the effect of many familiar pieces. The depth of expression it adds to certain phrases is wonderful. At the same time, it removes a certain heaviness and stiffness, as becomes apparent the moment the right expression is understood.

Many well-known numbers in the "Messiah" can serve as examples. See the 4th, 5th, and 6th bars in "Ev'ry valley shall be exalted"; the semiquavers in "But who may abide the day of His coming?"; the semiquavers in "He was despised"; the semiquavers in "Behold and see," which come on the words "and see" and "sorrow" (in the two places in this air where the second violin and the viola answer the voice, Handel has written the instrumental parts accurately, but the voice part in the conventional way); the semiquavers in "But Thou didst not leave"; the quavers in "If God is for us," &c.

In Bach's "St. Matthew" Passion there are still more numerous cases for the application of this rule. But the reader will find them out. This section shall end with two instrumental extracts from Bach. The first is the Sarabande from the sixth Suite for a five-stringed Violoncello, which is popular through arrangements for all sorts of instruments. The original is given, and a transcription for keyboard with the rhythm written out as it should sound, *or thereabouts;* for it must be remembered that this lengthening and shortening of notes is not bound to mathematical divisions of time. It is perhaps on account of this intended freedom in the execution that the composers did not write it down, as it would thus have assumed too stiff an appearance :—

Here follows another example—the Sarabande from the "Suite Française" No. 1, in D minor. This piece would be still more beautiful, were the proper ornaments added to it. But the question of ornaments must not be anticipated :—

CHAPTER IV.

ORNAMENTATION.

In modern music the ornamentation is practically all incorporated with the text. In the Old Music the ornamentation is sometimes left out altogether, or indicated more or less completely by means of conventional signs. The composer in either case had prepared his music for the ornaments; if we do not use them we are violating his intentions just as much as if we altered his text. It is not even a question whether we like them or not, or whether they are in or out of fashion; they form an integral part of the music. To omit them is just as barbarous as taking off the exuberant decoration of flamboyant Gothic architecture under the pretext that one prefers a simpler style. The ornamentation alters the melody, rhythm, and harmony of the music. Its study is, therefore, indispensable. Like everything in Art, and perhaps more than most things, it has been subject to "modes and fashions"; it would not be right, therefore, to use for a certain piece of music the ornamentation belonging to a different style.

It seems impossible to classify the ornaments logically; there are too many combinations and crosses between the various kinds. Their names, moreover, are a great source of confusion, the same name being often applied to different ornaments, and the same ornament appearing under several names. We shall use the best understood name, and give its principal English and foreign synonyms. Besides, we shall treat of only one kind under each several heading, considering the *thing itself* rather than the name. It is hoped in this way to minimise confusion.

C. Ph. E. Bach, in his "Versuch über die wahre Art das Clavier zu spielen," Berlin, 1753, has a valuable Introduction to the part treating of ornaments. We shall quote here some of its most interesting points.

"§ 1. It is not likely that anybody could question the necessity of ornaments. They are found everywhere in music, and are not only useful, but indispensable. They connect the notes; they give them life. They emphasise them, and besides giving accent and meaning they render them grateful; they illustrate the sentiments, be they sad or merry, and take an important part in the general effect. They give to the player an opportunity to show off his technical skill and powers of expression. A mediocre composition can be made attractive by their aid, and the best melody without them may seem obscure and meaningless.

"§ 2. But in proportion with their usefulness and beauty when properly applied, can they do harm when the wrong ornaments are employed, or their application is not well controlled.

"§ 3. Therefore we should commend those who clearly mark all the ornaments they intend in their pieces, instead of leaving them to the discretion of a possibly incompetent performer.

"§ 4. And here must we give due praise to those French composers who have carefully indicated in their pieces all that is needful for their correct interpretation. Some of the greatest masters of Germany have done the same, though perhaps not so thoroughly as the French . . . .

"§ 8. Those who have skill enough may introduce more ornaments than we indicate; but they must take care that the meaning and expression of the piece are not affected thereby. It must be understood that fewer graces should be used in pieces intended to express sadness, or innocence, than if other sentiments were involved. A man can combine the art of singing upon his instrument with such effects as are proper to instrumental music, and thus stimulate and keep the attention of the listener by constant variety. This can be done without confusing the vocal and instrumental styles. If the ornaments used are chosen with taste, there is no need to trouble whether the passage be singable or not.

"§ 9. In this matter, above all things there must be no exaggeration. The use of graces must not go too far. It is with music as with architecture: the finest building may be overloaded with ornamentation, like a dish which can be spoiled by too much spice. Many notes are good enough in themselves and need no ornaments; the latter ought only to be used on notes requiring special stress and prominence. If all the words of a discourse were equally emphasised, continual monotony would be the result. . . .

"§ 11. . . . Pieces in which the ornaments are indicated do not give any trouble; but when there are few or no signs, the piece must be ornamented according to its proper style. . . .

"§ 13. This matter is so intricate that one should as much as possible develop the ear by carefully listening to good music, and above all obtain a thorough knowledge of harmony. . . .

"§ 14. The singers as well as instrumentists, if they want to render their music properly must use many of the same ornaments as 'clavier' players; but they have not taken the trouble to put order in this matter. They indicate a variety of graces by the help of few signs and give trouble to themselves in that way."

An exception should be made in favour of the French viola da gamba composers such as Marin Marais, the Forquerays, De Caix d'Hervelois and others who have left us the most perfect texts imaginable. But the violinists, Senaillé, Leclair, &c., mostly use only one sign, a little cross or something such, which has to do duty for everything. That they had a strong prejudice against a carefully marked text is proved by the fact that when harpsichord players, like Rameau in his "Concerts en Trio," used a violin or flute, the same phrase which appears carefully ornamented for the harpsichord is left with only a few crosses for the other parts. In the "Pièces de Clavecin en Sonates avec accompagnement de Violon par Mondonville," Op. 3 (1734), the violin part is treated in that way; but the author has added the following note:—

"The ornaments of the violin must be treated like those of the harpsichord."

In the "Pièces de Clavecin avec Voix ou Violon," Op. 5, published a few years later, the ornaments of the voice or violin are marked with the same precise care as those of the harpsichord. The author had probably repented of his former lax practice.

Two more quotations from C. Ph. E. Bach, and we shall begin our study of the various ornaments in detail:—

"§ 16. As the French masters were so admirable in their way of playing ornaments and writing them, it is regrettable that people should begin to leave them aside. The result is that the signs so well known formerly are becoming strange, even in clavier pieces."

We might leave off here, for indeed this points to the beginning of the end, as far as ornaments are concerned! Still, the following quotation must be given, on account of its extreme importance:—

"§ 28. The fact that most of my examples occur for the right hand does not mean that the left should not have its fair share of them; I advise rather that all ornaments should be practised by both hands so that they may be played with the same ease and finish. Ornaments occur in the bass as well as in the treble. Moreover, the player is bound to *ornament all imitative phrases alike, wherever they occur.* The left hand must therefore be well practised to be able to do effectively all sorts of ornaments. Otherwise it would be better to have none at all, for they lose all their beauty when badly played."

SECTION I.

The Appoggiatura.

(Old English: *Forefall*, *Backfall*, *Beat*, *Half-Fall*. French: *Appoggiature*, *Port-de-Voix*. Old French: *Cheute*, *Chute*, *Coulé*, *Accent*. Italian: *Appoggiatura*, *Portamento*. German: *Vorschlag*, *Accent steigend*, *Accent fallend*.)

The appoggiatura is a very important ornament affecting both the melody and harmony. It originated with the lute-players, and was one of their favourite graces. Here are Thomas Mace's directions for its performance:—

Page 104. "The Back-fall Explained.

"A Back-fall, is only Thus: viz. Let your Note be what it will; It must 1st partake of the *Tone of another Note*, or *Half-note* above it, before it sound,

"As for example.

"Suppose I would *Back-fall a*, upon the Treble String, then I must first stop *c*, upon the same String, and strike it, as if I did absolutely intend *c* (only) should Sound; yet so soon as I have so struck *c*, I must, with the stopping finger (only) cause the *a*, to sound, by taking it off in a kind of a Twitch, so that the Letter *a*, may sound, (by reason of that Twitch, or Falling back) presently after the letter *c* is struck. . . ."

Mace, of course, employs the language of the lute tablature. As some might not be familiar with it, it may be well to explain that *a* means the open string, whatever its tuning, and *c* the second fret. As the frets are a semitone apart, there is a distance of a whole-tone between *a* and *c*.

a in that case is the G of the treble clef, and *c* the A above it. The result of Mace's explanations may therefore be transcribed thus :—

It is a short appoggiatura from above; the auxiliary note comes on the beat, and it is accented.

The *Half-Fall* is thus explained :—

"The Half-Fall is ever from a Half-Note beneath, and is performed by striking that *Half-Note* first; but so soon as that is struck, you must readily *Clap down* the *True Note*, (with the *proper finger*, standing ready) without any further striking. Explained thus. Suppose I would make a *Half-Fall* to *f*, upon the Treble (or any other string) I must place a Finger in *e* upon the same String, *and absolutely strike e*, as if *nothing else were intended;* but so soon as *e* has given its *perfect sound*, my next *Finger*, must fall *smartly* into *f;* so that *f* may Sound strongly, only by *that Fall;* which will cause a *Pritty*, *Neat*, and *Soft Sound*, without any other striking, and this is the *Half-fall*."

This translated gives us :—

It is an appoggiatura from below, the auxiliary note on the beat, and *stronger* than the true note, for it is impossible to make a sound as strong, with the finger of the left hand alone falling on the string, as when the note is plucked by the right hand. Guitar players will understand this.

Moreover, the auxiliary note *had* to be short, or else the vibrations of the string might have stopped by the time the next finger fell upon it, in which case the true note would hardly be audible But with the voice and many instruments it was possible to lengthen the auxiliary note at will, and as the effect thus produced was found pleasing the appoggiatura grew at the expense of the main note until it took one-half, two-thirds, and even the whole of its value.

In Bach's time the short appoggiatura was rarely used. It came back into fashion with the next generation. In the 19th century the long appoggiatura had become almost forgotten. Nowadays the majority of musicians still play all appoggiature short and mostly before their time, to the great detriment of the music. A general survey of the question, chronological as far as possible, is the only way to bring light on a point the importance of which could hardly be over-estimated.

Praetorius, in his "Syntagma Musicum," third volume, published at Wolffenbüttel in 1619, gives at page 233 a great many ornaments which he calls "*Accents*," among which are the following true appoggiature:—

The "black semibreves" being the sign of triple time, in our notation it would come to this :—

There is no sign given for the appoggiatura; it is ascending, and takes *one-third* of the value of the main note.

Its introduction was left to the player.

In Playford's "Introduction to the Skill of Music," first edition, 1654, the table of "Graces proper to the Viol or Violin" gives appoggiature from below and above. The first is called "Beat," the second "Back-fall." It will be remembered that Mace calls the first "Half-fall," and gives the name of "Beat" to another ornament. This is the sort of confusion we shall find over and over again all through the nomenclature of ornaments.

Here is Playford's diagram :—

The appoggiatura is played *on the beat*, and takes one-quarter of the value of the main note.

In Christopher Simpson's "Division-Violist," published 1659, there is a table of graces with the following note :—

"For these, I am obliged to the ever famous Charles Colman, Doctor in Musick."

Dr. Colman was a musician of repute; but no more so than Christopher Simpson. Why he should have had to advise Simpson on such a subject remains a mystery.

The table being an exact reproduction of that given in Playford, except that the examples are in the alto clef instead of the treble, we need say no more about it.

In Matthew Locke's "Melothesia," published in 1673, we find:—

The Fore-fall: ⁄. The Back-fall: ∖. No indications are given for their performance.

In Purcell's "Lessons," &c., 1696, the appoggiature are indicated thus:—

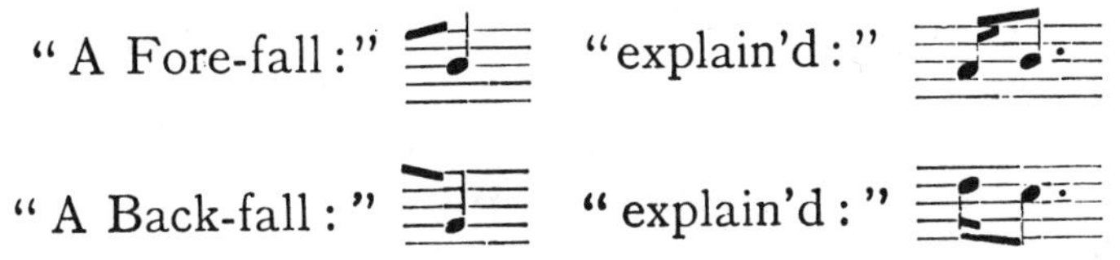

The names and signs are the same as Matthew Locke's; the execution agrees with Playford's, Dr. Colman's, and Christopher Simpson's. No doubt John Jenkins, William Lawes, Dr. Blow, and other English composers of the second half of the 17th century followed the same practice.

In J. C. de Chambonnières's "Pièces de Clavecin," First Book (Paris, 1670):—

the cross [+] used for the appoggiatura is the sign commonly used by other composers of the end of the 17th and all the 18th century for a trill, or indiscriminately for *all sorts of ornaments.* Hence confusion might easily arise. The two semiquavers B which form the appoggiatura make half the value of the principal note, thereby reduced to half its value. The repetition of the auxiliary note B is unusual. The engraved text is so clear that the existence of a mistake could hardly be supposed. Chambonnières uses the appoggiatura sign much more rarely than the other signs, and wherever it is marked its explanation as given above sounds well. However, the point is open to question.

De Machy, "Pièces de Violle en Tablature" (Paris, 1685), says:—

"The *port-de-voix* which is called *cheute* on the Lute and other Instruments is made *by anticipation* from one note to another."

The *cheute* of D'Anglebert, 1689, explained below, is a true appoggiatura, from below or above; but it is not made by anticipation. It is on the contrary clearly marked *on the beat*, and as part of the note to which it belongs.

There seem to have been at all times people who *anticipated* the ornaments, thus making them out of the note preceding the one to which they belonged. In our own time, it is the immense majority who do so. The best composers, the great masters, never did it; they frequently protested against it. And the reason is easy to understand. The auxiliary note is nearly always *a discord*, which when used with taste and *emphasised on the beat with the Harmony*, often produces rich and surprising effects; chords, in fact, which the composers would not have *dared* to write out plainly. The anticipation of the appoggiatura destroys all this.

Appoggiature not indicated by any sign are very frequently used as preparation to a trill or a mordent, in the first case from above, in the second from below. They come on the beat, and take from one-quarter to two-thirds of the value of the main note. (See section "Compound Ornaments.")

Marin Marais, in his "Pièces à Une et à Deux Violes," Paris, 1686, considers it so clear that shakes must be prepared by appoggiature of half their value that he indicates in his figured bass the *chord formed by the appoggiature* with the bass. See the following examples. (The comma *after* a note means a trill; the cross before the note a mordent, and the wavy line [〰] a vibrato. The implied appoggiature in question occur in the fourth and last bars):—

Marin Marais, Sarabande from Second Suite for two Viole da Gamba and Bass:—

The harmony indicated by the figures is:—

but the melody of the two Viols is written thus:—

It would make a horrible confusion with the accompaniment if the Viols did not play thus:—

Jean Henry D'Anglebert, in his "Pièces de Clavecin" (Paris, 1689), gives a "Marque des Agrémens et leur signification," from which the following examples are taken:—

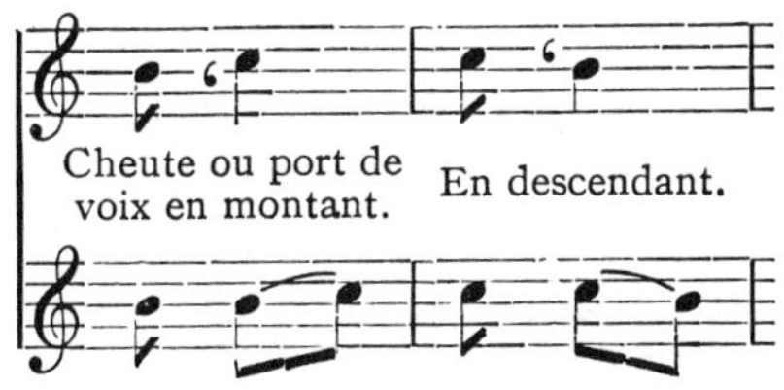

This is the appoggiatura, upwards and downwards, in all its perfection.

In François Couperin's "Pièces de Clavecin," Livre Ier. (Paris, 1713), "Explication des Agrémens, et des Signes," we find this:—

Unfortunately, Couperin is not logical; what he calls "Port de voix simple" is a *port de voix* combined with a *pincé* or mordent, of which latter this [✢] is the sign; and it is the *pincé* which is simple, not the appoggiatura. In the "Port de voix double" it is the *pincé* which is double!

On the other hand his "Port de voix coulée" is a true, simple, upward appoggiatura; it is "coulé," no doubt (*i.e.*, slurred, for *all* appoggiature must be slurred). (The second "e" of "coulée" ought not to be there; it was ungrammatical in 1713, just as it is at present.) Another serious fault with Couperin is that his "Explications" are always given in *small notes*, the values of which are uncertain.

Here are more details from the "Méthode" he published in 1717 (already cited):—

Page 22: "The auxiliary note of a *port de voix*, or of a *coulé*, must strike with the Harmony, that is to say, in the time that ought to be given to the note which follows it."

And again, page 19: "It is the value of the notes which should, in general, determine the length of the *pincés-doubles*, the *ports-de-voix doubles*, and of the *tremblements*."

This implies that his *ports-de-voix*, *i.e.*, appoggiature, have a proportionate relation with the value of the note to which they belong; but he omits to tell us what that proportion is.

The point is, fortunately, better treated by his contemporaries—D'Anglebert, already quoted, and Rameau, to follow.

John Sebastian Bach wrote in 1720 a book of instruction for his son, Wilhelm Friedemann. It is known as "Clavier-Büchlein vor Wilhelm Friedemann Bach." There is in it an "*Explication* showing the Signs, and how the various *Manieren* can be nicely played." (*Manieren* is the general name in German for Ornaments.)

Here follows the appoggiatura and its explanation:—

Bach calls it "*Accent*," a very good name for it, since it does accent the music more effectively perhaps than anything else could. "*Steigend*" and "*fallend*" mean, respectively, *rising* and *falling*. The above demonstrates that Bach's appoggiature are to be played *on the beat*, and that they take half the value of the note to which they belong. The rule is clear, and we possess no other instruction from Bach on the point. Moreover, it agrees with the practice of his contemporaries. These being the only examples he chose to write for the instruction of his son, it follows that they are representative of the majority of cases to be found in his music; and so it proves. The reader can find plenty of examples for himself all through Bach's works. Additional knowledge is, however, needed to meet the cases in which this rule cannot apply.

Besides the short curved line already seen, Bach has two other ways to indicate the appoggiatura: a double curve, from below or above, or small notes of various values—semiquavers, quavers or crotchets. These indistinctively indicate appoggiature, in most cases of half the value of the note to which they belong, but also of *longer* or *shorter* duration, or even *very short* ones, as the case may be. It being of immense importance for the right expression of Bach's music to be able to distinguish between these, we shall try to clear the point with the assistance of Bach's contemporary, Joachim Quantz, whose precepts, here condensed into rules, will help us materially.

1. The appoggiatura to a dotted note takes two-thirds of its value, the principal note coming in the time of the dot.

2. In $\frac{6}{4}$ time, an appoggiatura to a dotted minim tied to another note takes all the value of the first note, the principal note coming in the time of the second. In $\frac{6}{8}$ time the same rule applies to a dotted crotchet tied to another note.

3. An appoggiatura to a note followed by a rest takes the whole value of that note; the principal note is played in the time of the rest.

4. An appoggiatura between two notes of the same pitch must be played very short, on the beat.

5. An appoggiatura to a note of the shortest value used in the piece or passage where it occurs must be played very short.

6. An appoggiatura to a note forming a discord with the bass, augmented fourth, diminished fifth, seventh, second, &c., must be played very short or else the discord will be changed into a concord, and the harmony spoiled.

(A translation of the original wording, with further details, will be found later.)

The following examples show the application of these rules. The text used is that of the Bach Gesellschaft.

Rule I. "Suite Française" No. I, Menuet I.:—

The first appoggiatura follows Bach's only rule, the second our Rule I.

Sonata in E major for Violin alone, Menuet I.:—

"Das wohltemperirte Klavier," vol. ii., Fugue XV.:—

Another beautiful example exists in the introduction to the quartet and chorus "So ist mein Jesus nun," in the second part of the "St. Matthew" Passion; here it is:—

Rule 2. "Das wohltemperirte Klavier," vol. i., Præludium IV.:—

(The last bar of the above example will also serve as illustration for Rule 5.)

Rule 3. "Das wohltemperirte Klavier," vol. ii., Præludium VII. :—

This exquisite but unfortunate Prelude has been tortured by editors in all sorts of ways; some of them felt that the appoggiatura ought to be long, but they did not know how to work it out. It has been done thus:—

The case, however, is of the simplest. Would there were no more troublesome in Bach!

One shudders to think that had the "Preislied" from Wagner's "Meistersinger" been written in the 18th century, there would be barbarians at the present time who would play it thus:—

Rule 4. "St. Matthew" Passion, Part II., Aria for alto, "Erbarme dich," Violino solo part:—

The appoggiatura at N.B. must be played on the beat, and *very short*. This Aria also contains many characteristic cases of long appoggiature.

In the same work the soprano Aria, "Aus Liebe," has the following:—

The appoggiatura at N.B. must be played very short, for the ornament which precedes it does not alter the fact that the note E is practically *before* and *after* it. The appoggiatura E in the next bar must be played long, as a crotchet, in the usual way. The appoggiatura B in the last bar of this example could not be held until the semiquaver rest which follows the principal note, as it should be according to Rule 3, for the harmony would be spoiled thereby. It should be done as a quaver, as thus the plaintive expression of the passage will be preserved.

Rule 5. See the last bar of the example given for Rule 2.

Rule 6. "Das wohltemperirte Klavier," vol. ii., Præludium XIII:—

Execution.
(14)
(15)
(42)
(43)
Execution.
(42)
(43)
tr
(44)
&c.
Execution.
tr
(44)
&c.

The first appoggiatura, bar 1, follows Rule 1.

The appoggiatura in bar 15 follows the present Rule, No. 6. The B♯ principal note forms an augmented fourth with the bass; the appoggiatura C♯ would turn it into a perfect fifth and spoil the harmony. It must therefore be short. The same remark applies to bar 43; the interesting harmony which a long appoggiatura would spoil is the augmented second B—C×. In the next bar, number 44, the two appoggiature are subject to Rule 1.

Although the rules given above are sufficient to solve most appoggiature to be found in Bach's music, still cases will occur where the *spirit* rather than the *letter* of the rule must be sought, as its strict application would be unsatisfactory, or even impossible. Sometimes, the ornamented note is so long that were one-half of it given to the appoggiatura, the sound of the latter would have died out before the end, at least upon a clavichord or harpsichord, and obviously it could not be *slurred* into the principal note. Or again, the harmony might have changed so that the principal note would be meaningless.

A few examples will illustrate this :—

In the opening of the "Loure" from the fifth "Suite Française," the first appoggiatura, according to Rule 2, should be held the whole time of the *dotted minim* to which it belongs, its resolution coming in the time of the following note to which the ornamented note is tied. But the complications brought in by the bass, itself ornamented, render this impossible. In this case, however, one need not look far for the correct solution. The bass part starts in imitation of the treble, and by reason of the sequel the corresponding ornamented note is turned into a dotted crotchet, the appoggiatura to which, according to Rule 1, should have the value of a crotchet. As both appoggiature must be played alike to carry out the imitation, and the second, for obvious reasons, cannot be made like the first, the first must then be made like the second, and played as a crotchet. And, played thus, this appoggiatura sounds long, as it should; for it is long by comparison with the notes that precede it.

The effect of length is further emphasised by the shortening of the quavers which is imperative in that kind of measure, as explained in Chapter III., page 56.

"Loure," from the fifth "Suite Française":—

The next example is from Præludium XVIII., vol. ii., of " Das wohltemperirte Klavier."

The first appoggiatura in bar 2 would fall under Rule 3. the principal note would thus come in the time of the rest; but the resulting harmony would be impossible. The second appoggiatura in the same bar is an ordinary one of half the value of the main note; the nature of the passage makes it obvious that both appoggiature should produce the same rhythmical effect. The first must therefore be treated like the second. A positive proof that this is right is found at bars 44 and 45, where the harmony intended by Bach could not have been clearly expressed by appoggiature, and the passage appears written out in full. The slurs, which are original, leave no doubt as to the composer's intention:—

(2)
etc.
Execution.
etc.
(42)
(43)
(44)

The *Allegro* which follows the long passage in Arpeggios in Præludium III. from the same book contains a series of appoggiature which would either fall under Rule 2 (for this $\frac{3}{8}$ is in reality a $\frac{6}{8}$) or under Rule 1, if bar 6 is taken as a pattern, but are independent of either. At bar 3 the appoggiatura *must be a quaver*, or else the fourth C♯—F♯ would have no resolution. All the appoggiature must be treated alike to carry on the imitations; they must therefore be all of the length of a quaver. They are quite satisfactory thus treated; the effect of length is again produced by contrast with the preceding semiquavers:—

Pier. Francesco Tosi: "Opinioni de' cantori antichi e moderni o sieno osservazioni sopra il canto figurato" (Bologna, 1723). This book was translated into English by John Ernest Galliard. and published in London in 1742 under the title: "Observations on the Florid Song, or Sentiments of the Ancient and Modern Singers." A German translation by J. F. Agricola, a pupil of J. S. Bach, appeared in Berlin in 1757. It does not seem to have been translated into French until 1874, when an excellent translation with annotations was published by Théophile Lemaire under the title "L'Art du Chant."

It contains a chapter on the appoggiatura in which the *length* of this ornament is not even alluded to. It was so clear to everyone in those days! Galliard, in his translation, adds a note on this point which is worth quoting:—

"*Appoggiatura* is a word to which the English language has not an Equivalent; it is a Note added by the Singer, for the arriving more gracefully to the following Note, either in rising or falling. The French express it by two different terms, *Port de voix* and *Appuyer;* as the English do by a *Prepare* and a *Lead.* The word *Appoggiatura* is derived from *Appoggiare*, to lean on. In this sense, you lean on the first to arrive at the Note intended, rising or falling; and you *dwell longer on the Preparation than on the Note for which the preparation is made*, and according to the value of the Note."

In other words, the Appoggiatura is *longer* than the principal note.

Here are two interesting extracts from Tosi's book:—

"Among the ornaments of singing there is none so easy to teach and to learn as the appoggiatura. Besides its own charm, it possesses the unique privilege to be heard often without tiring the auditor, provided it does not go beyond the limits of good taste."

Tosi is right, the appoggiatura is not difficult to master, with good examples. But the difficulty for us is to get these good examples!

"As soon as the pupil will have mastered these precepts, the appoggiature will become so familiar to him with constant practice that, hardly out of his first lessons, he will laugh at those composers who write the appoggiature so as to pass for modern, or to seem to understand the art of singing better than the singers. If these composers are so talented, why do they not write also the 'passages' (divisions, variations) which are much more important and difficult than the appoggiature? If they write the latter not to lose the glorious title of 'Virtuoso alla Moda,' they ought at least to realise that it costs them much less trouble and study. Poor Italy! Tell me, I pray, are the singers of to-day incapable of knowing where the appoggiature ought to be made, if they are not pointed out to them? In my time, one's intelligence alone indicated them. Let an eternal blame fall upon him who first introduced these foreign puerilities into our nation which boasts to teach other peoples the majority of the fine arts, and particularly the art of Singing! How great is the weakness of those who follow such an example! What an insult to you, modern singers, who tolerate such instructions, at the most good for children. The foreigners deserve to be imitated, and esteemed, but only in such things as they excel in."

Some of the French composers—Chambonnières, Marais, D'Anglebert, Couperin, Rameau, and some of the Germans—Muffat, C. Ph. E. Bach,—were most careful to indicate in their music all they thought necessary for its perfect understanding. We are thankful to them now, not only because their music gives us less trouble as soon as their notation is understood, but because they help us to understand the works of those who, like J. S. Bach, Handel, and others, wrote without logic or system, or any apparent idea that their music would ever go beyond the limits of their own circle, where under their paramount influence no misunderstanding was possible. It is curious that so many people, like Tosi, should have actually resented precise notation. They wanted everything left to the performer but the skeleton of the music. The Italians were worse than the others on that point.

In Theofilo Muffat's "Componimenti Musicali per il Cembalo" (Vienna, ?1735) there is a very complete and exact table of ornaments at the end of the book. Muffat gives no names, only signs and their execution. Here are those concerning the appoggiature:—

From J. Ph. Rameau's "Pièces de Clavecin avec une Table pour les Agrémens" (Paris, 1731), we extract the following examples:—

Note the semiquaver tied to the auxiliary note, which shows that the finger must not be raised until the second note is heard. This is to ensure a perfect *legato*. It applies only to the harpsichord or clavichord; on the organ the effect would be intolerable.

Charles Dieupart's "Suittes de Clavecin" were published in Amsterdam and London, but without date. They may be ascribed to the period *c.* 1705. At the end of the "Suittes" is a Table of Ornaments in French and English. Here are the parts of it concerning appoggiature:

"A Treatise of Good Taste in the Art of Musick" was written by Francesco Geminiani, the famous violin virtuoso, and favourite of

King George II. The Privilege was granted in 1739, but the book is dated London, 1749. It contains a table of Graces, from which the following is an extract:—

"Of the *Superior Apogiatura.*

"The Superior Apogiatura is supposed to express Love, Affection, Pleasure, &c. It should be made pretty long, giving it *more than half the length* or time of the Note it belongs to, observing to swell the Sound by Degrees, and towards the end to force the Bow a little. If it be made short, it will lose much of the aforesaid qualities; but will always have a pleasing effect, and it may be added to any note you will:—

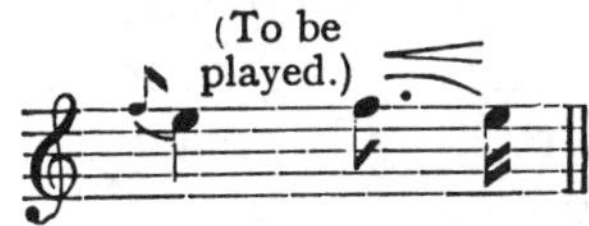

"Of the *Inferior Apogiatura.*

"The Inferior Apogiatura has the same qualities with the preceding, except that it is much more confin'd, as it can only be made when the Melody rises the Interval of a second or third, observing to make a Beat on the following Note:—

These explanations are good, but incomplete. It is well to swell the sound of the appoggiatura, but it obviously must be diminished again on the principal note, or the effect would be absurd and contrary to all that is known about it. It cannot be admitted that the appoggiatura when "made short . . . will always have a pleasing effect. . ." Try it on some of the expressive Bach examples already given, and particularly upon "So ist mein Jesus nun," at page 106. The effect is positively derisive.

In J. J. Quantz's "Versuch einer Anweisung," &c., Berlin, 1752, there is a rich store of information concerning the appoggiatura :—

Chap. 8., § 1. "The 'Vorschläge' (Italian *Appoggiatura*, French *Ports de voix*) are not only ornaments, but also a very necessary thing. Without them the melody would be often dry and plain. If a melody is to have a polished appearance, it must contain more concords than discords. However, when after several concords in succession comes a long concord, the ear might easily become tired. The discords must sometimes excite and re-awake it. This is what the appoggiature may help to do, because they change a third into a fourth, a sixth into a seventh, and resolve it on the following note.

"§ 2. They are written in small notes, so they may not be mistaken for ordinary notes, and they take their value from the notes before which they are found. It does not matter much whether they be semiquavers, quavers, or crotchets. However, it is usual to write them as quavers, and one uses semiquavers only before notes from which none of the value can be taken; for example, before one or more long notes, be they crotchets or minims, if they are of the same pitch :—

These semiquavers must be expressed very briefly, whether they come from below or above, and they must be played on the beat, in the time of the principal note.

"§ 3. The appoggiature, being a retardation from the preceding note, may be taken from above or below, according to the note which precedes (*see* Exx. 1 and 2). When the preceding note is one or two degrees higher than the one which has an appoggiatura, the latter must be taken from above (*see* Ex. 3). But if the preceding note is lower, it must be taken from below (*see* Ex. 4); and it is mostly a ninth resolved upon a third, or a fourth ascending to a fifth:—

"§ 4. The tongue should gently mark the appoggiature, swell them if the time allows, and slur the following note a little more softly. This kind of ornament is called 'Abzug' (French *Accents*), and comes from the Italians."

The fifth and sixth paragraphs treat of a kind of passing-note which the author calls "Passing appoggiature" and which are essentially different from true appoggiature. We shall consider these later.

"§ 7. Appoggiature are found on a long note on the accented beat which follows a short one on an unaccented beat (*see* Ex. 5). One must hold the appoggiatura half the value of the principal note as at Ex. 6.

"§ 8. If the appoggiatura belongs to a dotted note, the latter is divided in three parts, of which the appoggiatura takes two and the principal note only one, that is, the value of the dot. Thus the notes at Ex. 7 must be played as indicated at Ex. 8. This rule, as well as the one given in the preceding paragraph, is general, whatever may be the value of the notes, and whether the appoggiature come from above or below the principal notes :—

"§ 9. When in a six-four or six-eight, two notes are tied together, and the first has a dot after it, as happens in the Gigues, one must hold the appoggiatura the whole value of the dotted note (*see* Exx. 9 and 11). They are played as at Exx. 10 and 12, and do not follow the rule given in § 8. These kinds of measures must be considered in relation with the appoggiature as if they were binary, and not ternary measures :—

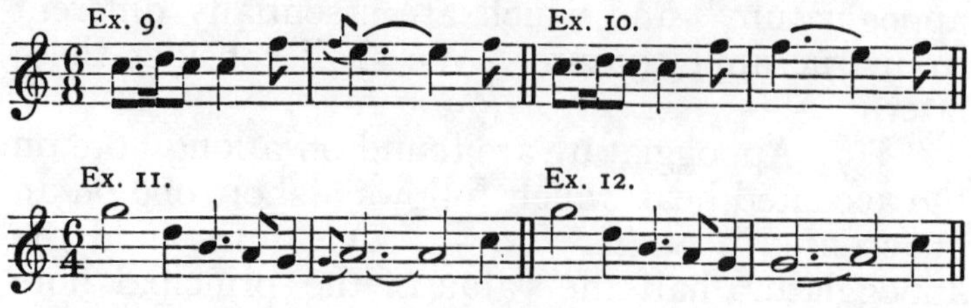

"§ 10. When there are shakes on notes which form a discord to the bass, be they augmented fourth, diminished fifth, or seventh, or second (*see* Exx. 13, 14, 15, 16), the appoggiature must be made very short, so that the discords may not be changed into concords. For example: If the appoggiatura of Ex. 15 were held half as long as the G♯ which follows with a shake, one would hear, instead of the seventh G♯—F, a sixth A—F, and in consequence there would be no more discord. This must be avoided as much as possible, so as not to spoil the beauty and pleasure of the harmony:—

"§ 11. When there is an appoggiatura to a note followed by a rest, you must give to the appoggiatura the whole time of the principal note, and to the latter the time of the rest, unless you absolutely must take breath. The three kinds of appoggiature at Ex. 17 are played as at Ex. 18:—

"§ 12. It is not sufficient to know how to play the appoggiature according to their nature, when they are marked; you must also know where to place them rightly when they are not written. Here is a rule showing how to do it. When after one or several short notes on the down or up beat comes a long note which is a concord, you must make an appoggiatura before the long note to keep the melody pleasant; the preceding note will show whether the appoggiatura must come from above or from below.

"§ 13. The following example comprises most kinds of appoggiature. To be convinced of their necessity and of the excellent effect they produce, you have but to play this example with the appoggiature as indicated, and to omit them afterwards; the difference of taste will then be distinctly seen. You will see also by this example that the appoggiature are mostly used before notes preceded or followed by quicker ones, and also that most shakes require an appoggiatura."

The first two appoggiature of bar 8 are of the "passing-note" kind, and so is the first of bar 13, although the latter might be treated as a long one. It may be remarked here that in doubtful cases the long appoggiatura is most likely to be the best. The "passing" appoggiature are explained at page 149.

Quantz gives a number of "Kleine Manieren" to adorn the appoggiature in this example; although they are not in order here, anticipating their respective explanations, it was thought better to give them, as otherwise his instructions would not be complete. Care should be taken to place the ornaments according to the letters in both examples. (*a*) and (*b*) are shakes: page 154. (*c*) (*d*) (*f*) (*g*) are mordents: page 209. (*e*) is a turn: page 224:—

Some interesting examples of appoggiature are found in Fr. Wilh. Marpurg's "Die Kunst das Clavier zu spielen," published at Berlin in 1750. A French translation, revised and augmented, and with engraved examples, appeared at Paris in 1755. We shall quote from the latter.

Marpurg began to introduce the method (afterwards perfected by C. Ph. E. Bach) of giving to the small note indicating the appoggiatura the value it really ought to have. These small notes appear therefore in the form of minims, crotchets, quavers, semiquavers, dotted notes of all values.

It is interesting to see in Marpurg's table the old signs—cross, comma, and lines indicating half-long appoggiature, as in Playford; Locke, Purcell, &c.; the small notes of indistinct value indicating long appoggiature, as in Couperin and Bach; and the small notes with a precise meaning as in C. Ph. E. Bach:—

Lentement.

C. Ph. E. Bach, in his "Versuch," &c., already quoted, has given an exhaustive treatise on the appoggiatura. The art of ornamentation, and particularly the use of the appoggiatura, had attained their fullest development with him. Many of his examples would never find place in music earlier than his. He himself has been so careful in noting down the exact performance of the appoggiature in his own music that it might seem unnecessary to reproduce all his instructions. He has shown not only how to interpret written appoggiature, but demonstrated by examples where they should be placed in incomplete texts. Besides, he confirms, enlarges, and deepens the precepts given by his forerunners. At the present time, however, when so much ignorance, and, —worse still, so many wrong notions prevail,— one could hardly fear to be accused of shedding too much light on the subject. As was said before, Marpurg, and probably others, had started the idea of writing the appoggiature with small notes of the value they intended them to have. C. Ph. E. Bach adopted and systematized this plan. As a result, we can always know how to play his appoggiature by examining the value of the small notes used as signs. He did not find it necessary, therefore, in the examples in his book, to write out in full, in measured notes forming part of the bar, how these appoggiature should be played, unless there was some special point to elucidate.

We shall do the same here; his examples will be reproduced as he gave them, excepting that the C clef on the first line will be replaced by the more familiar G clef.

And once again, at the risk of redundancy, let it be well understood that C. Ph. E. Bach's method of indicating the value of the appoggiatura does not apply to earlier composers, not even to J. S. Bach, his father!

"Chap. II. 2: On Appoggiature.

"§ 1. Appoggiature are among the most important graces. They improve the melody as well as the harmony. Their effect is grateful, for they smoothly connect the notes; by them such notes as might feel too long are shortened, and similarly they delight the ear by repeating a preceding sound. It is well known that in music the timely repetition of a sound is pleasant. In other ways, they bring variety to the harmony which without these appoggiature might seem too simple. It is possible to trace back all suspensions and dissonances to these appoggiature; and what would harmony be without both these things?

"§ 2. Appoggiature are partly written as ordinary notes, forming part of the bar, and partly indicated with small notes which do not seem to affect the value of the main note, although in the execution the latter always loses some of its value.

"§ 3. The little that need be said about the former will be mentioned later; we shall treat principally here of the latter. Both kinds occur as well from above as from below.

"§ 4. These small notes are either of various durations, or else always short.

"§ 5. In view of the first mentioned case, people began not very long ago to write these appoggiature according to their true value, whereas formerly they were all written as quavers (*see* Exx. 1, 2):—

"At that time appoggiature of such various durations had not yet been introduced. With the present taste, however, we could not well do without a precise notation, since the rules for determining their value are inadequate on account of the variety of notes to which they may belong.

"§ 6. We see from Exx. 3 and 4 that an appoggiatura may be a repetition of the preceding note or otherwise (Exx. 5 to 12), and that the following note may proceed by degree, ascending or descending, or by skip:—

* This example is one of the exceptions. The author does not explain it here, but in paragraph 16, where it is repeated.

"§ 7. We learn further from these examples (Exx. 1 to 12) how they should be performed. All appoggiature are played louder than the following note with its ornaments (if any), and are slurred with it, whether it be so written or not. These two points are in keeping with the spirit of the appoggiatura, since by their means the notes are smoothly connected together.

"The appoggiatura must also be held until the following note is sounded, so as perfectly to slur the two together. The expression, when a simple soft note follows an appoggiatura, is called 'Abzug' (French *Accent:* literally, 'dying off').

"§ 8. As the signs for the appoggiatura and the trill are almost the only ones understood by everybody, they are generally given. But as this cannot always be depended upon, one should try to learn where to place these varying appoggiature.

"§ 9. Besides what we have already seen in § 6, appoggiature of varying durations also occur in common time on down beats (Ex. 13), and on up beats (Ex. 14); in triple time on the down beat only (Ex. 15), and always before a fairly long note.

"They are also found before a final trill (Ex. 16), before a half-close (Exx. 17, 18, 19, 20), before a *caesura* (Exx. 21, 22), before a pause (Ex. 23), before the key-note following a trill (Ex. 24), or on the final note without a preceding trill (Ex. 25). We see by example (Ex. 24) that after a trill the appoggiatura from below is better than from above; therefore the case of Ex. 26 would not sound well.

"Long dotted notes sometimes bear this kind of appoggiatura (*see* Ex. 27). But even though they be marked with short notes, their tempo must still be moderate :—

"§ 10. Varying appoggiature from below do not often occur otherwise than where they are a repetition of the preceding note; but those from above are used in many other ways.

"§ 11. According to the usual rule concerning the value of these varying appoggiature, we find that they take half the value of the following note in common time (Exx. 28, 29, 30, 31) and two-thirds in triple time (Exx. 32, 33). But the following examples are worthy of remark (Exx. 34 to 39)."

(The author does not give the rules regulating these appoggiature; those concerning Exx. 34, 36, 37, 39 have been given by Quantz (at page 126, § 9). Exx. 34 and 38 can be understood if we notice that the *rhythm* of the figures would be obscured were the appoggiature treated in the usual way. They might be made short, but obviously the author desired the effect of a long appoggiatura. Therefore his is the only solution. In this way the *relative* value of the notes of the rhythmical figures at least is preserved, though their speed is doubled.)

"Exx. 40, 41, 42, frequently occur. The method of writing them is not the best, since the rests cannot be observed. It would be better to add dots or use longer notes:—

(The following paragraphs concern *short* appoggiature only; the kind called by the author "unchanging," because they are always short. He might have called his "varying" appoggiature *long*, since they are always so, though not always of the same length, and the others *short*, thus avoiding all possibility of misunderstanding. Anybody would see the difference between *long*

and *short*, whilst the terms *varying*, *variable*, &c., have already caused some to muddle up the whole affair. However, he did not do so, and it was thought best to keep as near as possible to the original text.)

"§ 13. It is only natural that the unchanging *short* appoggiature should occur frequently with short notes. *See* Exx. 43, 44, 45, 46:—

They are written as semiquavers, demisemiquavers, or even shorter notes, and are played so rapidly that the following note hardly loses any of its value. However, they are also used before long notes; sometimes when a note is repeated several times in succession, Exx. 47, 48, and otherwise also, Ex. 49; before a *caesura*, in connection with a short note, Ex. 50; with syncopations, Ex. 51; with tied notes, Ex. 52; in slurred passages, Exx. 53, 54, 55. The character of the principal notes in these examples remains unaltered:—

"Ex. 56 with appoggiature from below sounds better when the appoggiature are played as quavers. It remains to be said that in all examples concerning *short* appoggiature, the latter must remain short, even when the example is played slowly.

"§ 14. When the appoggiature fill up skips of thirds, they are also short (Ex. 57). In an *Adagio*, however, the expression is more flattering if they are played as a quaver forming part of a triplet, and not as semiquavers. The division of the time is shown at Ex. 58:—

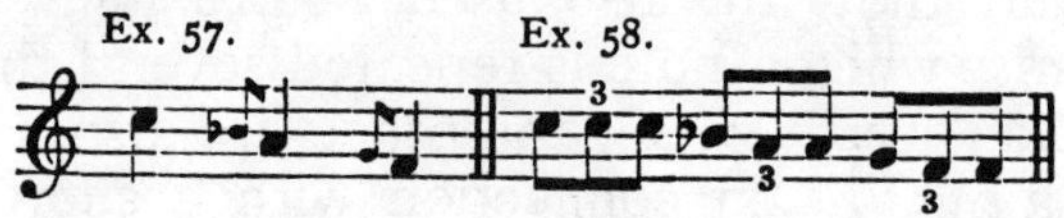

"Sometimes for certain reasons the conclusion of a phrase must be interrupted; the appoggiatura must then be very short:—

"The appoggiature before triplets are played short (Ex. 60) so that the character of the triplet may not be obscured and a confusion brought about with the sort of figure shown at Ex. 61 :—

"When the appoggiatura forms an octave with the bass it cannot be long, or otherwise the harmony would be too weak (Ex. 62); but if it were a *diminished* octave, it might be made long (Ex. 63) :—

"If a note rises a second and immediately returns, either by an ordinary note or by an appoggiatura, a short appoggiatura will gracefully spring on the middle note (Exx. 64, 65) :—

"In Exx. 66 to 92 there are many appoggiature on all kinds of notes in duple and triple time. In Ex. 66 a long appoggiatura would also be possible.

"As *staccato* notes must always be played more plainly than *legato* notes, and as the appoggiatura must always be slurred with the following note, it stands to reason that in all the examples the *legato* is understood.

"Let it be said, moreover, that with all ornaments a moderate tempo is required, because ornamentation is not effective if the speed is too great.

Ex. 66.
Ex. 67.
Ex. 68.
Ex. 69.
Ex. 70.
Ex. 71.
Ex. 72.
tr
Ex. 73.
Ex. 74.
Ex. 75.
Ex. 76.
Ex. 77.
Ex. 78.
Ex. 79.
Ex. 80.
Ex. 81.
Ex. 82.
Ex. 83.
Ex. 84.
Ex. 85.
Ex. 86.
Ex. 87.
Ex. 88.
Ex. 89.
Ex. 90.
Ex. 91.
Ex. 92.

"In Ex. 93, where a short note is followed by a long note of *uneven value*, an appoggiatura would not sound well. We shall see later another kind of ornament which would be more effective :—

"§ 16. Besides the directions already given regarding the value of appoggiature, there are cases where the passionate feeling of the phrase demands an appoggiatura longer than usual, and consequently of more than half the value of the following note (Ex. 94) :—

"Sometimes the duration of the appoggiatura is determined by the harmony. If, in Exx. 95, 96. the appoggiature were played as crotchets, the fifth and the third quaver of every bar would be very crude, whilst in Ex. 97 plain consecutive fifths would be the result :—

"In the following example (Ex. 6, reproduced from p. 134) the appoggiatura must be no longer than a quaver, otherwise the seventh thus produced (G—F) would sound too crude:—

"§ 17. In using appoggiature, as well as other ornaments, care must be taken not to injure the purity of the composition. For this reason it would not be right to imitate Exx. 98 and 99. It would be better, therefore, to write all appoggiature according to their true value:—

(Note: the two consecutive octaves in Ex. 98 and the two consecutive fifths in Ex. 99.)

"§ 18. All these appoggiature, with their 'Abzug,' especially when they occur frequently, produce a singularly good effect in very expressive places, because they die away as it were in a *pianissimo* (Ex. 100):—

(Note: the cross + is equivalent to *tr.*)

"In other instances, however, they might weaken the melody, unless the following note receives a lively ornament, or they are themselves ornamented.

"§ 20. When an appoggiatura has been ornamented it is preferable to leave the following note plain; such simplicity agrees well with the *morendo* effect proper to it. A plain appoggiatura, on the contrary, may have its main note ornamented (see Ex. 101 for an example of the latter and Ex. 102 for the former):—

"§ 20. As these ornamented appoggiature often require additional small notes, they introduce other ornaments which are explained later; it is usual in such cases to write the appoggiatura in full as part of the bar (see Ex. 103). In slow movements the appoggiatura as well as the main note may at times be ornamented (see Ex. 104):—

"§ 21. Appoggiature are often written in full, so that neither they nor the main note may be ornamented:—

"§ 21. Although the notes following an appoggiatura lose some of their value, yet they do not lose their ornament, should one be placed over them (Ex. 106). On the other hand the ornament must not be marked over the note which indicates the appoggiatura. The sign should be placed where it belongs. If the ornament is to be executed between the appoggiatura and the main note, it must be placed between them (Ex. 107):—

"§ 23. Before appoggiature from above, which have been written out in full, additional appoggiature both long and short can sometimes be used when the preceding note is repeated (*see* Exx. 108, 109), but not when the written appoggiatura stands before the final note of a phrase. Ex. 110 shows the bad effect of such a case":—

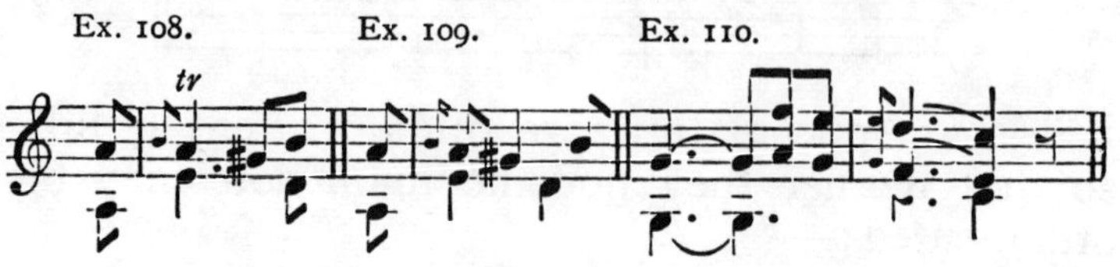

(Here the author has gone too far and himself given a bad example, for the appoggiature at

Exx. 108 and 109 weaken the harmony and fall under the rule he has exemplified at Ex. 62, and which Quantz has expressed better (see page 126, § 10). But at that time the appoggiatura fashion had become a craze. When rules are given for applying appoggiature to appoggiature, it ought to be time to stop.)

"Written-out appoggiature from below cannot admit additional appoggiature, whether from above or below (Ex. 111); but they could be followed by one (Ex. 112):—

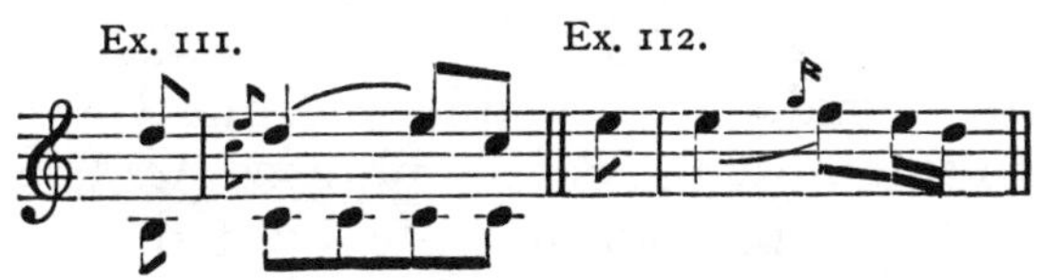

"§ 24. There are other faults concerning appoggiature which we shall consider here. The first is when, after a short trill, an appoggiatura is introduced from above at the close (see Ex. 26 *ante*)." [It is not clear why the author reiterates here the rule already given in connection with that example.] Should the trill come after an appoggiatura, the following note descending (Ex. 113) or ascending (Ex. 114) could stand an appoggiatura:—

(NOTE: The + is equivalent to *tr*.)

"The second fault is when the appoggiatura becomes separated from the main note either because it has not been sustained enough or has been joined to the preceding note and taken out of its time (Exx. 115, 116) :—

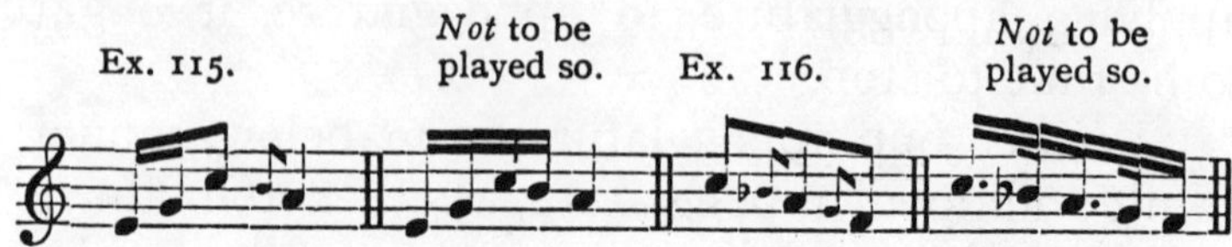

"§ 25. From this last fault have proceeded those hateful 'springers' (German *Nachschläge*) which are so abnormally fashionable and, alas! are often added to the most melodious phrases (*see* Exx. 117, 118). If such appoggiature are wanted, they may be rendered more tolerable by being played as indicated below :—

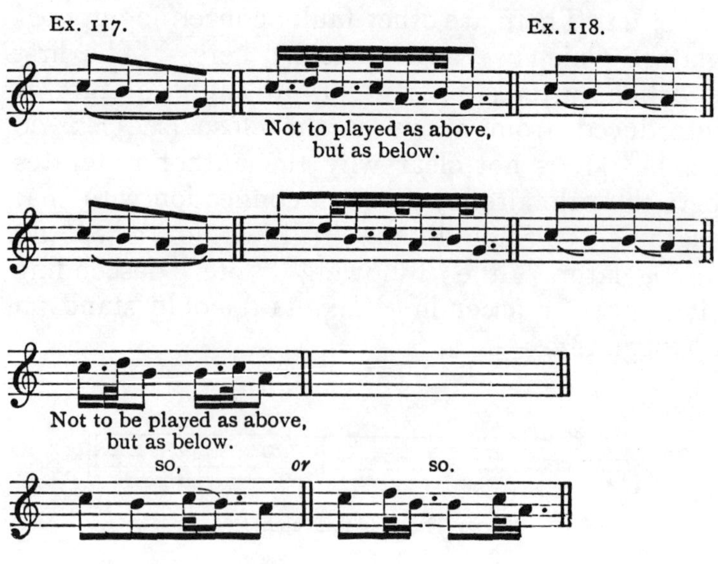

"It will be seen from these examples that you can avoid such faults by turning these *Nachschläge* into *Vorschläge* (appoggiature proper)."

(*A protest.*—The rendering condemned by the author at Ex. 116 is used by many excellent musicians, J. S. Bach included. It is nothing else but the "Passing appoggiature" to be seen later. The "hateful *Nachschläge*," as he calls them, have been in use under the names of Springer, Acute, Sighs, Accents, Aspiration, &c., from the beginning of the 17th century, and probably earlier. That C. Ph. E. Bach should dislike them is allowable; he was not forced to use them in his works. But his advice that they should be turned into something else when they occur elsewhere cannot be approved of. He shows himself distinctly in advance of his time in taking such liberties with other people's music.)

Passing Appoggiature.

These ornaments, probably because they were marked with the same signs as appoggiature, have been confused by nearly all writers with the true appoggiature, although they are quite different in nature. Quantz speaks of them as follows:—

"Chap. viii., § 5. There are two kinds of appoggiature. The first are played like accented notes on the accented beat; the others like unaccented notes on the off beat. The first could be called "beating" (German *anschlagende;* French *frappant*), the second "passing" (German *durchgehende;* French *passager*).

"§ 6. The passing appoggiature are found when several notes of the same value descend by skips of thirds (see Ex. 1). They must be played as seen at Ex. 2 :—

"One must hold the dots, and accent the first of the two slurred notes, that is to say, the second, fourth, sixth, &c. This kind of figures must not be confused with those where the dot comes *after* the second slurred note, and which express almost the same melody (see Ex. 3). In these figures, the

second, fourth, and the following short notes strike on the accented beat, like *discords* against the bass; and so they are played boldly and quickly. On the contrary, the passing appoggiature in question demand a flattering expression. If, then, the appoggiatura in Ex. 1 were made long and accented, and its value taken out of the following note, the meaning would be completely altered and become like that of Ex. 4. This would be quite in opposition to the French style of playing, from which these appoggiature are derived, and contrary to the intention of their inventors, who have won general praise with regard to them."

The passing appoggiature are amongst the "Accents" in Prætorius's tables, already mentioned (page 95) (see Exx. 5, 6) :—

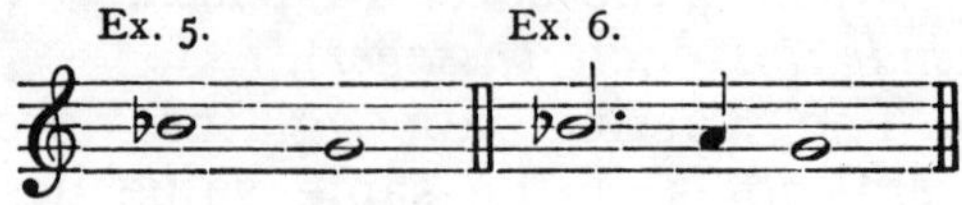

Marpurg, 1750, already quoted, turns the hooks of the small notes indicating the *passing appoggiature* to the left, pointing towards the preceding note out of whose time they are to be taken, to distinguish them from true appoggiature. He also uses them in ascending passages. His examples are as follows:—

Leopold Mozart, "Gründliche Violinschule," 1756, says: "Passing appoggiature (*Durchgehende Vorschläge*). These appoggiature do not take their time from the main note following, but they must be made out of the time of the preceding note (Ex. 9):—

(The signs ⊔ ∧ will be understood by violinists as meaning *up* and *down* bows.

Daniel Gotlob Türk, in his "Klavierschule oder Anweisung zum Klavierspielen für Lehrer und Lernende, mit Kritischen Anmerkungen" (Leipzig, 1789), the latest book worth consulting about old music, gives the execution of such figures both as true appoggiature and as *passing appoggiature* (Ex. 10, *a*, *b*).

He says in a note: "Formerly these *Nachschläge* were indicated by small notes with their hooks reversed" (Exx. 10, 11, 12):—

We shall now consider a few passages in J. S. Bach's works where the passing appoggiature occur:—

Das wohltemperirte Klavier, vol. ii., Præludium XXIII.

&c.

Another is the " Aria " which served as theme for the thirty variations known as " The Goldberg " :—

The first appoggiatura in bar 2 is of the passing kind. It fills up a skip of a third and is on the unaccented beat. The second in the same bar is of the ordinary kind, a long one; it comes before a long note on an accented beat.

At bar 7 Bach has written in full the short appoggiature he wanted, for fear one might play them as passing-notes, and destroy the meaning.

At bar 12 the case is similar to that of bar 2. There would naturally be an appoggiatura on the C♯, to start the ornament.

At bar 18 the *passing* appoggiature would not fit; the first one must be *on the beat*, since the time it would have to take if played before the beat is already filled. The passage answers to that in bar 7. On the G, second beat of the bar, occurs a long appoggiatura subject to the ordinary rule for dotted notes. The G, last note in the bar, has to be turned into a semiquaver to keep the relative values of the figure ♩. ♪. (See C. Ph. E. Bach, § 11, page 137.) It would have to be shortened in any case, according to the usual lengthening of dots in such movements.

In bar 25 the conditions are the same as in bar 2.

SECTION II.—The Shake or Trill.

Half-shakes, Sudden shakes. Italian: *Groppo*, *Trillo*, *Tremoletto*. French: *Tremblement*, *Cadence*, *Trille*, *Pincé renversé*. German: *Triller*, *Pralltriller*

These names have been used for various kinds of ornaments. The shake we shall consider here was the chief grace of Chambonnières, Purcell, Couperin, Rameau, J. S. Bach and his sons, and practically all the musicians of the 18th century. It continued well into the 19th century; in fact, until the advent of the pianoforte virtuosi.

Its chief characteristics are :—

1. A principal note, part of the harmony, and an auxiliary note a whole-tone or a semitone above it.
2. The rapid alternation of these two notes so arranged rhythmically that the accent falls upon the upper note, at least at the beginning.

The shake is closely allied to the appoggiatura from above. It can be used in the same places, the latter often serving as a preparation to it. It is derived from the "Divisions" and "Groppi" of the 16th century. Sylvestro di Ganassi, in his Treatise upon the Flute, entitled, "La Fontegara, &c.," published at Venice in 1535, has examples of perfect shakes amongst his "Divisions." Here is one :—

GANASSI, 1535.

A shake identical with this one, showing the same number of notes and the same termination, exists not only amongst J. S. Bach's own examples but in those of almost every writer. from D'Anglebert to the end of the 18th century. It should be remarked that the number of repercussions was left to the player's discretion, in the early days when the shakes were, or rather appeared to be, written out in full, as well as in later times, when they were indicated by a sign or even not marked at all.

Diego Ortiz' "Trattado de glosas, &c.," Rome, 1553, has the following shake :—

DIEGO ORTIZ, 1553.

Luigi Zacconi, "Practica di Musica," Venice, 1592, has the following ornament, which to the eye is a prolonged shake, but if one considers the "ground" upon which it works, is a *mordent* upon the B, a real shake upon the A, and becomes a *mordent* again upon the G♯:—

LUIGI ZACCONI, 1592.

Girolamo Diruta, "Il Transilvano," Venice, 1597, has real shakes amongst his divisions. The second in the following examples is identical with Bach's "Doppelt Cadenz," and was frequent in the 18th century:—

G. DIRUTA, 1597.

The example from Andrea Gabrieli's "Canzon Ariosa," 1605 given below, shows a true shake:—

Canzon Ariosa, 1605. A. GABRIELI.

Written-out shakes occur frequently in the virginals and organ music of the period 1530-1650; but these are surrounded by other ornaments which, although resembling shakes, do not possess their chief characteristic.

The ornaments *under the slurs* (*a*), (*b*), (*c*), (*d*) in the following extracts from John Bull's "Queen Elizabeth's Pavan," are all true shakes, but the others are not. In the first bar, during the third beat, the ornament is a *mordent;* the change in the harmony on the fourth beat would make it a true shake if it were continued beyond its written value, which would be quite in order, according to the custom of the time.

In the second bar, the first half of the third bar, and such other places, we find only divisions resembling shakes:—

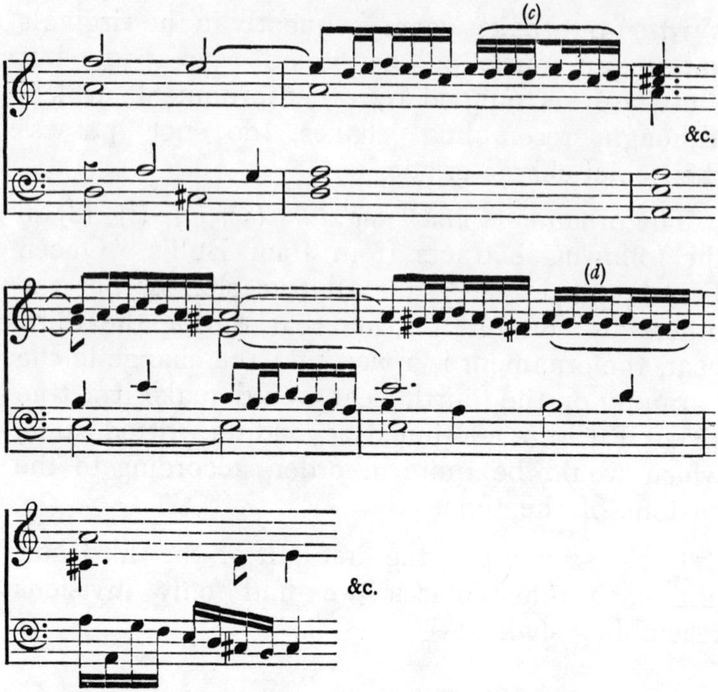

These shakes are not common in the English music for other instruments at that period. The virginal players were leaders of the fashion. Here is an example from Daniel Norcombe (*e*). It is one of the three or four to be found amongst twenty-nine important sets of Divisions by him :—

Divisions on a Ground. DANIEL NORCOMBE, *c.* 1605.

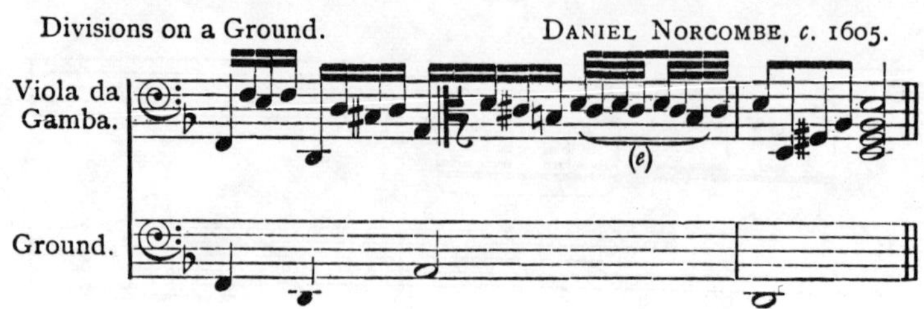

Later, these shakes became more common. The Divisions of Christopher Simpson contain a great many.

Among the "Groppi" of Prætorius, 1619, are some true shakes. (See Ex. (*a*).) At Ex. (*b*), as the theme varies from one to the other of the two notes forming the shake, it results that during the first crotchet there is a true shake, during the following minim a mordent, and a shake again in the following crotchet:—

With Frescobaldi, 1615, the conditions are the same as with the English virginal writers. There are true shakes, fully written out, and many divisions resembling shakes. A small *t* frequently found on *short* notes is the sign for an ornament which in most cases requires the upper auxiliary, but starts on the main note and therefore is not a true shake. Most of the shakes we have seen, so far, occur on closes where the harmonic conditions resemble those of a later period. The earlier music, based on descant and counterpoint, does not lend itself to appoggiature and shakes. These ornaments can only flourish upon a concordant harmony, which they transform and enrich by adding to one of the elements of the chord the flavour of the discord next above it: the fourth to the third, the sixth to the fifth, the seventh to the sixth, the ninth to the octave.

The divisions, on the contrary, do not alter the notes of the subject or counterpoint. They repercuss and embroider them, they fill the spaces between them with passing-notes, but they have to start from and return to them. It is possible, and indeed frequent, to play both the subject and the division together, an impossible thing with the ornaments of the succeeding period.

From the middle of the 17th century the shake began to establish itself, and a long list of documents containing precise instructions on the subject is available. It begins with Playford's "Introduction to the skill of Music," 1654:—

(NOTE.—The *Backfall* is an appoggiatura. The *Elevation* is a slide, preparing a turned shake. In the *Cadent* the beginning is again a slide, but the end of the shake is plain.)

The first shake is not finished: its sequel is left to the imagination; the second finishes in an appoggiatura from below, of medium length, as is usual with the English composers of that time.

In Christopher Simpson's "The Division Violist," 1659, table of graces by Dr. Colman (see page 96), the shakes are the same as above.

With the lute-players the shake was a very important grace; their plain shake, however, began on the main note and was not therefore a true shake. It is described at page 202. But their shake was often combined with an appoggiatura, and then it became a true shake. Here is what Thomas Mace (1676) says about the *Backfall shaked*, as he calls it. He is representative of the other lute-players of that time:—

Page 104: "Now you must know that the Back-fall may be either Plain or Shaked; if Plain, you have done it already, by the last Direction.

"If *Shaked*, then *Thus*, viz.

"When you have given it that *Twitch*, (I have not a fitter word to give it) you must *Shake* it, either with the *Loud*, or *Soft* Shake afterward, as if it had not been *Back-fall'd;* and This, is likewise sufficient for It."

In the "Pièces de Clavecin" of Chambonnières, Paris, 1670, the following shake is given:—

The indentations of the sign, which begin larger than they finish [sign] indicate graphically the true performance of the shake, which should begin slow and gradually increase in rapidity.

Le Bègue, in his "Pièces de Clavecin," Paris, 1677, gives the same shake as Chambonnières.

De Machy, in his "Pièces de Viole," Paris, 1685, says:—"The shake (*Tremblement*) must be prepared according to the value of the note, and played evenly." In other words, it begins with an appoggiatura.

In Jean Rousseau's "Traité de la Viole," Paris, 1687, we find these explanations :—

"De la Cadence.

"Il faut premièrement remarquer que par le mot de Cadence, j'entends le *Tremblement* . . ." which means, "You must first remark that by the word "Cadence" I mean the "Tremblement."

Then why call it a Cadence? "Tremblement" is the right name; yet "Cadence" survived! Jean Rousseau continues :—

"There are two kinds of shakes: the *prepared* shake and the *unprepared* shake. The prepared shake is when the finger which must play the shake rests a while, before shaking, upon the note immediately above the one to be shaked."

In other words, the shake begins with an appoggiatura. On short notes the shake should be unprepared, or the preparation very slight.

Jean Henri D'Anglebert, in his "Pièces de Clavecin,' Paris, 1689, gives the following examples :—

D'Anglebert, 1689.

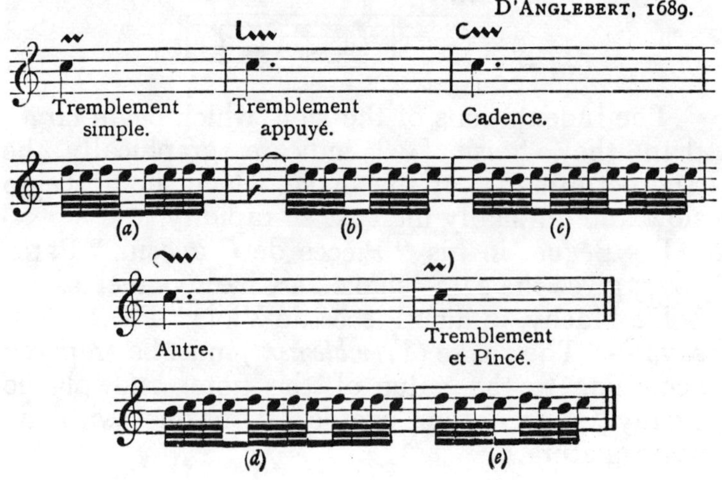

The sign at (*a*) [~] is short; but nevertheless it stands for a long shake.

The sign [~] is graphic, and suggests the prepared shake.

The two "Cadences" (*c*) and (*d*) are shakes prepared by a turn.

The "Tremblement et Pincé" is a shake with a *Turn* as termination. This form is very frequently used.

In Henry Purcell's (Posthumous) "Lessons for the Harpsichord or Spinet," 1696, the following explanations are given:—

"*A shake* is mark'd thus:  explain'd thus: 

"A *plain note and shake* thus:  explain'd thus: 

"The mark for the *shake turn'd* thus:  explain'd thus: 

Purcell's "*plain note and shake*" shows an appoggiatura, of more than half the value of the note, followed by a shake. This is interesting, because his plain appoggiature are only given *one quarter* of that value (see page 97). It shows that the *long* appoggiatura was used in his time.

The "*shake turn'd*" shows a termination which became very common later.

In the "Pièces de Viole" of Marin Marais, 1686, and De Caix d'Hervelois, *c.*1725, the shakes are indicated by a comma, thus :—

This sign was employed later by Couperin, Rameau and others for a *mordent.*

Sebastien de Brossard, in his "Dictionnaire de Musique," Paris, 1703, says :—

"*Trillo*, plural *Trilli*, which is often marked in abbreviation by a *T*, or by *Tr*, or simply by a small *t*, as well for the voices as for the instruments. It is often the mark that one must beat very quickly alternately, or one after the other, two sounds next to one another, like F E, or E D, &c., in such a way that one begins with the higher, and finishes with the lower, and this is properly the 'Cadence' or 'Tremblement' in the French way. But, it is also very often. . . . " (and the author proceeds to tell us what the old Italian *Trillo* was: a completely different thing, as we shall see hereafter (page 196).

Hotteterre-le-Romain, in his "Principes de la Flute Traversière," Paris, 1707, has an excellent definition of the shake, and additional remarks upon it which are worth quoting; he calls the shake "Cadence" :—

"To render the idea of a shake clear to those who do not conceive it, it can be defined: 'The agitation of two notes at the distance of a whole-tone or a semitone from one another, and beaten several times in succession.' One begins with the higher note and finishes with the lower, and only articulates the first: It is the Finger which continues it.

"The number of repercussions is regulated by the length of the note. Above all you must be in no hurry to start the shake; but on the contrary hold it, about half the value of the note, principally in grave movements. The least you can give to short shakes is three movements of the finger, as on crotchets in quick movements."

Three movements of the finger on the flute, as on stringed instruments, make six notes, since one is produced by lifting as by lowering the finger.

François Couperin, in his first book of "Pièces de Clavecin," 1713, shows the following shakes with their signs:—

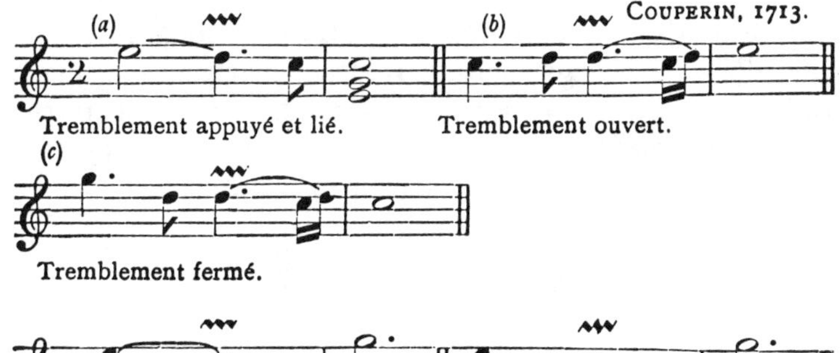

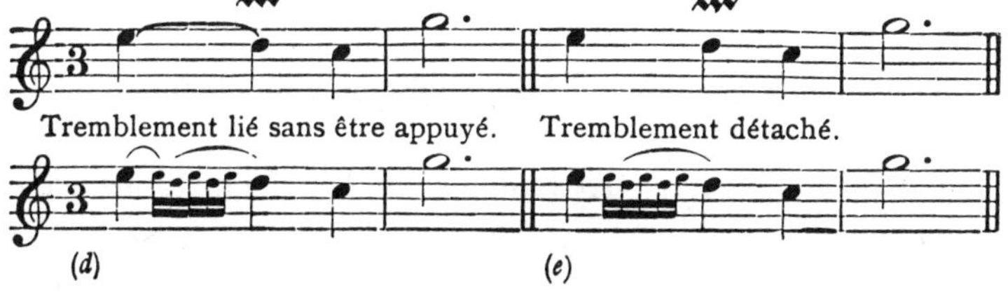

Couperin's logic was not on a par with his musical talent. The "Tremblement ouvert" (*b*) and "Tremblement fermé" (*c*) are the same ornament; the next following note goes up in the first and down in the second, but the shake is not affected thereby.

The "Tremblement lié sans être appuyé" (*d*) is "appuyé" (prepared) too, or else his explanation needs explaining. It is to be regretted that his explanations are written in small notes, the value and position of which are uncertain. But in his "Méthode" he elucidates the point.

Couperin, "Méthode," page 23:—

"Although the shakes are marked equal in the table of graces of my first book, they must, however, begin slower than they finish: but this gradation must be imperceptible.

"On whatever note a shake may be marked, one must always begin it on the whole-tone or half-tone above.

"The shakes of a value at all considerable comprise three things, which in the execution appear only one and the same thing. 1°. The prepare, which is made upon the note above the essential. 2°. The shake. 3°. The stopping point:—

"With regard to the other shakes, they are arbitrary. Some are prepared; others are so short that they have neither preparation nor stopping point. They can even be aspired."

"Aspired" with Couperin, means cut short, abruptly interrupted. An effect of this kind, for example:—

In the "Klavier Büchlein für Wilhelm Friedemann Bach," J. S. Bach gives the following shakes:—

The following signs indicative of shakes are also found in Bach's works: *tr*, [sign], *t*, +, [sign]. They have no particular shade of meaning, being only the consequence of his lack of system.

The shakes given above agree perfectly with all we have seen, from Playford downwards, and all we are going to see later. They are so exactly like those of D'Anglebert's table (page 162), names, explanations, signs, even the short sign [sign] for a long shake, that they were probably copied from it.

Bach's ornamentation agrees entirely with the general practice of his time. He did not innovate anything or fail to employ all that was good in that direction. It is impossible, therefore, to justify any exception about the execution of shakes or other ornaments in his music. The fact that one has been taught a certain passage in a certain way, and that by grinding at it for years and teaching it to others it has become so incrusted in one's mind that a new reading produces a shock, does not alter the question.

For example, the shake in the Fugue in D minor, No. VI., from Vol. i. of "Das wohltemperirte Klavier" should be played as shown below:—

It should moreover be reproduced exactly wherever the subject occurs. It is the right way and also the most beautiful.

Some might question the termination of the shake. But without it, it would be shorn of much of its beauty. It seems clear, moreover, that Bach had that effect in his mind, for in the ninth bar, the last in our example, and the two following ones, he puts the sign ∾, which means a turn, instead of the *tr* and 𝆖 which he uses in other places.

The following extracts from the chapter on "The shake," in Tosi's "Opinioni," 1723, are taken in part from the original, and from Galliard's translation:—

"He who possesses the *shake* in all its perfection, even if he were deprived of all other ornaments could always easily come to the closes [cadenzas] where this grace is most essential; but he who cannot do it, or does it badly, can never be a great singer, however perfect he may be in other respects.

"The shake being of such importance to the singer, the Master must strive, by means of examples executed by the voice or instrument, to help the pupil to acquire a beautiful Trill—equal, distinct, easy and of moderate speed. . . .

"There are eight kinds of shakes. The first is the major shake, made from two sounds a whole tone apart. Ex. (*a*) :—

"The second is the minor shake, composed of a semitone. Ex. (*b*). The third is the half-shake, or short shake. Those who can do the first two kinds will easily master this one, by beating it a little quicker, and stopping almost as soon as it is begun. It is more effective in lively than in pathetic airs. Ex. (*c*) :—

"The fourth is the rising shake, which is done by making the voice ascend from semitone to semitone by imperceptible gradations.

"The fifth is the descending shake, which reverses the former process." [Our notation is incapable of expressing these two shakes in writing. Tosi says they were already obsolete in his time. He did not approve of them. One wonders what they did sound like. Judging from the description, nothing in modern music approaches them in point of dissonance. There might be a new spell of fashion for them.]

"The sixth is the slow shake whose name expresses the nature; by itself it is only an affected tremolo; if it gradually merges into the first or second kind it could hardly please after the first time. Ex. (*d*)":—

[Nevertheless, this shake has been used by many eminent musicians from Couperin, already seen, to others who will follow.]

"The seventh is the redoubled shake which consists in interpolating a few notes to arrest the progress of a major or minor shake, making several shakes out of one. Ex. (*e*):—

"This shake is effective when the interpolated notes are sung boldly. If it is done softly on high notes, by a beautiful voice perfect in it, and not used too often, it cannot displease even the envious. The eighth is the trillo-mordente or shake with a beat, which is one of the most agreeable ornaments in the art of singing; Nature teaches it rather than art. It is born more rapidly than the others, but hardly born it must die. It is most useful when properly introduced amongst divisions, and he who understands the art of singing rarely fails to introduce it after an appoggiatura. He who despises this shake must be guilty of more than ignorance. See Ex. (*f*) :—

"For a shake to be beautiful, it must be prepared; but the preparation is not always possible, sometimes the time does not permit it, nor the taste of the singer; however, it is necessary in final cadences and many other places.

"The shake is subject to many faults which one must know how to avoid. In former times, very long shakes were in favour; but nowadays, with the improvements in art, it is left to trumpet players, or those who do not mind running the risk of bursting, for a *Bravo!* from the people. If done too often, it cannot please, however well it may be executed. It is unpleasant if unevenly beaten. It makes one smile if it sounds like laughter or the bleating of a goat. The perfect shake is produced by a movement of the larynx; that produced on the interval of a third is disagreeable; the slow shake is tedious, and if it is not perfectly in tune it is horrible. The shake being absolutely necessary, the master must encourage the pupil to practise it upon all the vowels and throughout the whole compass of the voice. . . . .

"When the pupil has perfectly mastered the shake, the master must find out whether he has the same skill in stopping it, as some people seem incapable of doing so. As to finding out where the trill should be used, besides the cadences, it is an art that only practice, taste and intelligence can teach."

In Theofilo Muffat's "Componimenti," &c., ?1735, the signs are clear and logical, and the explanations accurate. No names are given to the ornaments:—

(*a*) (*b*) are plain shakes;

(*c*) (*d*) (*e*) shakes prepared with appoggiature of various lengths;

(*f*) (*g*) (*h*) (*i*) are shakes with terminations showing also the introduction of necessary accidentals;

(*k*) (*l*) (*m*) (*n*) are shakes prepared by a slide;

(*o*) (*p*) show the combination of slide and termination:—

TH. MUFFAT, ?1735.

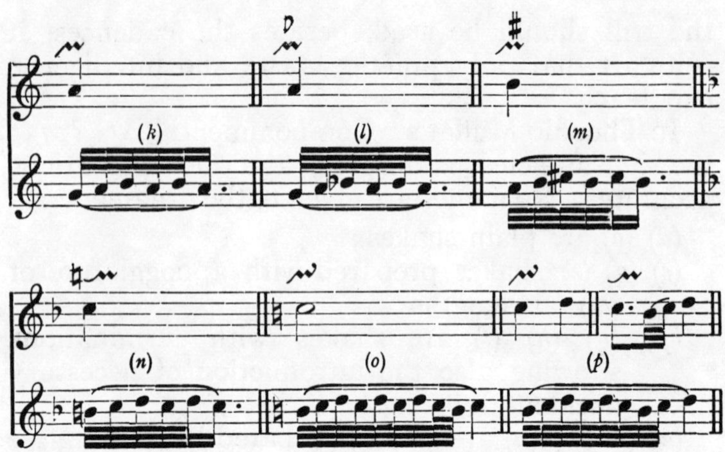

The shakes in J. P. Rameau's "Pièces de Clavecin," 1731 are explained thus :—

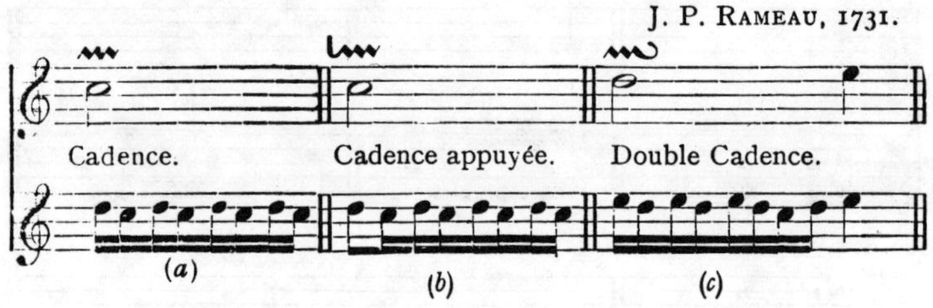

The example (*b*) would be better written as follows :—

and this is probably what the author means. However, it makes little difference, since the speed and number of notes in the shake were informal after the start. The following remark and

examples given by Rameau are interesting:—
"The note slurred to one having a shake or mordent serves as a beginning to each of these ornaments." (See Exx. (*d*) and (*e*):—

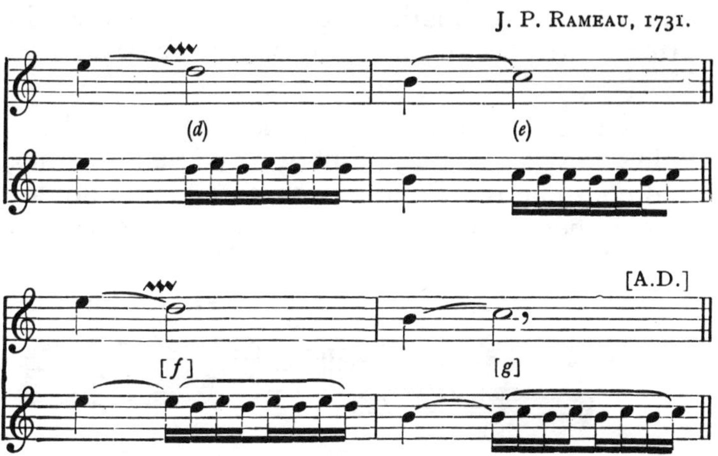

Here again the explanations are not well written; moreover, the sign for the mordent (,) is omitted. The writer suggests the reading given at (*f*) and (*g*).

In Ch. Dieupart's "Suittes de Clavecin," *c.* 1705, the following ornaments are given together with their French and English names:—

The " Treatise on Good Taste " of F. Geminiani (1749) contains the following remarks concerning the shake :—

" The plain shake is proper for quick movements ; and it may be made upon any note, observing after it to pass immediately to the ensuing note. Ex. (*a*).

" The turned shake being made quick and long is fit to express gaiety ; but if you make it short, and continue the length of the note plain and soft, it may then express some of more tender passions." Ex. (*b*) :—

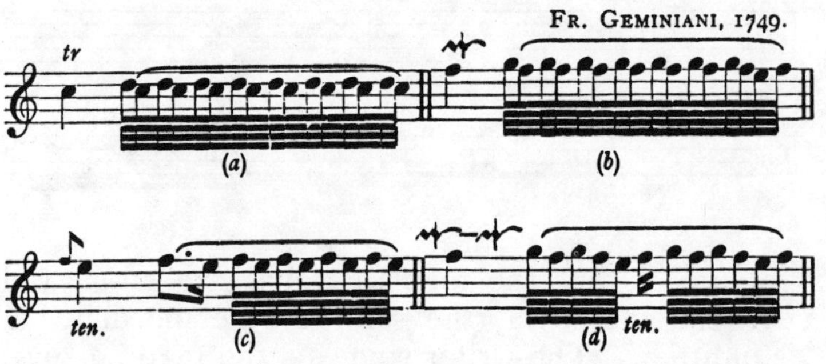

Geminiani is not logical. He speaks of the shake in an *Allegro*, and gives a preposterous number of repercussions ; just the shake for an *Adagio*. At (*c*) he shows an appoggiatura on a crotchet, and writes an ornament of a longer value ; it is true that he puts *Ten.* under that crotchet. But at (*d*) he gives an example of the *redoubled shake* which is interesting. (See Tosi, page 171.) Geminiani's sign for it, too, is worthy of remark. The line [—] indicates the *holding* of the plain note without ornament.

The sign used by Couperin and Rameau for the *suspension* is employed in J. C. Mondonville's "Pièces de Clavecin avec Voix ou Violon," 1748, to indicate a prepared shake :—

Mondonville gives the following explanation, but does not excuse his misappropriation of the sign :—

"That sign means that the shake must be prepared."

J. Quantz, in his "Versuch," &c., 1752, has an exceedingly valuable chapter on the shake, from which we shall quote the most part.

"§ 1. The shakes give an incomparable brilliancy to the execution, and are, like the appoggiature, absolutely indispensable. Should an instrumentalist or a singer possess all the skill and taste conceivable, if he cannot make a good shake, he will not be considered as a perfect artist. Some are given by nature what others can only acquire after much practice. One person can shake with all his fingers, another only with a few, and to a third the shake will be the torment of his life. It might be believed that it depends more upon the nature of the nerves than on the will. Intelligent practice, however, can do much to improve matters, provided one does not wait until the shake comes of itself; and that one begins early, taking all possible care to attain perfection on that point before the fingers have reached their complete development.

"§ 2. All the *shakes* must not be made with the same speed. One must consider not only the place where one practises, but that where the performance will take place. The echo of a large hall will confuse the movements of the shake and it may become blurred. If, on the contrary, one plays in a small stuffy room, where the auditors are very near, a rapid shake will be better than a slow one. Besides, one must make a difference according to the piece played, and not confuse everything as so many people do. In a sad piece, the shake should be slow; but more rapid in a merry one.

"§ 3. As to the slowness or quickness, nothing must be exaggerated. The *very slow shake*, which is only used in the French style of singing, is as bad as the *very rapid shake*, which the French call *chevroté* (goaty). Even though some of the most famous singers might render it quite fascinatingly, one must not be influenced by that. And although some think this goaty shake an enviable accomplishment, they do not consider the fact that a moderate and even shake is far more difficult to do than one of extreme but indistinct rapidity; the latter should rather be accounted as a fault.

"§ 4. The *shake of a third*, which is made with a third instead of a second, has been in use formerly; and there are still Italian violinists and oboe players who use it. But it should not be used for either voice or instruments (unless it be on the bagpipe). A shake must only occupy the interval of a tone, or semitone, according to the mode and note from which the shake originates.

"§ 5. For a shake to be perfectly beautiful it must be equal, that is to say, its speed must be even and at the same time moderate; for this reason, on instruments, one must not lift the finger for one beat higher than for another.

"§ 6. It would be difficult to indicate the precise speed of a good shake. I believe, however, that a *long* shake at the close of a piece would be neither too fast nor too slow, if within one beat of the pulse the finger did not do much more than four movements, and consequently *eight* of these notes which may be seen at Ex. 1 :—

Ex. 1.

In a quick and merry piece, the short shakes can be made a little quicker; one could then, during the time of a pulse beat, lift the finger once or twice more. It must be clearly understood, however, that this can happen only to short notes, and amongst other short notes. It could be further remarked, about the speed of shakes, that it must differ according to whether the notes be high or low. Speaking of the harpsichord, I should say that if you take the speed already explained between the notes :—

you can make it a little quicker between :—

slower between :—

and slower still in the lower octave. Applying this to the voice, I conclude that a treble should shake quicker than an alto; a tenor and a bass slower still. The shakes on the violin, viola, violoncello, and violone will be equal to those of the four voices. The flute and oboe can shake as quickly as the treble, and the bassoon take the speed of the tenor. It is open to anyone to adopt or reject my advice; and though such subtleties may be regarded as useless by some of my readers, I know that those who have a delicate taste, ripe judgment and much experience, will not be altogether against me.

"§ 7. Every shake begins with an appoggiatura which is before its note and is taken from above or below, as explained before. The end of every shake consists of two little notes near the note of the shake and are joined to it in the same speed. See Ex. 2. They are called in German '*Nachschlag*' (after-blow). Sometimes these two little notes are written (see Ex. 3); but when there is only a single note (see Ex. 4), both the appoggiatura and the termination are implied. Without them the shake would be neither perfect nor brilliant :—

QUANTZ, 1752.

"§ 8. The appoggiatura of a shake is sometimes as quick as the other notes of the shake; for example, when a new phrase begins with a shake, after a rest. This appoggiatura, whether long or short, must always be accented; but the shake and termination must be slurred.

"§ 13. When a shake precedes a close, be it in the middle or at the end of a piece, one cannot after the shake and its termination introduce an appoggiatura before the final note; for example, if you are shaking on a D, to end on a C, and before this last C you introduce a D appoggiatura, the effect will be stale and the expression low. This fault would not be committed by a musician of taste."

This is all perfectly clear and to the point. If, however, Quantz were writing at the present time, he would not be so imprudent as to give such an example as his Ex. 1, where the shake apparently begins by the lower note. Of course, he only intends to show the number of repercussions; and he has already explained without the possibility of a doubt that all shakes begin with an appoggiatura. Nevertheless, one in search of an excuse to play shakes the wrong way might quote this example. It has been done.

In Chap. viii. (Appoggiature), § 14, Quantz mentions amongst the "Kleine Manieren" which may ornament the appoggiatura, and "are employed by the French to add brilliancy to their pieces," two "*Demi Tremblements*" (half-shakes). They are shown amongst the examples on page 129, Exx. (*a*) and (*b*), and require no further explanation.

Few of the examples given in F. W. Marpurg's "Die Kunst das Klavier zu spielen" (1750-55) offer anything new. Several are alike; the signs only differ. The last example shows a *long* appoggiatura treated according to the general rule, which makes the shake seem short, and late in coming:—

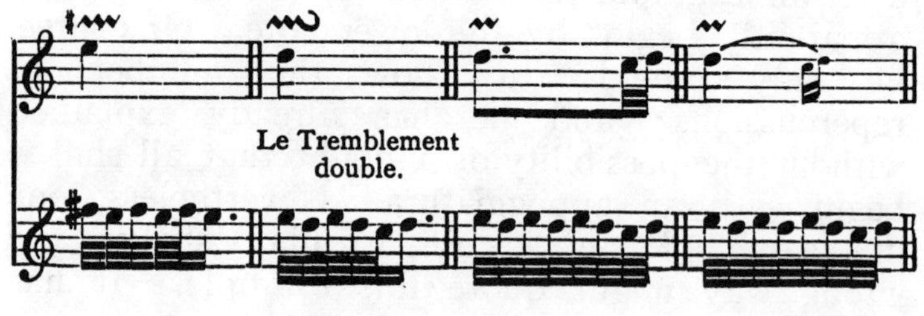

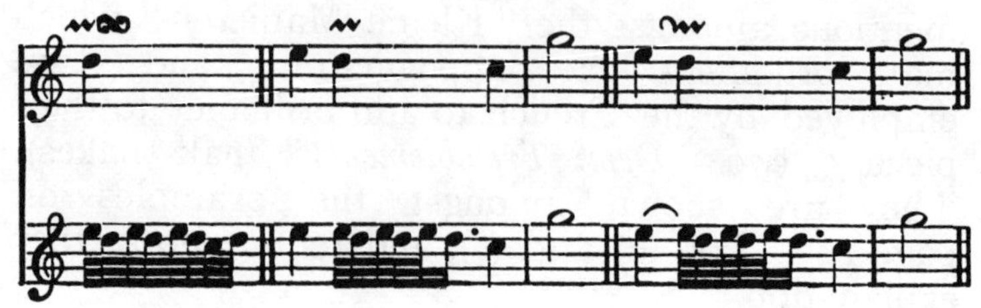

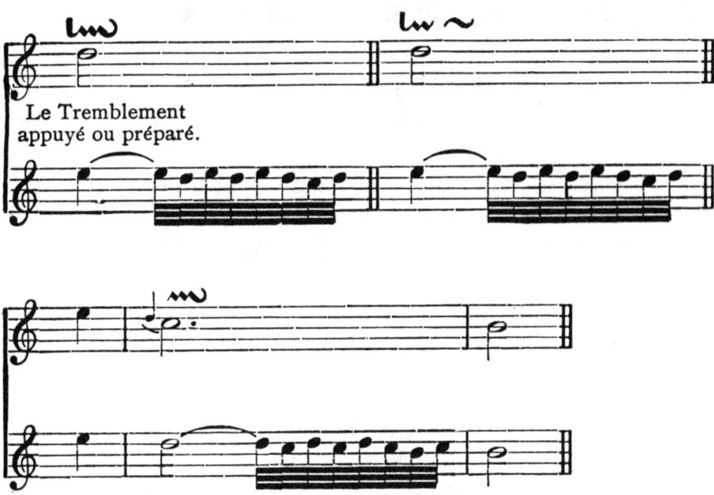

We need not give *in extenso* the long chapter on the shake contained in C. Ph. E. Bach's "Versuch" (1753), most of which would only be a repetition of what we have seen already. The following quotations, many of them compressed, must suffice:—

"§ 1. The shake is now used much more freely than formerly.

"§ 2. It should be applied most carefully, especially in expressive pieces.

"§§ 3, 4. Four kinds of shakes are used in the art of clavier playing; each has a particular sign. However, they are frequently all indicated by *tr.* or by a cross.

"§ 5. The correct sign for an ordinary shake is 𝆖 :—

"On long notes the sign is lengthened:—

"The shake begins with the note above. It is therefore superfluous to add a small note unless a long appoggiatura is intended:—

"§ 6. Sometimes two little notes from under are added to it. They are called *Nachschlag* (Termination), and add much brilliancy to the shake:—

They are also indicated by the sign ∿∿|, but it resembles so nearly that for a long mordent, that I think it would be better to use the sign ∿∿ only, to avoid confusion.

"§ 7. Trills are the most difficult of ornaments. All cannot succeed with them. They should be started in youth. Their execution must before all be smooth and swift. A quick shake is always preferable to a slow one. In sad pieces, the shake can be done somewhat slower; but otherwise a rapid trill adds much to the beauty of a piece. As to strength and weakness, this must be adjusted according to the feeling of the phrase in which the trill occurs.

"§ 8. In practising the trill, one must lift the fingers evenly, but not too high. One should begin it slowly, and gradually get it quicker, but always even. The nerves must be lax, otherwise a goaty and unequal trill will be the result. The higher note, when it occurs for the last time, should be snapped (*geschnellet*); that is to say, after the stroke, the finger is sharply curved, the point glides towards the front of the key, and is abruptly withdrawn.

"§ 13. A shake on a tolerably long note should always have a termination, whether the following note be higher or lower. If the following note proceeds by skip, the termination must be added (Ex. 5). On short notes, the termination will go better when the following note rises a second (Ex. 6), than when it descends a second (Ex. 7):—

"In very slow movements, the shakes in Ex. 8 might have terminations, although the quick notes after the dots could serve for that purpose. The correct execution of such shakes, with terminations, will be shown in the following paragraph, when dotted notes are considered. There is no obligation, however, to give a termination to these shakes, if they are properly sustained:—

"§ 14. Dotted notes, followed by a short note ascending, should have a termination to their shake:—

Ex. 9.

But whereas the last note of the termination is usually joined to the following note with the greatest rapidity:—

it is not so in the case of dotted notes, because a very small space must be left between the last note of the termination and the note following:—

This space need only be just long enough for one to hear that the termination and the following note are two separate things."

[C. Ph. E. Bach is at some pains to explain all this, because he has not as yet explained the execution of dotted notes, of which it is merely a consequence, Moreover, he has omitted to note in his example (Ex. 11) the little space he speaks of. This space, or rest, is also a consequence of the dot. The case being of interest, the writer ventures to give a more thorough solution of Exx. 8 and 11 :—

Ex. 12.

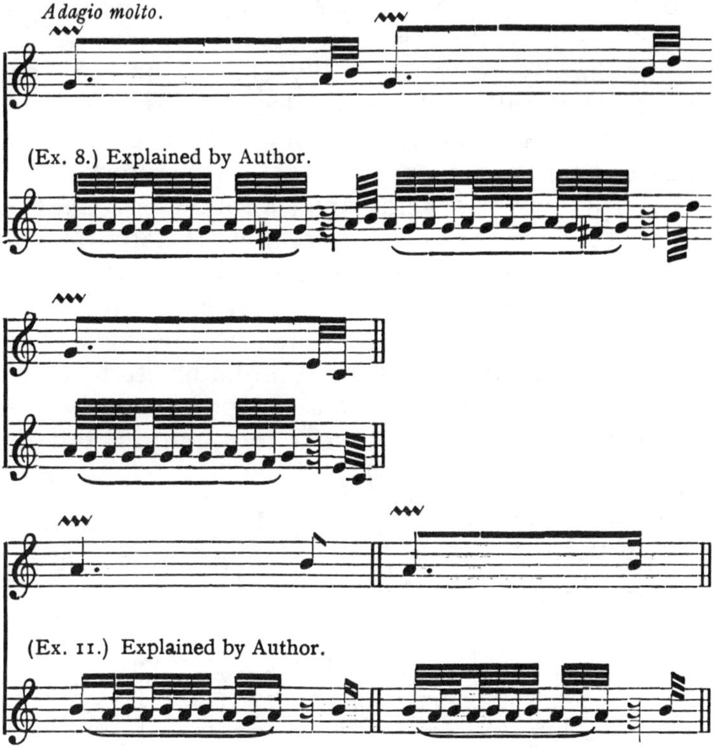
Adagio molto.
(Ex. 8.) Explained by Author.
(Ex. 11.) Explained by Author.

"§ 14 (*continued*). It is wrong to combine the termination of the shake on a dotted note with the quick note following (see Ex. 13). If the composer wants such an interpretation, he should write it out clearly :—

Ex. 13.

(wrong.)

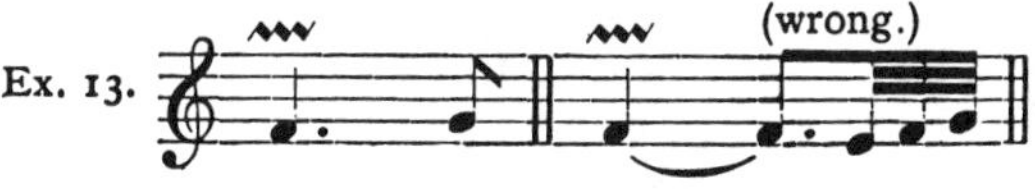

"§ 15. Since the termination must be played at the same speed as the shake, it follows that the second finger of the right hand, and the thumb, are not suitable to play shakes with a termination, as the crossing of fingers necessary for the termination could hardly be done nimbly enough, and the end of the best trill could be spoiled thereby.

"§ 16. The shake without termination suits descending passages (Ex. 14) and short notes (Ex. 15); when several shakes follow one another (Ex. 16); when one or several short notes follow, which take, as it were, the place of the termination (Ex. 17). According to the above, the tempo of an example such as Ex. 18 must not be very slow In triplets, also, the termination had better be left out (Ex. 19). In *very slow* tempo the first three shakes might possibly have a termination, but the last never":—

[In Ex. 15, the notes with shakes, being dotted, must be treated as explained at § 14. There must be a rest between them and the following note. The same remark applies to Ex. 17 *a*, *d*, *e*, and *f*.]

"§ 17. A moderately good ear would in itself be sufficient to decide whether shakes ought to have a termination or not. I have given these numerous examples to help beginners and for the sake of thoroughness."

As we are all beginners we ought to be thankful to him! Note the implied information in the following paragraph, *that phrases under a slur should not be ornamented.*

"§ 20. Amongst the faults of which the shake is often the innocent cause, the first to be exposed is this: in such phrases as those of Ex. 20:—

many burden the first note with a trill, *although the slurs usually placed over such passages ought to deter them* from doing so. However strong might be the temptation, such notes must not have trills. It is indeed singular that by corrupted taste the best and most melodious phrases should be spoiled. Most of the faults occur with long sustained notes. People are wont to enliven them with shakes. Their spoilt ear requires continual excitement. It perceives nothing except a clatter. One can see from this that such faults are committed by those who are incapable of singing mentally, or of starting a note impressively and sustaining it. On the clavichord as well as on the harpsichord, the sound continues if the notes are not played too short. One instrument may be better than another in this respect. In France, where the clavichord is so remarkably little known, most of the pieces are written for the harpsichord. Nevertheless, the French music is full of bindings and slurs indicated by curved lines. Supposing the tempo is too slow or the instrument too bad to sustain the sound, it is always worse to try to revive a note, overdrawn and exhausted, by a trill, than to lose something of the latter part of that note, which loss can be more than counterbalanced by skilful playing. In music many things occur which require the help of the imagination, because they cannot be clearly heard. For example, in a concerto with a full accompaniment, the soloist always loses such notes as must be accompanied fortissimo, and those which are in unison with the tutti. Intelligent listeners supply whatever is thus lost, through their imagination, and it is these listeners that we should endeavour to please before all.

"§ 21. Other faults occur when a lame termination is appended to a trill (Ex. 21) [the Trill (*a*) would not fit at (*b*) (see par. 14]; when a superfluous note is added to the termination, which at once renders it objectionable (Ex. 22) [the bad note is marked thus +]:—

when the trills are not sustained in spite of the rule that all trills (except half-shakes, *i.e.*, Prall-Trillern) must be continued during the full value of the notes on which they are; when a trill which requires a preparation is jumped on without the required appoggiatura, or when the latter is not properly connected with the trill; when insolent, noisy shakes are made, in a phrase which should be languid and weak; when, finally, one feels bound to underline every note of some length with a trill, one commits faults as hateful as they are common. The latter are those silly little trills which have been already alluded to in the Introduction, § 10."

Here is the passage is question. The author has been mentioning the stiffening of the left hand resulting from continually playing in octaves when accompanying on the figured bass:—

"The master seeks to compensate this stiffness of the left hand in the right hand, by teaching his pupils, particularly in the Adagios and most expressive pieces, the fine art of richly decorating every corner with a sickening surfeit of silly little trills, alternating with pedantic old ornaments and runs both inappropriate and out of place, in which the fingers seem to have gone crazy.

"§ 22. The shake from below is indicated as shown at Ex. 23 (*a*); its execution is explained at (*b*). It is also sometimes indicated as at (*c*) and (*d*):—

or with the mark for a plain shake, in which case the player may employ it if he chooses.

"§ 23. As this shake requires many repercussions, it is only proper to long notes.

"§ 24. Ex. 24 shows how the termination can be used after a long shake:—

Ex. 24.

"§ 26. In a succession of skips, the ordinary shake is best, on account of the sharp definition required, which introductory notes from below or above would impair:—

Ex. 25.

"§ 27. The shake from above is indicated as shown at Ex. 26 (*a*); its execution is given at (*b*):—

Ex. 26.

"§ 30. The Half-shake, or Sudden shake (Prall-Triller) is indicated by clavier players, and executed as shown in Ex. 27, where the example clearly demonstrates its effect and peculiarity:—

Ex. 27.

"§ 31. As the half-shake connects the note upon which it stands with the preceding note, it follows that it cannot be used on separated (staccato) notes. . . . .

"§ 32. This is the most indispensable and enjoyable, but at the same time the most difficult of all ornaments. If not perfectly played, it either does not come out or seems lame and poor, which is the very reverse of its nature. One cannot slowly demonstrate its performance to a pupil. It must spring with a bound; this springing alone makes it effective. It should be done according to the directions of § 7, but with such extraordinary rapidity that the notes can hardly be distinguished one from another. In this way, such a remarkable sharpness is obtained that the sharpest ordinary trill would seem dull in comparison. Like the short appoggiatura, this sudden shake can be made on short notes. It is performed so rapidly that it does not seem to take away the smallest fraction of the value of the principal note, which must still absolutely coincide with the time-beats. After all, this shake does not sound nearly as frightening as it would appear were all its small notes written out in full. It renders the execution sprightly and brilliant. If necessary, one could dispense with all other shakes, replacing them by other light ornaments without harm to the performance; but these sudden shakes cannot be dispensed with. However well were all else done, if they were missing one could not feel satisfied.

"§ 33. Since the sudden shake must above all be played easily and rapidly, those fingers which can trill best should be used for it. It follows that liberties must often be taken with the usual method of fingering in order to get the best trills;

but, in so doing, one must take care lest the execution of the passage should suffer:—

"§ 34. These sudden shakes cannot be used otherwise than before a descending second, which may come through an appoggiatura or a principal note (Ex. 30). They are often used on short notes (Ex. 31), or on such notes as have been shortened by an appoggiatura (Ex. 32). When they happen upon a pause of the usual kind, one keeps the appoggiatura very long, and terminates very abruptly, with a sudden shake, immediately afterwards withdrawing the fingers from the key (Ex. 33):—

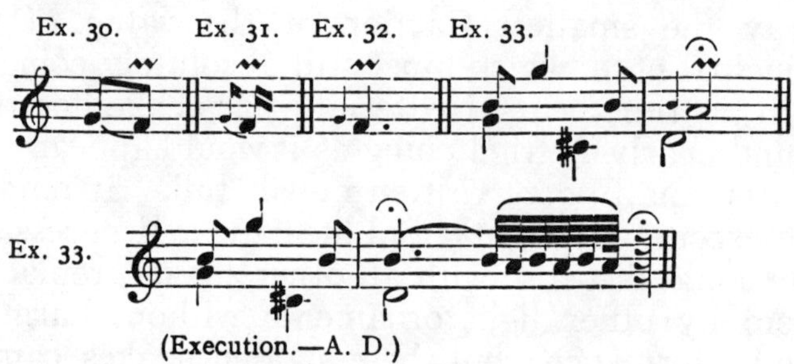

"§ 35. The sudden shake is often found in passages where three or more notes descend:—

"§ 36. Apropos of the execution of these shakes, it may be remarked that upon the *piano-forte*, to play them softly is of the most extreme difficulty. The requisite snapping (*Schnellen*) of the fingers cannot be done without some violence, which involves hard blows upon this instrument. To make matters worse, this shake, whether alone or in company with a turn, often comes after an appoggiatura, and consequently *must* be played *piano*. This difficulty arises with all *Schnellen*, and particularly here, where the sharpest kind of *Schnellen* is required. I doubt whether it would be possible to avoid hardness upon the pianoforte, in playing these shakes, even with the greatest amount of study."

The half-shake or sudden shake was a great favourite with C. Ph. E. Bach. It was not so much in favour in former times. The sign ⁓ which he specializes for it was frequently used to indicate ordinary shakes. It is found, however, in the works of Couperin, J. S. Bach, and others, in places where only the half-shake could be placed. Couperin and Tosi have explained it. It is the "*tr*" of Frescobaldi, and one of the meanings of the sign ⩵ so frequently used in the English virginal music. Its shortness fits it admirably for the contrapuntal style, as it does not obscure the main note.

Here ends the study of the Shake. Succeeding writers, such as Leopold Mozart, Türk, and others, do not bring any new light on the subject. The shakes from "Dom Bedos's" plates will be seen, one might almost say "heard," in the Appendix; those of Beethoven were just like them, for there was no change until the pianoforte virtuoso, Hummel, about 1820, preconised the trill beginning with the main note.

SECTION III.—THE TREMOLO, CLOSE-SHAKE. *Organ-shake*, *Vibrato*, *Sting*, *Old Shake*, *Modern Shake or Trill*.

Italian: *Trillo*, *Tremolo*, *Tremoletto*, *Vibrato*, *Ribattuta*.

French: *Martellement*, *Balancement*, *Verre Cassé*, *Plainte*, *Langueur*, *Battement*, *Tremblement sans appuyer*.

German: *Mordent*, *Bebung*, *Schwebung*.

These ornaments give emphasis to a note by repeatedly interrupting or altering its sound. If the pitch is unaltered we have the old Italian *Trillo*, *Organ-shake*, or *Tremolo*. If the pitch is slightly altered, as can be done with the voice, wind and stringed instruments, and the clavichord, we have the *Vibrato*, *Close-shake*, or *Bebung*.

As keyboard instruments other than the clavichord are incapable of producing this effect, they imitate it by alternating the principal sound with that of the next note. If the note above is used we have the *Tremolo* or *Tremoletto* of the early Italians, which is the same thing as the common *modern shake*, but must not be confused with the shake of the Bach period. When the note below the principal is used, the *Beat* or *Mordent* is produced. This ornament, on account of its great importance, will be treated separately hereafter.

The following example of a *Tremolo* or *Old Shake* is found in Zacconi's "Practica di Musica," 1592:—

In Diruta's "Il Transylvano," 1597, mention is made of light repercussions of the key producing a true *Tremolo* and intended to make up for the shortness of sound of the virginals.

The following Old Shakes are taken from the examples of *Tremoli* and *Tremoletti* given in that book:—

Giulio Caccini, in the Preface to his "Nuove Musiche," 1601, gives explanations of the vocal *Trillo* and *Ribattuta*, which are quoted in the following extract from Prætorius.

Michael Prætorius's "Syntagma," Book iii., 1619, page 237:—

"*Trillo:* Is of two kinds: The *first* is performed in unison (*i.e.*, on one single note), when many notes are very quickly repeated one after another:—

The other *Trillo* is performed in various ways. And indeed it is impossible to learn to execute a *Trillo* in the right way from written directions. Let it therefore be done *viva Praeceptoris voce et ope*, and have it sung and executed before a person, which is the only way to learn it, as one bird learns from the others, by imitation. For this reason, I have never seen it explained by any Italian authors, only excepting Giulio Caccini; they only indicate the proper places for it by a *t*, *tr*, or *tri*. Nevertheless, I have thought it necessary to give a few examples so that the hitherto ignorant 'tyro' may see and understand to a certain extent what is meant by a *Trillo*:—

Ex. 2.

Ex. 3.

"And these ornaments are found in Claudio Monteverde."

In Ex. 3, the first four notes show the *Ribattuta*, which we shall see later.

The following examples show how the *Trillo* should be placed, and some of the ornaments which may be used before and after it :—

At page 235, Prætorius explains the *Tremolo* and *Tremoletto* mostly by examples, but also with these few interesting words (Ex. 8) :—

"*Tremolo*, or *Tremulo:* is nothing else but the shaking of the voice over a note : the organists call it *Mordanten* or *Moderanten :*—

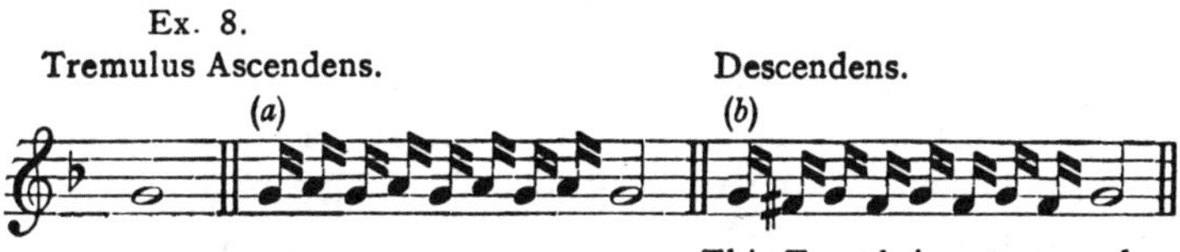

This *Tremulo* is not so good as the *ascendens*.

"And these are used more for the organ and *Instrumenta pennata* than for men's voices."

The *Instrumenta pennata* are virginals.

The example at (*b*) is a true mordent. Prætorius says that it is not so good as the *ascendens* at (*a*); but this is not the opinion which prevailed later, for in the 18th century the *ascendens* had become quite obsolete, whilst the *descendens* was very frequently used. Exx. (*c*) and (*h*) are the plain notes; the others the *tremoletti*.

Playford, in his "Introduction," 1654, explains the *Trillo* and *Groppo*, after Caccini, which explanations need not be repeated; but he also gives elucidations of his own, well worth quoting:—

"Our author being short in setting forth this chief or most usual Grace in singing, called the *Trill*, which, as he saith very right. is by a beating in the Throat on the vowel (*a'h*) some observe that it is rather the shaking of the Uvula or Pallate on the Throat, in one sound, upon a Note; For the attaining of this, the most surest and ready way is by imitation of those who are perfect in the same; yet, I have heard of some that have attained it by this manner, in singing a plain Song, of 6 notes up and 6 down, they have in the midst of every Note beat or shaked with their finger upon their Throat, which by often practice came to do the same Notes exactly without. It was my chance lately to be in company with three gentlemen at a Musical Practice, which sung their parts very well, and used this Grace (called the Trill) very exactly. I desired to know their Tutor, they told me I was their Tutor, for they never had any other but this my *Introduction:* That (I answered) could direct them but in the Theory, they must needs have a better help in the Practick, especially in attaining to sing the *Trill* so well. One of them made this Reply, (which made me smile) I used, said he, at my first learning the Trill, to imitate that breaking of a Sound in the Throat, which Men use when they Leur their Hawks, as *he-he-he-he-he;* which he used slow at first, and by often practice on several Notes, higher and lower in sound, he became perfect therein. The *Trill* or shake of the Voice, being the most usual Grace, is made in Closes, Cadences, and other places, where by a long Note an *Exclamation* or *Passion* is expressed there the *Trill* is made in the latter part of any such Note; but most usually upon binding Notes in *Cadences* and *Closes*, and on that Note that precedes the closing Note. Those who once attain to the perfect use of the *Trill*, other Graces will become easie."

In the "Table of Graces proper to the Viol or Violin," given in the same book, the following explanation of the Close shake is given. This is the vibrato proper; the notation shows that a slight variation in pitch is intended:—

(Observe the dot used as a sign for this Grace.)

Christopher Simpson, in his "Division-Violist," 1659, gives the same example as above, and explains its performance thus:—

"§ 16. *Close-shake* is that when we shake the Finger as close and near the sounding Note as possible may be, touching the String with the Shaking finger so softly and nicely that it make no variation of Tone. This may be used where no other Grace is concerned."

The Latin name for Close shake is *Tremor pressus*.

In § 15 he explains the tremolo thus:—

"Some also affect a Shake or Tremble with the Bow, like the Shaking-stop of an Organ, but the frequent use thereof is not (in my opinion) much commendable."

Thomas Mace in "Musick's Monument," 1676, has the following delightful explanations of Lute Shakes:—

Page 103: "The *Shake*, is 2 ways to be performed, either *Hard*, or *Soft*, the *Hard*, (or *Tearing-Shake*) is thus done, *viz.* If you shake any *String Open*, you must first strike it with some *Right Hand Finger*, and then be ready with the *Fore-Finger*, of the *Left Hand* to pick it up, with the very Tip (near the Nail) of your Finger; and so, by often, and quick picking up in that manner, or (more plainly) Scratching It, in a *Smooth*, *Nimble*, and *Strong Agitation*, you will have performed It.

"The *Soft-Shake*, is done, in all respects, like the former, except the *Tearing*, and *Scratching;* and only by *Beating the String Strongly*, and with a *Quick Motion*, in the same place, as you did the other; which always must be in *b*, or *c* Frett; and if it be done Evenly, and Strongly, it gives a very Pleasant Grace unto your Play.

"Some there are, (and many I have met with) who have such a Natural Agility (in their nerves) and Aptitude, to that Performance, that before they could do anything else to purpose, they would make a *Shake*, *Rarely well.* And some again can scarcely *ever Gain a Good Shake*, by reason of the *unaptness of their Nerves*, to that action; but yet otherwise come to *Play very well.*

"I, for my own part, have had occasion to *break*, *both my Arms;* by reason of which, I cannot make the *Nerve-Shake* well, nor *Strong;* yet, by a certain *Motion of my Arm*, I have gain'd such a *Contentive Shake*, that sometimes my Scholars will ask me, *How they shall do to get the like?* I have then no better *Answer* for Them, than to tell Them, They must first *Break their Arm*, as I have done; and so possibly, after that, (*by Practice*) they may get *My manner of Shake.*"

Page 109: "The *Sting*, is another very Neat, and Pritty Grace; (but not *Modish* in These Days) yet, for some sorts of *Humours*, very *Excellent;* and is thus done, (upon a *Long Note*, and a *Single String*) first strike your *Note*, and so soon as It is struck, *hold your Finger* (but not too Hard) stopt upon the Place, (letting your *Thumb loose*) and *wave your Hand* (Exactly) *downwards, and upwards, several Times, from the Nut, to the Bridge*, by which *Motion*, your Finger will *draw*, or *stretch* the String a little *upwards*, and *downwards*, so as to make the Sound seem to *Swell*, with pritty *unexpected Humour*, and gives much *Contentment*, *upon Cases*."

This is the true vibrato, and the effect of it is very much like that of the *Bebung* on the clavichord.

De Machy, in his "Pièces de Viole," 1685, says: "The *Aspiration*, also named *Plainte*, is made by varying the finger upon the fret. Some people will call this *mewing* by allusion."

This is the *Vibrato* proper; but why does he call it *Aspiration*, a name which other musicians of the time give to an entirely different thing; and which, moreover, is not at all suggestive?

"The *Tremblement sans appuyer* (shake without pressing) is made with two fingers held close to one another, and pressing only very slightly upon the string."

This is the Close shake of Playford, Simpson, and many others; but again under an unusual and misleading name. De Machy is most troublesome in that way.

In his "Pièces à Une et à Deux Violes," 1686, Marin Marais calls the Close shake with two fingers upon the frets, "Pincé ou flattement," and indicates it by a suggestive wave line ~~~. The true vibrato, with one finger, which is principally used beyond the frets, he calls "Plainte," and indicates thus ⌇; also a very good sign.

Jean Rousseau, "Traité de la Viole," 1687, says:—

"The 'Batement' is made when two fingers being held close together, one presses upon the string, and the other beats it very lightly.

"The 'Batement' imitates a certain sweet agitation of the voice; this is why it is used on all notes long enough to permit it, and it must last as long as the note. [This is the Close shake.] The 'Langueur' is made by varying the finger upon a fret. It is usually made when the note has to be played with the fourth finger, and that the time permits it. This grace is used instead of the "Batement," which cannot be made when the little finger is pressing."

This is very clear; but Jean Rousseau was not giving sound advice when saying that the vibrato should be made upon every note long enough to permit it! This practice has unfortunately been carried down to the present day.

The "Balancement" in the following example from Michel l'Affilard, "Principes très-faciles pour apprendre la musique," *c.* 1691, shows a true tremolo, indicated by the sign which viol-players use for the vibrato:—

Brossard, in his "Dictionaire de Musique," 1703, Article "Trillo," sign *tr.*, after describing the true shake under that name, adds:—

"But, it is also very often, in Italian music, the sign that one must beat several times on the same note, first somewhat slowly, then ending with as much lightness and rapidity as the throat can make. Example :—

"And this is properly the veritable Italian 'Trillo,' at least as far as it can be noted down in writing, for it must be admitted that our example can only give a very coarse idea of it, in comparison with the quickness with which it can be done, and that a good master can teach better than all that could be written about it."

Hotteterre-le-Romain, in his "Principes de la Flute Traversière," explains very clearly how to make the vibrato on the flute. He calls it "Flattement" or "Tremblement mineur." The effect produced by following his directions is a waving of the sound, which is alternately flattened a little and brought back to its normal pitch.

P. F. Tosi, in his "Treatise on Singing," 1723, mentions the vocal *Trillo* in a way which shows that it had become comparatively rare at that time. He did not like it, if we may judge from this :—

"What might not be said of him who invented the prodigious art of singing like the crickets ? Who ever could have imagined, before the introduction of that fashion, that ten or twelve quavers in a row could be rolled one after another by a certain shaking of the voice, which has for some time passed under the name of *Mordente fresco ?* :—

He will be still more strongly inclined to detest the invention of laughing in singing, or that of singing like the hens after they have laid an egg. Is there no other little animal worthy of being imitated, so as to cast a little more ridicule on our profession?"

This is the last we hear of the vocal *Trillo!*

Francesco Geminiani, in "A Treatise of Good Taste, &c.," 1749, treating of the "Close Shake" Sign (ꟿ), says: "This cannot possibly be described by notes. To perform it, you must press the finger strongly upon the string of the instrument, and move the wrist in and out slowly and equally. When it is long continued, swelling the sound by degrees, drawing the bow nearer to the bridge, and ending it very strong, it may express majesty, dignity, &c. But making it shorter, lower, and softer, it may denote affliction, fear, &c., and when it is made on short notes, it only contributes to make them sound more agreeable; and for this reason it should be made use of as often as possible."

Here again is a piece of doubtful advice, for it would lead to continual vibrato, and then how could it express majesty, and fear and affliction in the proper places if it is used all the time?

But we have now finished with the vibrato. It is the "Bebung" which will monopolise our attention. It is that form of vibrato peculiar to the clavichord, and one of the points which give to that instrument its wonderful fascination. J. S. Bach occasionally indicates it thus: ⁀. . . . .⁀, but he has left no instructions for its performance. The occasions to use it abound in his music. Marpurg calls it "Balancement," and indicates it as above. C. Ph. E. Bach, in his "Versuch," &c., explains its performance thus:—

"A long and expressive note requires a 'Bebung,' during which the finger remains on the key and evenly rocks it; the sign for it is thus:—

This explanation is hardly sufficient, but we shall get additional light elsewhere. In his Preface, § 11, C. Ph. E. Bach speaks of the harpsichord, pianoforte, and clavichord, and comparing the two latter, he says:—

"But, I believe, nevertheless, that a good clavichord, except that its tone is weaker, has all the beauties of the pianoforte, and in addition the 'Bebung' and the power of sustaining the sounds, for after playing a note I can still give a fresh pressure."

There is therefore a difference between the "Bebung," a vibrato, and the "Tragen der Töne," which is not a re-striking, but a reviving of the tone produced by allowing the tangent of the clavichord almost to leave the string for a space of time so short that the ear cannot appreciate it, the finger remaining all the time on the key. The clavichord players, however, did not often make a distinction between the two effects, and used the word "Bebung" for both. In practice, the first often leads to the second.

Türk's "Klavierschule," 1789, has a paragraph on the "Bebung" which is very valuable:—

"§ 88. The 'Bebung' (French: *Balancement;* Italian: *Tremolo*) can only be employed with good effect on long notes, and in pieces of a sad character. It is usually indicated by the sign given at (*a*), or by the word *tremolo*, as at (*b*). The execution would be about as shown at (*c*) and (*d*):—

"One keeps the finger on the key as long as the value of the note requires, and endeavours by gentle, frequently repeated pressures to reinforce the tone. I need hardly remark that there must be a relaxation after each pressure, but the finger must not leave the key.

"This ornament can only be done on the clavichord, and indeed upon a very good one.

"One must not use the Bebung too often, and guard against the hateful exaggeration coming from too violent pressure."

SECTION IV.—Mordent, Beat (Open Shake, Sweetening).

Italian: *Mordente*, one of the *Groppi* and *Tremoli*, *Acciaccatura*.

German: *Mordant* or *Mordent*, *Beisser*, *Zusammenschlag*.

French: *Martellement*, *Pincement*, *Pincé*, *Battement*, *Mordant*.

This ornament consists of the rapid alternation of a note with the next note below it. The interval may be a semitone or a whole-tone, according to the scale. The main note is played first, and bears the accent. There may be one or more repercussions. As this ornament does not alter the melodic or harmonic character of the principal note, but rather emphasises it, it is equally suitable to the early contrapuntal and to the later harmonic music. The note above the principal is sometimes used instead of the note below; the ornament then becomes very similar to the common modern shake, but this form had become obsolete in the 18th century.

Nicolaus Ammerbach, in his "Orgel—oder Instrument — Tabulatur," 1571, explains the mordent excellently in this way:—

"In an ascending phrase, for example E to F, E will alternate with D and F with E.

"In a descending phrase, F to E, F alternates with G, and E with F":—

NICOLAUS AMMERBACH, 1571.

The true mordent and the old shake are very clearly differentiated here, and the rule given can be applied very frequently in the music of that period.

Diruta, in "Il Transilvano," 1597, has mordents amongst his *Groppi*, but they are more like divisions than mordents proper, for instead of stopping on the principal note, they lead straightway to the following:—

Prætorius's only example of a mordent was shown at page 199.

The lute-players called the mordent *Tiret*, *Pincé*, *Beat*, *Beisser*. Here is Thomas Mace's (1676) explanation of it:—

Page 105: "The *Beate*, is your *Letter* struck; (be it what it will) and so soon as it is struck, that sound must be *Falsifyed*, always into a *Half Note* beneath, by taking up your Finger, (as if you would *Back-fall* the *False Note*, from that stopped Letter) and *strongly*, so *shaked*, *and again;* yet, at last, the same Finger, must *rest down*, in the 1st *True note*. As for Example.

"If I would make a *Beate* upon *d*, on the 4th String, I must at the *same time*, (together with that *d*) stop *c*, on the *same string;* and, so soon as I have struck the *d*, I must *Twitch it up*, and by the *Twitch*, cause the *c* to Sound, and so continue in that *Quick Motion*, as if I did only intend to *Shake* the *c*; yet, so strongly knocking down my Finger into *d*, *that at every Knock*, or *Motion d* may be equally heard with *c*; and when I have thus continued *Beating*, so long as my Time will allow me, I must then give the last knock into *d*, with all the strength I can; so that *d* must be *Eminently heard* at the very last: For you must know this, that whatever your *Grace* be, you must in your *Fare-well*, express the *True Note* perfectly, or else your *pretended* Grace, will prove a *Disgrace*."

The "Table of Graces proper to the Viol or Violin," in Playford's "Introduction," 1654, and that in Christopher Simpson's "Division-Violist,"

1659, both give the following example, which is a mordent preceded by an appoggiatura :—

Chambonnières, in his "1st Book of Pieces," 1670, was the first to use the sign ⁓ for a mordent. It was used later by Couperin, J. S. Bach, and many other composers :—

In the "Harpsichord Pieces" of Monsieur Le Begue, Paris, 1677, the sign and execution of the mordent are the same as in Chambonnières. The name *pincement* became *pincé*, and the latter form remained in use in France until the 19th century.

In the Introduction to the "Pièces de Viole" of De Machy, 1685, the mordent, which is there called "martellement," is thus explained :—

"The Martellement is to lift the finger from the letter or note, as soon as it is heard, and to put it down again *at the same time*."

It is of course impossible to lift the finger and put it down again at the same time; but the author intends to emphasise the extreme rapidity which is one of the most important features of this ornament.

De Machy also explains the "double martellement" as being made in the same way, only doubled.

Marin Marais, "Pièces de Viole," 1686, calls the mordent "Batement," and marks it by a cross; so does De Caix d'Hervelois ("Pièces de Violes," *c.* 1725). Antoine Forqueray le Père (*c.* 1700) also uses a cross, but calls the mordent "Pincé."

Jean Rousseau, in his "Traité de la Viole," 1687, describes the mordent, which he calls "martellement," like De Machy, thus:—

"The martellement is done when the finger playing a note first beats two or three times more quickly and lightly than for a shake, and remains on the fret afterwards.

"The martellement is always inseparable from the appoggiatura, for the appoggiatura must always be terminated by a martellement. It is an ornament which the voice does naturally by a slight agitation of the throat, in finishing an appoggiatura, and the instruments must imitate it."

It should be remarked that the author is exaggerating when he says that every appoggiatura must be followed by a mordent. It is frequently done, after an appoggiatura from below; but after one from above a shake is preferable, and both appoggiature were often used plain by Rousseau's contemporaries.

Henry d'Anglebert, "Pièces de Clavecin," 1689, uses a comma after the note to indicate the mordent, which he calls "Pincé." It is clear from his examples that the number of repercussions was to be greater on a long note :—

G. Muffat, Preface to the pieces for viols entitled "Florilegium," Augsburg, 1695, gives the following explanation of the mordent :—

In the Rules for Graces of Purcell's "Harpsichord Pieces," 1696 (posthumous), the following explanation of the mordent is given: "A beat mark'd thus ; explain'd thus" :—

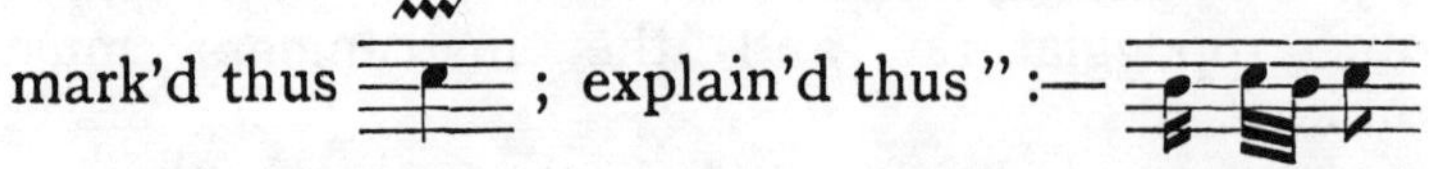

This is a mordent preceded by an appoggiatura.

"The Compleat Flute Master, or the whole Art of playing on y^e^ Rechorder," anonymous, London, *c.* 1700, has a quaint way of dividing his shakes into "close shake" and "open-shake," the former being the true variety, the latter the mordent. These appellations are logical enough on the flute, for a shake must finish with the shaking finger closing the hole, whilst the mordent, being made with the note below, must end with the shaking finger off the hole. The signs are:—

"A close shake thus =, an open shake, beat, or sweetning thus +. After a close shake keep your finger down, after an open shake keep your finger up."

François Couperin seems to have considered the mordent, which he calls "Pincé," as the most important grace; for he gives it the first place both in the Table of Graces prefacing his "First Book of Harpsichord Pieces" (1713), and in his "Méthode" (1716). Unfortunately, Couperin employs small notes of undetermined value to explain his *Pincés*, and the way he writes them at times might be construed by some as an excuse to play them *before* the note. But the explanations given in his "Méthode" leave no doubt as to his intentions. The following examples are taken from the "Explanations" of his "Harpsichord Pieces":—

The flat before C in Ex. 5 lowers the C♯ a semitone; it thus becomes C natural, not C *flat*.

The following examples and explanations are taken from Couperin's "Méthode," 1716:—

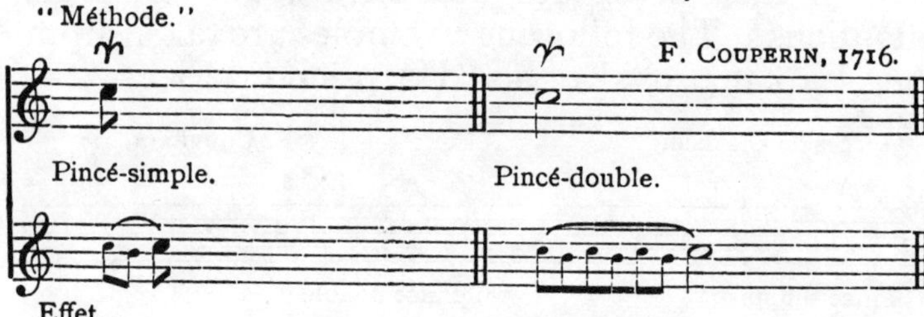

"Every *mordent* must be stopped on the note upon which it is posed; and to make it clear I use the word 'Stopping-place,' which is marked here below by a star; thus the beats, and the note upon which one stops, *must all be comprised in the value of the principal note*:—

"The *pincé-double*, in the playing of the organ and harpsichord, takes the place of the *martèlement* [vibrato] in the bow instruments."

Theophilo Muffat, in his "Componimenti," has the following very complete and perfect examples, which leave nothing doubtful and require no explanations. He also places the mordent first amongst his ornaments:—

TH. MUFFAT, ?1735.

J. Ph. Rameau, "Pièces de Clavecin," 1731, uses the comma to indicate mordents (*pincés*).

He places it to the right of the note, whilst the same comma placed on the left side of the note indicates the appoggiatura :—

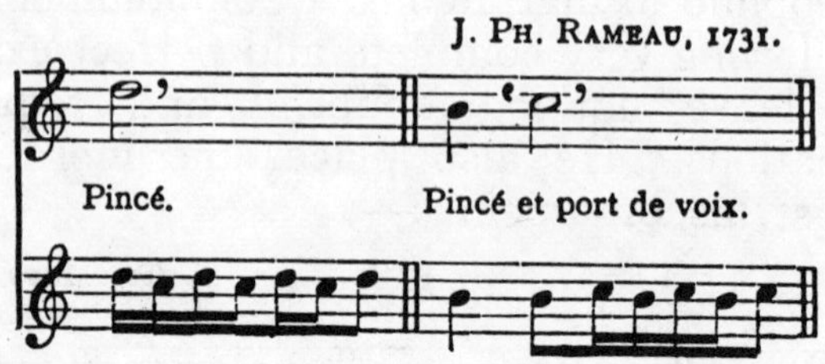

Ch. Dieupart (1731), Johann Mattheson (1739), and Mondonville (*c.* 1748), use the same sign and interpretation as Rameau. Marpurg (1755) has a very complete table like Muffat, but gives nothing new. It is rather interesting to see him show so late the old English sign 𝄚; but he perhaps gives it for the sake of completeness.

J. S. Bach, in the explanations of ornaments written for his son, W. Friedemann Bach, 1720, has the following mordents :—

Very little need be said about these. Bach obviously wanted them to be very rapid, and on the beat. The number of repercussions was left to the player when the principal note was long enough for more than one. He sometimes used the sign ⁓|⁓ for a mordent, and it probably meant a long mordent; but considering his lack of system, this cannot be depended upon. The context should be studied before deciding. His use of the sign ⁓⁓| for a "trillo und mordant" (really a shake with the common termination) is unfortunate for two reasons: the first is that the sign could easily be mistaken for the mark of a long mordent, as the difference in the position of the perpendicular stroke, from the right end of the wavy line to the middle, is so slight; and the second because the termination of the shake thus indicated is not a mordent, though it resembles one.

J. J. Quantz ("Versuch," &c., 1752), Chap. viii., § 14, comprises the mordent amongst the "Kleine Manieren" which may ornament the appoggiatura, and are "used by the French to add brilliancy to their pieces." The examples have been given at page 129, Exx. (*c*), (*d*), (*f*), (*g*). He calls the first two "Pincés," the last two "Battements." The reason of this difference in names is not clear. We shall quote his § 15 entirely:—

"To give vivacity and brilliancy to notes proceeding by skip, when an appoggiatura is not practicable, one may also use Battements. The first kind of battement [Ex. (*f*)], is made on the flute with the tongue and finger movement at the same time, and can be used on quick or slow notes equally well; but the last kind [Ex. (*g*)], is more suitable for moderately slow notes than for quick ones. It is necessary, however, that the demisemiquavers be played with the utmost possible speed, and for this reason the finger must not be lifted high."

One must not try too literally to use the "tongue and finger at the same time," for then the lower note only would sound. But, like De Machy, he means to impress the student with the necessity of playing the mordent with extreme rapidity.

C. Ph. E. Bach, in his "Versuch," &c., 1753, devotes four pages and some thirty examples to the mordent. As it is unnecessary to repeat what has already been fully said, we shall only quote those passages which contain something new. In the following examples, the sign 𝆖 means a short mordent; 𝆖 a mordent of any length over three notes.

"§ 3. There is a special way of making the mordent when it has to be very short. One plays the two notes together (Ex. 1), immediately releasing the lower and holding the upper one only. This manner is not to be despised, but it must be used much more rarely than the other mordent. It occurs only *ex abrupto—i.e.*, without connection—at the beginning of a phrase or after rests.

(This is the Pincé étouffé, Acciaccatura, or Zusammenschlag):—

"§ 6. The mordent following an appoggiatura must be played soft, according to the rule for the execution of the appoggiatura.

"§ 7 The mordent is used to fill up sustained notes; also as shown in the above examples on notes tied over (Ex. 2), on dotted notes (Ex. 3), on syncopations (Ex. 4). In the latter case the mordent may be repeated on successive or alternate notes. In the last two examples the mordent is best introduced on the first syncopation (Ex. 5), or on the first repetition of a preceding tone (Ex. 6). In such syncopations the mordent not only fills up, but at the same time adds brilliancy to the notes.

"§ 8. In such figures as Exx. 2 and 3, if the tempo is so slow that even a long mordent is not sufficient to fill up, one may divide these long notes and re-strike them, playing as shown in Exx. 2*a* and 3*a*. Such liberties, however, must be used with caution; one might thereby mar the composer's design.

"This fault will be avoided when players realise that with proper pressure and holding of the notes, the tone of our instrument [the clavichord] can be sustained much longer than they think. The long mordents should not be allowed to hinder the ringing of prolonged sounds, which happens when they are continued too long, or applied indiscriminately to every note of some length. After a mordent intended to fill up, a short space of time must always be left over, for the best performed mordent becomes nauseous if it is directly connected, like a shake, with the following note.

"§ 9. To skipping and detached notes, the mordent adds brilliance. In such cases it is generally played short. One finds it over notes which are important harmonically to establish the key (Ex. 7), with certain passages in broken chords (Ex. 8), and over the middle note of full chords (Ex. 9), where, if the note is long enough, the long mordent can be used (Ex. 10). This ornament occurs sometimes on staccato dotted notes, when the dots are not held (Ex. 11), and where rests follow thereon (Ex. 12); also when after several short notes a longer one follows (Exx. 13, 14):—

"§ 10. Amongst all ornaments the mordent is the most frequently used in the bass, although its sign is rarely marked there. It is used on ascending notes (Ex. 15), on skips (Ex. 16), particularly when the bass jumps down an octave, whether there be a cadence or not (Ex. 17).

"§ 11. The mordent, like the shake, takes the accidentals required by the key. Often an accidental is added for the sake of incisiveness (Ex. 18) :—

C. Ph. E. Bach, 1753.

"§ 12. In order that after a short note the necessary fingers may be equally free and ready for a mordent, a special fingering is necessary (see Ex. 18). These fingerings demand a moderate tempo, and are justified by the short duration of the dotted note (*i.e., the dot becoming a rest*), by dint of which, after settling the 4th finger, the thumb and 2nd finger are alike prepared for the execution of the mordent. There is time enough, with the long note of the 3rd finger, to carry the hand a little to the right. Should such passages occur without dots, or in quick time, the usual fingering would be preferable.

"§ 13. We have seen that the mordent, specially when it is long, is employed to *fill up* long sustained notes. When so used after a shake, the long note must be divided so as to ensure the separation of the mordent from the shake, for *one ought never to crowd ornaments behind one another.*

"In Ex. 19 the right way to treat such cases is shown. The duration of the mordent depends on the tempo, which, of course, cannot be fast, or else this expedient would not be needed at all :—

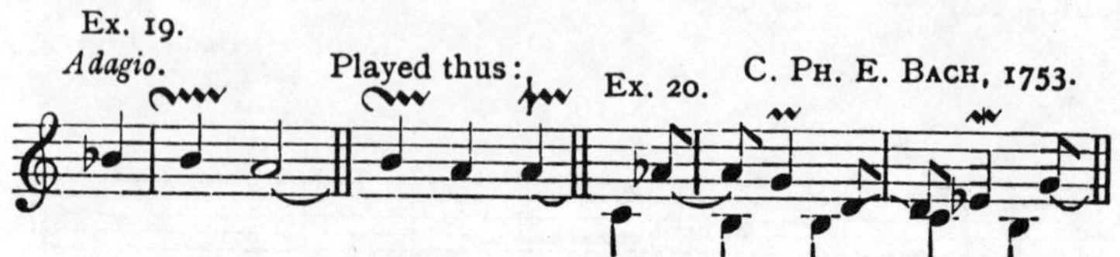

"§ 14. The mordent and the half-shake are the reverse of one another in this respect, that the latter can only be made on descending seconds whilst the mordent can never be used thus. They both fit well on seconds; the mordent when they ascend, the half-shake when they descend. This is clearly demonstrated in Ex. 20."

The later writers, having nothing new to teach us, need not be quoted. It is only when we come to Hummel, 1828, the great pioneer of confusion and ignorance on this, our subject, that we find a new departure. The mordent is left out altogether from his explanations of graces, and its name given to another ornament.

SECTION V.—THE TURN, SINGLE RELISH.

Italian: *Circolo mezzo.*

French: *Doublé, Cadence, Tour de Gosier, Double-Cadence, Cadence sans tremblements.*

German: *Doppelschlag.*

The turn consists of four notes: the note above the principal, the principal, the note below, the principal again. Sometimes the order is reversed: the note below comes first, the note above third. This ornament has been in favour from the earliest times to the present day. It is pretty, easy to perform, and can be placed almost anywhere. It can be abused; in fact, it has been much abused. The following explanations, though not exhaustive (a volume could be written upon it), ought to be sufficient to ensure its reasonable and effective employment. It is often found as a termination to the shakes in the 16th century. Examples can be seen in "Ganassi," 1535 (page 155); Diego Ortiz, 1553 (page 155); G. Diruta, 1597 (page 156), &c.; in fact, most shakes end with a turn. But it is also frequently used by itself, among the divisions, under the form called by the Italians *circolo mezzo*. In this case the turn begins on the principal note, and either returns to it (Ex. 1), or leads to the third above (Ex. 2), or to the third below (Ex. 3). Sometimes the principal note is held, when time allows, and the turn ornaments the end of it, connecting it with the sequel (Exx. 4, 5):—

Chambonnières, "Pièces de Clavecin," 1670, gives the following example:—

In the original the last C is made a semiquaver, an obvious mistake.

Thomas Mace, "The Lute," &c., 1676, page 107, says: "The *Single Relish* ∴ is generally done upon the *Ascension* or *Descension* of a 3d. Thus:—

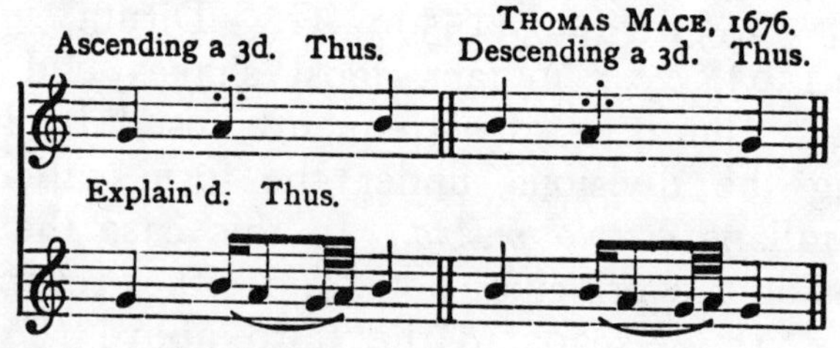

"Note, That the 2d Note, upon which you perform the *Relish*, has a *Back-fall*, which would always be performed very *strongly and smartly*, before you attempt the other *2 Notes;* which is *All* that is needful to be express'd, concerning the *Single Relish*."

In other words, the short appoggiatura which begins the turn must be well accented.

J. H. D'Anglebert, "Pièces de Clavecin," 1689, has several forms of turns, exhibiting side by side the old "division" turn, and the form that was almost exclusively employed in the Bach period

In Ex. 1 the first four notes are a true turn, introducing a shake.

In Ex. 2 the turn is inverted.

In Ex. 3 we have the old turn, starting on the main note and descending a third, followed by an inverted turn introducing a shake.

In Ex. 4 it is again the old turn, followed by a true turn introducing a shake.

In Ex. 5 the turn is simple, and employed in the most usual manner.

In Ex. 6 the turn is also simple, but it is played a little after the beat, thus giving special emphasis to the harmony note :—

There is a fundamental difference between the turns shown in Exx. 3 and 4 and the true turns of the other examples.

On account of the emphasis given to the third below the principal note, which comes as a longer note after shorter ones, the first turn will fit well only when the main note is the third above the bass; it might be used on the fifth, if the B was made flat, but it will not do on the octave from the bass, with a common chord. The other turn, on the contrary, will do equally well in all cases.

George Muffat, in the "Florilegium Primum," 1695, has an interesting turn:—

"The sign for the turn, being placed after the main note, ornaments the latter part of it. The quaver D becomes transformed into a semi-quaver, according to the rule for the playing of short notes after dots. The following shake would of course begin with an appoggiatura, E."

In Purcell's "Lessons for the Harpsichord," 1696 (posthumous), we find this amongst the "Rules for Graces":—

"A mark for the turn thus:—

explain'd thus—

the mark for y^e shake turn'd thus—

explain'd thus—

"

The turn is perfect in both examples. The main note is played first, in the first example, which retards the turn a little, as in Ex. 6 of D'Anglebert.

In Loulié's "Principes de Musique," 1696, the jerky character of the turn is interesting. The ternary rhythm should not, however, be taken too literally. No more is meant than the alternation of short and long notes :—

François Couperin, "Pièces de Claveçin," 1713, only gives the following examples of the turn, and he does not mention it in his "Méthode":—

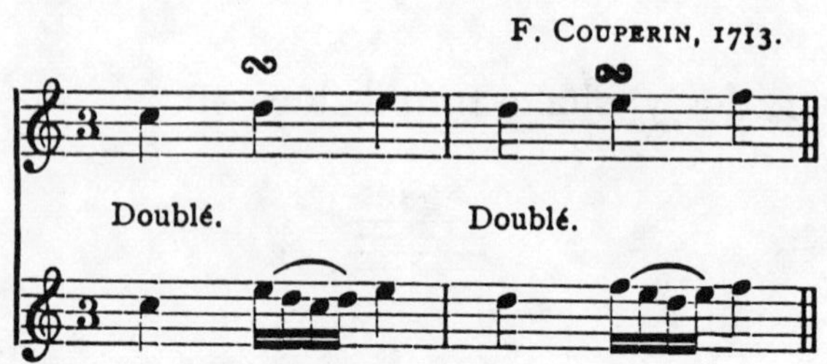

In his music the sign for the turn is occasionally placed after the principal note, which should in such cases be played first, the turn being introduced later.

Couperin also uses the compound sign ∾, which is somewhat forbidding in appearance. It only means the usual shake ending with a turn, of which we have seen many examples already.

J. S. Bach, in the explanations of ornaments written for his son, W. Friedemann, in 1720, has the following examples of turns; they are substantially the same as D'Anglebert's (page 227), and need no special comment:—

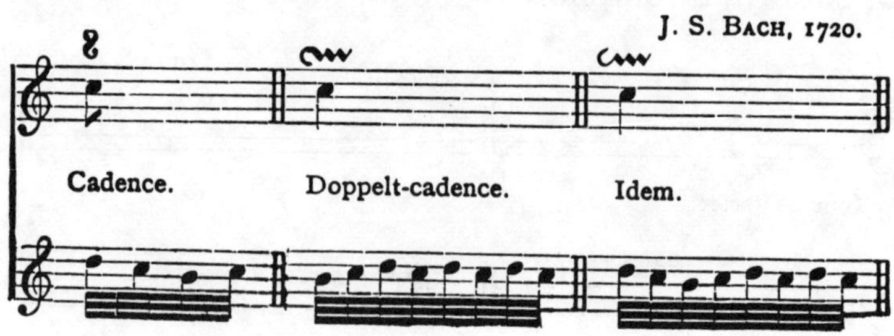

In practice, the horizontal sign (∾) for the turn appears more frequently than the vertical (8); the meaning is the same. When the sign is placed between two notes, the turn is played after the first note, and connects it with the following note. The combination ∾ occasionally appears in Bach's music. It should be played as explained above in connection with Fr. Couperin.

Th. Muffat,?1735, has nothing new to show.

J. Ph. Rameau, 1731, calls the turn "Doublé," and treats it like Couperin.

Charles Dieupart, "Pièces de Claveçin" [1731], gives the following example:—

This is the old turn which starts on the main note and goes down a third, as in Chambonnières and D'Anglebert, and he uses no other. This points to an earlier date than is generally ascribed to his pieces. They were published without a date, and the date of birth of Dieupart is unknown. He died in 1740. There is no reason why his "Pièces" should not have been written about 1700, which would agree well with the style of the music.

Fr. W. Marpurg, in "Die Kunst das Klavier zu spielen," Berlin, 1750, shows the following turns:—

In Ex. 1, first bar, we see the turn on the end of a note, and in the second bar the written-out execution of the double sign, already mentioned. In Ex. 2 we see the special sign indicating a turn which starts on the main note, the old "Groppo" of *c.* 1600.

In the French version of this work, published in 1755, the various kinds of turns, with their different notations, are given as follows:—

In Ex. 3 the turn is shown in two different rhythms. The first for quick, the second for slow movements.

In Ex. 4 the inverted sign indicates an inverted turn. It is logical enough, but in practice the two signs are not easily distinguished from one another. The context shows sufficiently well whether the direct or the inverted turn should be used; in doubtful cases, the former would naturally be preferred. Ex. 5 seems to restrict the upright sign to the inverted turn; in practice, it means either one or the other.

Exx. 6, 7, 8, 9 show turns indicated wholly or partly by means of small notes, which, of course, does not alter their execution. In Ex. 10 we have the old Groppo again.

Ex. 11 shows the turn coming after an appoggiatura or a slur; its first note is held, not repeated, in such cases.

Quantz mentions the "Doublé" (page 81, paragraph 14), but has nothing special to say about it.

C. Ph. E. Bach devotes twelve pages of his "Versuch, &c.," 1753, to the turn, and gives some seventy examples not included in the twelve pages.

It would be of little use to quote all, most of which we know already well enough. The following extracts will suffice:—

"Von dem Doppelschlage, § 7. This beautiful ornament is too convenient; it fits almost anywhere, and consequently is often abused. Many seem to believe that the whole grace and charm of clavier-playing consists in introducing a turn at every moment. It is therefore necessary to learn its proper use, for in spite of its handiness, there are many tempting opportunities to place it where it should not be.

"§ 8. The turn is used principally to add brilliance to the notes; thus it commonly happens that notes which for expression should be simply sustained, are found uncomfortably long by those who do not understand the right touch and style, and are therefore spoiled by a turn.

"§ 9. If one considers that this ornament represents, in shortened form, an ordinary shake with termination, one can already get some idea of its proper use.

"§ 10. The turn being played quickly, in most cases, and its upper note *snapped* in the manner previously described (page 185), it is a mistake to use it on a long note instead of an ordinary shake, for the note is thus left too empty.

"§ 11. An exception should be made when, in slow time, for the sake of expression, or at a close (Ex. 1), or again after an appoggiatura from below (Ex. 2), instead of a shake one makes a *soft turn*, and holds its last note until the next:—

"§ 12. By reason of its resemblance to a shake with a termination, the turn goes better in ascending than in descending passages. One can even easily ornament all the notes of an ascending scale of one octave or more with plain turns; but not a descending one. This occurs frequently in music for the violin and other instruments of a like nature. The notation is then as at Ex. 3, the execution as at (*a*) and (*b*), according to the tempo:—

"§ 17. The sign for the turn is very little known outside of clavier players; yet this ornament is absolutely necessary. It thus happens that in instrumental music the sign for the shake, or even that of the mordent, is used to indicate a turn. In the following examples, there are many places where a turn is better and more convenient than a shake :—

In Exx. 4, 10, 18, 19, no other ornament but a turn could be used.

"In Exx. 13, 14, 15, and 16, where the third note is a repetition of the second, a shake would be right in slow or moderate tempo, and a turn in quick time.

"In Ex. 17, in slow time one might add a passing appoggiatura after the turn.

"§ 18. In Exx. 18 and 19, which are recitatives, and in which the last note of the turn must not be sustained, in imitation of speech, a turn is expressly demanded. As the sign for the shake could not possibly be placed there, if one knows of no other, the ornament has to be left to the discretion of the player."

The later writers bring no new information of importance on the turn; but in Türk's "Klavierschule," 1789, the following useful warning is given:—

"The quick turn (*geschnellter Doppelschlag*) begins with the principal note. It is often written as at (*a*). It must be played as indicated below; not as at (*b*). The principal note must not be played twice in succession":—

SECTION VI.

The Slide, Elevation, Double Backfall, Wholefall, Slur, Bearing.

French: *Coulé. Flatté.*
German: *Schleifer.*

This ornament consists of two additional consecutive notes below the principal, the lower of which is played first, with an accent and in the time of the principal.

The note C being given, to make a slide to it, start on A a third below, and play smoothly the three notes A, B, C, being careful not to begin before the time appointed for C. Sometimes the slide is inverted, the two additional notes being above the principal instead of below.

The slide is a very old ornament. It has been in and out of fashion several times. It was much abused early in the 17th century, if we may believe this passage:—

Playford's "Introduction to the Skill of Music," 1654:—

"There are some that in the *Tuning* of the first *Note*, Tune it a *Third* under: Others Tune the first *Note* in his proper Tune, always increasing it in Loudness, saying, that this is the good way of putting forth the *Voyce* gracefully.

"Concerning the first: Since it is not a general Rule, because it agrees not in many Cords, although in such places as it may be used, it is now become so ordinary, that instead of being a Grace (because some stay too long in the third note under, whereas it should be but lightly touched) it is rather tedious to the Ear; and that for Beginners in particular it ought seldom to be used: but instead of it, as being more strange, I would chuse the second for the Increasing of the Voyce."

This passage in Playford was taken from Caccini's "Nuove Musiche," the 2nd edition, 1607. The slide, therefore, must have been common at that time in Italy, although it is not often found in contemporary treatises. Here, however, are a few examples:—

Prætorius, as we know, was quoting Italian authors. It is worthy of notice that in all his examples, except the last, the first note of the slide is held and accented in the manner condemned by Playford, the very manner which became the rule in the 18th century.

Later, in "Playford's Introduction," among the "Graces for the Viol or Violin," already quoted, we find the following examples of perfect slides with the signs indicating them:—

Christopher Simpson, in the "Division Violist," 1659, says:—

Page 11: "Sometimes a note is Graced by sliding up to it from a Third below, called an *Elevation*, now something obsolete. Sometimes from the Third above, which we call a *Double Back-Fall*. This Sliding a Third, is performed commonly upon one String."

In the Table of Graces which follows, and which is written by "the ever-famous Charles Colman, Doctor in Musick," the signs and explanations given are precisely the same as those of Playford.

Thomas Mace, in "Musick's Monument," 1676, has the following:—

Page 105: "The *Whole-fall*, is a *Grace*, much out of use, in *These our Days;* yet because, in some Cases it is very *Good*, and *Handsome*, and may give *Delight*, and *Content* to many, who think fit to use It; know, it is *Thus Performed; viz.* It gives *Two* False Letters, before the *True intended Letter* comes in.

"Explained thus.

"Suppose I would give a *Whole-fall*, to the Letter *d*, upon the *5th String:* Then I must first strike *a*, upon that *String;* and then *fall my Fore-finger hard*, upon *b*, on the *same string*, and so closely after, (holding *b* still stopt) fall my 3d or *Little Finger*, as hard into the True intended Letter *d;* and thus the *Performance is Finished;* yet always observing, (that for an *Equality*, *and Evenness*, *in these 3 sounds*) (which is a thing *Chiefly* to be Regarded) you must take *Care*, that you strike not the first *so Loud*, as that the *strength* of the *Finger*, is not sufficient to cause the other 2 *following Letters to Sound as Loud, as the first which was struck.* Therefore, ever at a *Whole-fall*, strike the first Note of the 3, *Softly;* so may you with the more *Ease*, and *Certainty*, make the *next 2*, *as Loud;* for a Man cannot fall a *String* so Loud, as he can strike it."

This is the language of Lute Tablature. The notes mentioned correspond to *e*, *f*, *g*. The example in ordinary notation would come to this:—

"Musick's Monument," 1676. THOMAS MACE.

The sign used is the same as Playford's and Simpson's. It is the all-covering cross which for over a century indicated all kinds of ornaments in all kinds of music.

In Chambonnières's Table (1670), the "coulé" is a perfect slide to the ear; the fact that the first note is held down does not alter the effect so long as that note is part of the harmony.

In Purcell the notation is the same as Chambonnières's, only that the first note of the slide is not held down. Purcell calls it the slur;

a misleading name, since it conveys other meanings besides that intended.

D'Anglebert, 1689, shows various aspects of the slide. The examples of these three composers are quoted side by side, their resemblance being thus rendered the more striking:—

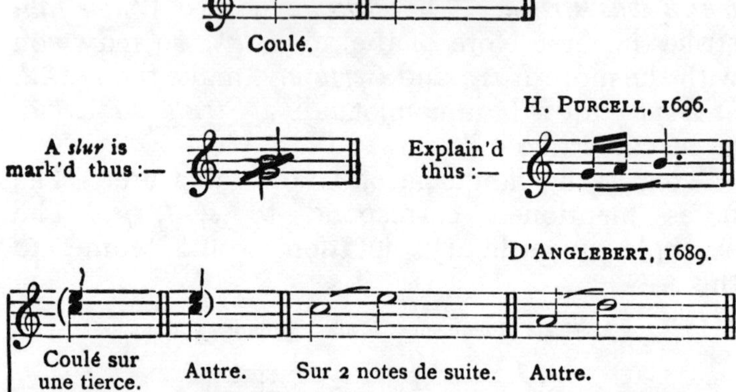

In G. Muffat's "Florilegium," 1695, the slide is similar to the preceding examples, the sign only being different:—

The composers of music for the viola da gamba, violin, flute, &c., of that period make a frequent use of the slide; but they indicate it in small notes, as may be seen in the works of Marin Marais, De Caix d'Hervelois, the Forquerays, and others, Some, like Senaillé, Schenck, &c., use the cross +, which means so many things that it is hardly better than no indication at all.

In all the examples of slides we have seen so far the ornament is played in the time of the principal note. This rule, however, was not followed by everybody. There always were some who played the graces *before* the notes to which they belong, in opposition to the practice of the great masters. Among them we find Johann Gottfried Walther, a contemporary and friend of J. S. Bach. Here are his examples:—

The slides are at (*a*), (*b*), (*c*). If played as they should be, with an accent on the first note diminishing the tone towards the principal, they sound neither graceful nor flowing, the one at (*c*) especially. They do not agree with the idea conveyed by the French word "flatté." They might, however, be considered as passing-notes, in which case they should be played evenly and the effect would be good; but then they would no longer be slides, and the sign ought not to be thus misused; it creates a confusion which may prove difficult to remove.

The sign ⁓ used by Walther had been previously employed by Joh. Kuhnau, *c.* 1689. J. S. Bach made frequent use of it; but during the 18th century the tendency has been more and more towards indicating the slide by means of small notes in preference to signs.

Franz Xaver Murschhauser, "Prototypon," &c., 1703, gives the following sign and explanation of the slide among his "Signa quaedam nonnullis explicanda":—

J. D. Heinichen, "General-Bass," 1728, has the following signs and explanations of the slide:—

Observe that the position of the oblique cross x in the stave indicates the note upon which the slide begins; also that the first note of the slide is six times longer than the principal note!

In the works of François Couperin the slides are generally written in small notes, and conform to his constant practice of playing ornaments in the time of the principal note to which they belong. In the Table of Graces which precedes his first book of pieces, his explanation of the "Tierce coulée" seems to place the ornament before the main note :—

This, however, should not be taken literally. Couperin's notation was often lacking in precision.

J. Ph. Rameau does not mention the slide.

In Th. Muffat's Table we find the following turns :—

Fr. Wilh. Marpurg gives the following slides :—

J. S. Bach has not included the slide in the list of ornaments he wrote for his son Friedemann. It is, however, frequently found in his works, sometimes written out in full, or in small notes, or indicated by the sign ∾. In the *Andante* of the Sonata in D major for harpsichord and viola da gamba there are many slides either written out as at (*a*) or indicated by a sign as at (*b*) :—

In the Aria for alto with violin obbligato from the second part of the "St. Matthew" Passion, "Erbarme dich," there are many slides indicated in small notes as at (*c*), or written out in full as at (*f*) and (*g*). The slide-like figures at (*d*) and (*e*) must not be confused with true slides, being only the termination of a shake which in the first case (*d*) is not even marked :—

Bach, as we know, was not careful in his texts. If, however, we consider the slides fully written out in his works, the way in which both these and the ones indicated by small notes or the usual sign fit the harmonies, and the constant practice of Bach concerning ornaments, as shown by his examples, it becomes evident that his slides must be played out of the time of the note which follows them.

In Chap. xvii., § 2, of J. J. Quantz's "Versuch, &c.," 1752, which is written for violin players, the following passages are given :—

"§ 21. When, in a slow movement, one finds additional small quavers, the first of which is dotted (see Ex. 1), they take the time of the principal note which follows them, and the latter gets only the time of the dot. They must be played lovingly, and in the manner shown at Ex. 2. The double-dotted note must be played with a down bow, *crescendo*, the next two slurred, *diminuendo*, the last *staccato*, with an up bow.

"§ 23. The two small semiquavers, Ex. 3, belong to the French style rather than to the Italian. They must not be played as slowly as those mentioned before, but on the contrary, with precipitation, as shown in Ex. 4":—

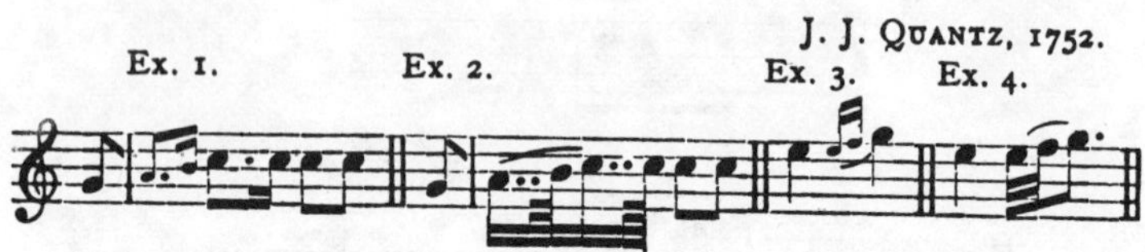

In C. Ph. E. Bach's "Versuch, &c.," 1753, we find mixed with the true slide an ornament of three notes which, being really an inverted turn, finds its proper place amongst the turns, and need not detain us further.

The following compendium of C. Ph. E. Bach's precepts and examples concerning the slide will be found useful:—

"The slide is used with or without a dot (Exx. 1 and 5).

"Slides are indicated by two little demisemiquavers; in *alla breve* time semiquavers are sufficient (Exx. 1 and 2). This ornament is also indicated by a sign (Ex. 3), or written out in full (Ex. 4).

"The slide with a dot conveys a pleasant feeling. Its time arrangement varies more than that of almost any other ornament; in the pieces I give as examples for study I have therefore written this ornament very carefully.

"The following examples exhibit a variety of slides, with their execution. In the case of Ex. 13, the arrangement shown at (*a*) goes better with the bass than that at (*b*).

"These examples show the proper places for using the slide. In the case of discords (Exx. 9, 10, 11, 12), or bare octaves (Exx. 14, 15), some ornament must be used, and there is no other which would do as well as a slide.

"The notes following a slide generally descend, but at Ex. 14 it is shown that the melody might continue on the same note. All that pertains to the playing of this ornament is shown at Exx. 7 and 8. We see there that the dotted note must be loud, whilst the little note which leads to the principal should be soft. The dot on the last note of the slur shows that the finger must be lifted before the value of this note is finished; in consequence, the dot which follows the first note becomes a rest, as may be seen at Exx. 12 and 13":—

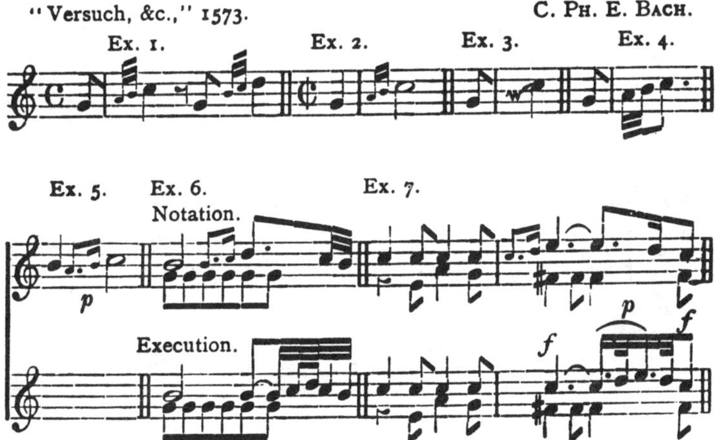

Ex. 8.
Notation.
Ex. 9.
Execution.
f
p
f
(a)
(b)
Ex. 10.
Ex. 11.
Notation.
Execution.
Ex. 12.
Ex. 13.
Notation.
Ex. 14.
Execution.
(a)
(b)

SECTION VII.

The Springer (or Spinger). Accent. Acute. Sigh.

French: *Accent. Aspiration. Plainte.*
German: *Nachschlag.*

The Springer or Accent consists of a short auxiliary note introduced at the end of the principal, and connecting it with the following note. This additional note is generally the next above, but sometimes the next below, the principal.

Prætorius, "Syntagma," &c., 1619, gives the following examples of accents:—

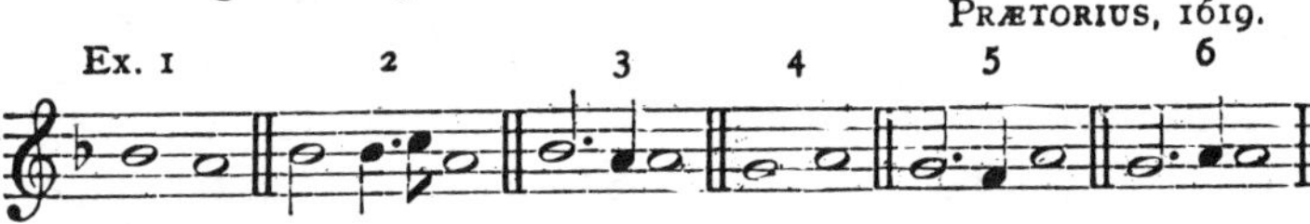

Exx. 1 and 4 are the plain notes; the others show the accents. In Exx. 3 and 6, the auxiliary note being the same as the following, the accent becomes an anticipation.

In Playford's "Introduction," &c., 1654, the following sign and explanation of the Springer are given in the Table of Graces:—

Ch. Simpson, in his "Division Violist," 1659 (page 11), says:—

"There is yet another Plain or Smooth Grace called an *Acute* or *Springer*, which concludes the Sound of a Note more acute, by clapping down another Finger just at the expiring of it."

The sign and explanation in his Table of Graces are the same as Playford's.

Th. Mace, in "Musick's Monument," 1676, calls this ornament "Spinger"; as he uses the same spelling constantly through his work, the omission of the "r" cannot be attributed to a misprint. His sign is the same as Playford's ⁀.

Mace's explanations are as follows:—

Page 108: "The *Spinger*, is a *Grace*, very *Neat, and Curious*, for some sort of *Notes;* and is done *Thus*, viz.

"After you have *Hit your Note*, which you intend to make the *Grace upon*, you must (just as you intend to part with *your Note*) *Dab* one of your *next Fingers lightly upon the same String, a Fret, or 2 Fretts below*, (according to the *Ayre*) as if you did intend to *stop the String, in that Place, yet so Gently, that you do not cause the String to Sound, in that Stop*, (so dab'd;) but only so, that it may *suddenly take away that Sound, which you last struck;* yet give some *small Tincture of a New Note;* but not *Distinctly to be heard*, as a *Note;* which *Grace* (if *Well done, and Properly*) is very *Taking, and Pleasant.*"

This is not really possible on any instrument but the lute. The guitar might give some idea of it, though its strings are too thick and too tight to produce the effect in perfection. Its particular grace can only be imitated on other instruments by playing the auxiliary note very softly and smoothly, and making it as short as possible.

Jean Rousseau, in his "Traité de la Viole," 1687, calls this grace "l'Aspiration," and gives many rules for its use. His directions for performance are worth quoting; they are excellent, and may be applied to all bowed instruments.

Page 90: "The Aspiration is made when at the end of a note one lets a finger fall upon the note which is situated immediately above it, in the same bowing, and upon which the bow must suddenly stop."

Rousseau does not give any sign for the Springer. In his examples, the cross indicates a shake:—

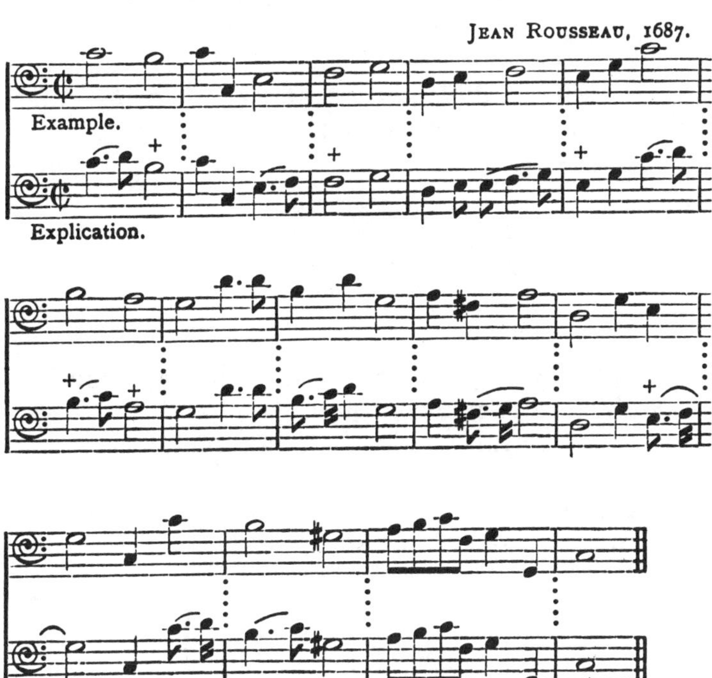

"Florilegium," 1695. G. MUFFAT.

LOULIÉ, 1696.

Fr. Couperin calls the Springer "Accent," and gives the following example :—

"Pièces de Clavecin," 1713. FRANÇOIS COUPERIN.

In the works of J. S. Bach, the Springer or *Nachschlag* is frequently found; but almost always written out in full. There is, however, a passage in the first Sonata for harpsichord and viola da gamba which seems to have a *Nachschlag* indicated by means of a short curve .—

Allegro moderato, bars 6, 7.

If the sign is correct, the execution would be :—

But considering that this *Nachschlag* destroys the syncopation, a characteristic feature of the phrase; that the same phrase occurs over and over again in the same movement, both in the viola da gamba part and in that of the harpsichord, but that the doubtful sign appears only once, it is probable that it is a mistake, and therefore had better be ignored by the performer.

C. Ph. E. Bach incidentally mentions the *Nachschlag*, but only to condemn it. It seems that some of his contemporaries abused it. No doubt the ornament in itself is weak, and if introduced too frequently would render the music insipid. But judiciously employed, it is full of grace and charm, and many phrases of Corelli or Tartini could not live without it.

The last author we need mention about the Springer is Fr. Wilh. Marpurg, who gives many interesting examples of it.

By the way, he further confirms the principle that graces were universally played in the time of the note which follows them. The aspiration and the portamento being the only two ornaments which do not follow this rule, to make sure that the little note which indicates them should not be treated as an appoggiatura and taken out of the following note, Marpurg turned the hooks of the little notes backwards to render confusion impossible. This device may be seen in Exx. 2. 3, 5, 8, and 9 of the following examples:—

In Exx. 6 and 7 the ornament is more akin to a portamento than an aspiration.

SECTION VIII.

The "Anschlag" or Doppelsvorschlag.

French : *Port de voix double.*

This ornament consists of two notes situated the one a second below, the other a second above, the principal. These two notes may be played more or less quickly, but always softly, and in the time of the principal. Sometimes the first note may form an interval greater than a second below the principal; but in such cases it must be a repetition of the preceding note. There is no English name for this ornament. Its French name, *Port de voix double*, is not appropriate, since it gives the idea of an appoggiatura with its accent on the auxiliary note, whilst there must be no such accent in the *Anschlag*. The word "Anschlag" literally means "striking at."

No sign was used for this ornament: only small notes.

It is first mentioned by Quantz in his "Versuch," &c., Chap. xiii., § 41:—

"The two small notes at (*a*), (*b*), (*c*), (*d*), (*e*), (*f*), (*g*), which form a skip of a third, are an *Anschlag*, which singers use in wide intervals, to find surely a high note. If you wish to make no other grace, you may use this *Anschlag* on all rising intervals, from a second to an octave, before long notes on accented or unaccented beats. But it must be joined very quickly, though softly, to the note. The note itself must be a little louder than the small notes. At the second, fourth and seventh, (*a*), (*c*), (*f*), the *Anschlag* is more agreeable than with the other intervals; it sounds better, therefore, when the auxiliary note is a semitone below the principal. Although the *Anschlag* expresses tender, sighing and pleasant feelings, it would not be advisable to use it too often. It must be rarely employed, for what is most pleasant is easiest to remember, and too much of one thing, however good, soon palls upon one":—

The *Anschlag* is occasionally found in J. S. Bach's works; but with one exception it is always written in full.

The exception is in the Saraband of the unfinished Suite for clavier in F minor: "Bach Gesellschaft," 36th year, page 230, bars 5, 6:—

And yet this is not a true *Anschlag*, for the skip between the two auxiliary notes is larger than a third, and the first note is not a repetition of the preceding main note. It should, however, be treated as an *Anschlag*.

Fr. Wilh. Marpurg, in his "Principes du Clavecin," 1755, gives the following examples:—

In Ex. 5 we see an inverted *Anschlag*, a very rare ornament.

In Ex. 6 the *Anschlag* is dotted. Its nature is much altered thereby, as the dotted note must perforce be accented. It is questionable whether it should be called an *Anschlag* in that form.

C. Ph. E. Bach, in his "Versuch," &c., 1753, has a chapter on the *Anschlag*. Some of the rules and examples are valuable, and complete the preceding information :—

The small notes in Ex. 1, when there is a skip of more than a third, are not played so rapidly as at Ex. 2; but they must always be played softer than the principal note.

The *Anschlag*, when it consists of the seconds below and above the principal, may be used in quick passages where no other ornament would be satisfactory (Ex. 3) :—

In slow time the *Anschlag* will do very well in such cases as Ex. 4, for it will soften the discord of the augmented second.

SECTION IX.

THE ARPEGGIO. BATTERY. BROKEN CHORD.

French : *Arpégé. Harpégement. Harpégé.*

German : *Harpeggio.*

Italian : *Arpeggio. Harpeggiato.*

The Arpeggio consists in playing the notes of a chord severally in succession instead of together.

Its name is derived from the Harp, on which instrument it is natural and effective to break the chords. In modern music, the chords, when broken, are nearly always broken upwards, beginning with the lowest note. In the old music many other forms were used. The player had to find out the best arrangement, and he was supposed to know how to fill up the time of each Arpeggio chord according to the style of the piece he was playing.

Frescobaldi, in the third paragraph of the Preface quoted at page 4, says :—

"The beginnings of the Toccate should be played *adagio* and *arpeggiando ;* the same applies to the syncopations and discords, even in the middle of the pieces. The chords should be broken with both hands so that the instrument may not be left empty ; this battery can be repeated at pleasure."

This clearly tells us what to do, but not how to do it. Plenty of information is, however, available from other sources, and it is hoped the sequence will make everything clear. Meanwhile, here is the beginning of Frescobaldi's eighth Toccata, first as it stands in the original, then as it might be interpreted. The long bars of the original are divided in the interpretation, to facilitate reading :—

"Toccata Otava"—Original text. FRESCOBALDI.

&c.

The same, interpreted :—

The lute players were experts in the art of breaking chords to fill up the harmony; so much so that the French called "parties luthées" those inner parts filled with arpeggios, so much used in the instrumental music of the period 1650-1750.

In Mace's "Musick's Monument" (1676) there is much valuable information on arpeggios.

A certain kind of close broken chord, very effective not only on the lute but on other instruments, is called by Mace "Raking play," and explained thus:—

Page 101. "Begin to Rake (or smoothly stroak) all those 1st Six Strings at the Treble String, laying on your 1st Finger, at the same time you lay on your *Bass;* Then, just as you hit the *Bass* with your *Thumb*, draw all over your *Fore-finger*, *very gently*, till you have hit the *Sixth String*, and you will hear a very *Full Consort*, of 7 Parts. . . . "

Here is the effect of this arpeggio :—

the two middle C's being played on the lute on two different strings, are heard successively.

In the third part of the book, which treats of "The *Generous Viol* in its Rightest Use," we find the following excellent advice for the playing of broken chords upon bowed instruments :—

Page 249 ". . . [The fault] of the *Right Hand* is that whenever they should strike a full stop, They seldom Hit the Lowest String, which is the very Substantiality of that stop ; it being the Ground to all those Upper Parts; and without which the rest of that Stop is (generally) all False Musick. Therefore I advise, ever when you come to a *Full Stop*, be sure to give the Lowest String a good full share of your Bow, (Singly, by It self, before you slide it upon the Rest) and Leave it likewise with a little Eminency of Smartness, by swelling the Bow a little, when you part with that String. This will make your Play very Lovely."

In that part of the book which treats of accompaniment on the Theorboe we find a rich store of ornamented arpeggios. Some of them also contain elaborate divisions. The following examples are selected amongst the simplest :—

In Chambonnières's "First book of Pieces," 1670, the arpeggio is given thus:—

Note the difference between the signs for upward and downward arpeggio: and

In the "Pièces de Clavecin composées par Monsieur Le Bègue," Paris, 1677, the sign and execution of the upward arpeggio are the same as in Chambonnières; but there is no mention of a downward arpeggio.

In Purcell's pieces, broken chords and arpeggios occur very frequently; but they are nearly always written out in full. The beautiful "Ground" in C minor is made up almost entirely of such broken chords:—

Among the "Rules for Graces" which preface the first edition of Purcell's "Lessons for the Harpsichord," we find this :—

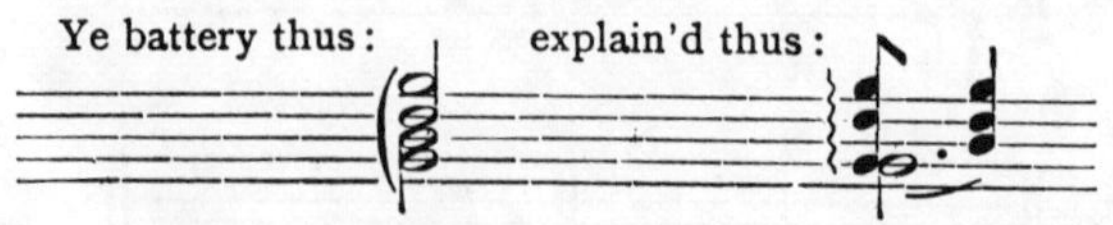

It is not clear. There must be some mistake about it. The word "battery" means arpeggio; there is no doubt on this point (see "Dieupart," page 269); *batterie* in French still means a broken chord at the present time. But the sign [(] used by Purcell was generally understood to indicate passing notes, and the explanation contains none. Moreover, the wavy line itself needs explaining.

Happily, this sign is rarely used by Purcell. It occurs in the fourth and last bars of the "Almand" of his second Suite in G minor, as follows :—

In the first case (bar 4) a mere breaking up of the chord would leave a gap in the bar; and, moreover, would hinder the progress of the melody and spoil its rhythm. The solution indicated is therefore preferable. In the last bar a downward breaking of the chord is right, for there also an upward arpeggio would destroy the rhythm, and would not satisfactorily conclude this majestic piece.

D'Anglebert rightly calls Exx. 3 to 6 "Arpégé"; but the first two are named "Cheute," which is one of the names of the appoggiatura. The additional notes, B in Ex. 1, B and D in Ex. 2, are appoggiature, and may have been foremost in his mind on account of the alteration they produce in the chords.

In Brossard's "Dictionaire de Musique," 1703, we find:—

"*Harpeggiato* or *Harpégé*. It is when the notes of a chord are played *not* together, but one after another, beginning with the lowest, of which the tone must, however, be held":—

F. Couperin gives these arpeggios:—

In the "Avertissement" of Marin Marais, "Pièces de Viole," third Book, Paris, 1711, we see ". . . . That sign [—] which is found by the side of chords, indicates that they must be separated, beginning at the bass and continuing until the treble; this may be called 'harpégement.' It is most essential in certain pieces, as in 'La Guitarre' and 'Le Moulinet.'"

NOTE.—[×] indicates a mordent, and [,] after the note a shake.

The following examples are taken from Dieupart's Table :—

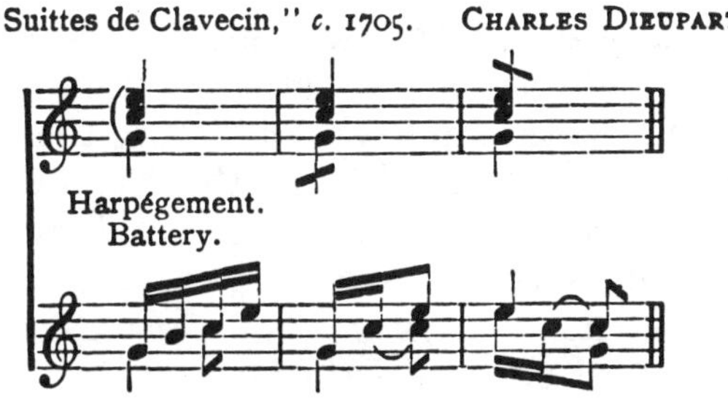

The French word "*Harpégement*," with its English equivalent "Battery," should be noted in conjunction with Purcell's "Battery" (see page 266). Here the sign [( ] indicates a figured arpeggio, whilst the oblique line is applied to the plain broken chord.

Rameau's arpeggios are as follows :—

Exx. 1 and 2 are like the examples of D'Anglebert. Other composers of the same period, such as Dandrieu and Muffat, have the same sign and explanations. It would be superfluous to quote them. At Ex. 3 the combination of the oblique line and the wavy vertical line, to indicate a figured arpeggio, should be noticed. Rameau is the only composer who uses it, and it is very common in his works. Ex. 4 is most interesting in showing how to fill empty places with "parties luthées."

In the advice to players prefacing the "Concerts en Trio" of Rameau (1741), there is a direction to the viol player which is most useful in indicating how to treat arpeggios containing important inner parts. Rameau says that in places where the violist cannot conveniently play two or more notes together, he must play them arpeggio, *finishing upon the one on the side of which the melody continues.*

This is the key to the interpretation of many arpeggios of Bach; as, for example, those in the "Chromatic Fantasia," which lose so much of their meaning and beauty when played in the usual way.

Unfortunately, original examples of the interpretation of complicated arpeggios are not common. Two interesting instances occur in the "Fantazia" of C. Ph. E. Bach, explained by his disciple Rellstab in "C. Ph. E. Bach's Anfangstücke, &c.," 1789. We can understand from these what freedom the performer was allowed in such cases, even to the extent of temporarily altering the bass of the harmony, as may be seen in the working out of the first two chords:—

p
ten.
ten.
decrescendo.
ff
ten.

But this very freedom increases our difficulties. Some arpeggios of Bach, where the changes of harmonies occur at irregular intervals, and which contain figures in the inner parts, require much experience and study for their interpretation. In Preludio xxi., from the first volume of "Das wohltemperirte Klavier," which is a free fantasia similar to those of C. Ph. E. Bach, the following passage occurs at bars 16, 17, 18 :—

The first chord obviously requires breaking, though not so marked. The ear could not understand from which part the melody continues, unless the A is played last, and held. In bar 17, third and fourth beats, the expressive inner part C, D, E♭ (right hand), is answered in imitation by the F, G, A♭, of the left hand. To render this effect, some such an arrangement as given below must be resorted to. It implies freedom of rhythm. The little notes follow one another very quickly, but still there must be time to play them :—

SECTION X.

Expressive Rests.

Crackled chords, The Tut, Détaché, Aspiration, Suspension, Silences d'Articulation, Son Coupé, Staccato.

These names refer to rests which are substituted either at the beginning or end of notes for an equivalent part of their value. In modern music, notes with a dot or a dash over them are only held for about a quarter of their value in the first case, and less in the second. The meaning of the dash is the same now as it used to be; but the dot was never employed in that sense until late in the 18th century. It meant that notes so marked were to be played evenly, as we have seen at page 75. Various signs indicated these rests; but in most cases there were no signs. The player had to know where and how they should be introduced.

The lute players were fond of suddenly stopping the sound of a note. The "Tut" and the "crackling" of chords were favourite devices. Here is what Thomas Mace has to say on this subject:—

"Musick's Monument," page 109: "The *Tut*, is a *Grace*, always performed with the *Right Hand*, and is a *sudden taking away the Sound of any Note*, and in such a manner, as it will seem to cry *Tut;* and is very *Pritty*, and *Easily done*, *Thus*.

"When you would perform *This Grace*, it is but to strike your *Letter*, (which you intend shall be so *Grac'd*) with one of your *Fingers*, and immediately *clap on your next striking Finger, upon the String which you struck;* on which doing, you suddenly *take away the Sound of the Letter*, which is that, we call the *Tut;* and if you do it clearly, it will seem to speak the word *Tut*, so plainly, as if it were a *Living Creature, Speakable.*"

Mace's sign for this grace is a double dot before the letter [: *a*].

Page 170: " To *crackle* such 3 *Part-Stops*, is only to *divide each Stop*, with your *Thumb*, and 2 Fingers; so as not to *loose Time;* But give *each Crochet* Its *due Quantity;* and to add Prittiness; Cause them to *Sobb*, by *Slacking your Stopping-Hand*, so soon as they are *Struck;* yet not to *unstop them*, but only so much as may *Dead the Sound* on a sudden. This gives Great Pleasure in such Cases."

The following explanations of D'Anglebert are obvious, since the accent required for the first note of either the *tremblement* or the *pincé* could not be given unless it were preceded by a silence:—

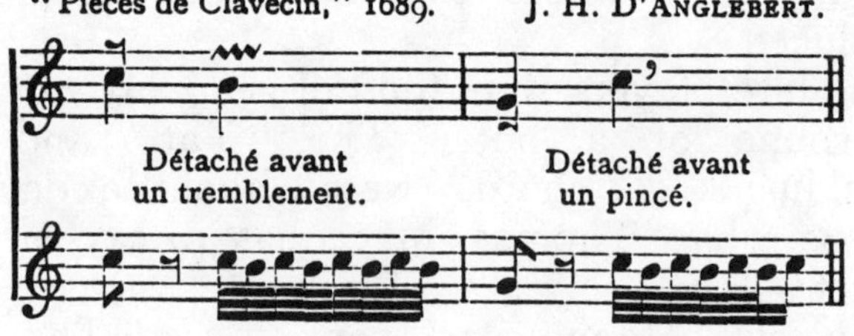

The dash does not indicate a real staccato; it only shortens the note by one quarter of its value:—

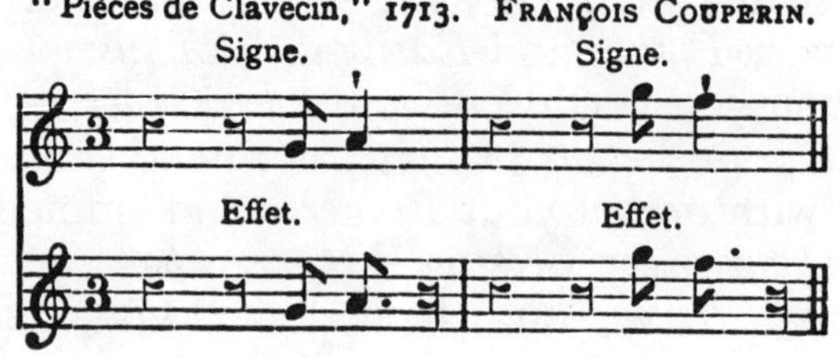

The Suspension is an interesting ornament:—

"Pièces de Clavecin," 1713. FRANÇOIS COUPERIN.

The *Tempo rubato* effect it produces is very characteristic and charming. It should be tried in "Les Laurentines" and "La Tendre Fauchon," from Couperin's first book of pieces, and in "La Castellane," from the second. One might look in vain for "suspensions" in the majority of modern editions. They have been removed, together with many other beautiful ornaments. Failing the original edition, which is very rare, the reprint issued under the supervision of Brahms and Chrysander may be used, for it is truthful in almost every detail.

Fr. Couperin, in "l'Art de Toucher le Clavecin," page 15, comments upon expressive rests in the following way. His ideas and phrases are occasionally lacking in clearness, but the passage deserves careful consideration. The translation is as literal as possible:—

"The sounds of the harpsichord being definite, each one in particular, and in consequence incapable of being either swelled or diminished, it has seemed almost incredible till now that any soul could be given to that instrument. However, having improved by study the natural talent Heaven gave me, I have become so fortunate as to touch the persons of taste who have heard me play, and to form pupils who, perhaps, surpass me.

"The effect I propose is due to the cessation, and to the suspension of the sounds, properly used, and according to the character of the melody.

"These two devices, by their contrast, leave the ear in suspense, so that in places where bowed instruments swell their sounds, the suspension of those of the harpsichord seems, by contrary means, to produce upon the ear the desired effect.

"I have already explained, in notes and rests, both the *Aspiration* and *Suspension*, in the Table of Graces of my first book of Pieces. I hope that the idea I have given of them will not prove useless to people of taste and feeling.

"These two names of 'Aspiration' and 'Suspension' may seem new; at any rate, if anyone boasts of having practised either of them, I don't think anyone will resent my having broken the ice, in giving to these graces names appropriate to their effects. Moreover, I thought it was better to understand one another in an art so highly esteemed and widely practised as harpsichord playing.

"For the 'Aspiration' you must detach the note upon which it is marked, but less quickly in tender than in light and rapid pieces.

"As to the 'Suspension,' it is hardly used in any but in slow and expressive pieces. The silence which precedes the note upon which it is marked must be regulated by the taste of the player."

Th. Muffat in his "Componimenti," ?1735, gives the following example:—

Rameau uses these devices freely. Here are his explanations :—

" Pièces de Claveein." J. PH. RAMEAU, 1731.

There being as yet no reliable reprint of his pieces, the following examples will prove valuable. There are complicated ornaments combined with the suspensions. The student who has persevered so far should find no difficulty in solving them :—

" L'Entretien des Muses." J. PH. RAMEAU.

(The quavers slightly unequal.)

(The quavers slightly unequal.)

Premier Menuet, " Pièces en Concert."
Harpsichord. J. PH. RAMEAU.

We now come to these " Silences d'Articulation " for which there does not seem to be an English name, although they are absolutely indispensable to music. The wind instruments with their breathing and tongueing, the bowed instruments with their bowing, cannot help using them. In the pianoforte, the enormous emphasis given to the beginning of the notes by the blow of the hammer, to a certain extent replaces them, and at the same time points out one of the causes of the general deficiency of phrasing conspicuous in modern pianoforte playing, for these silences are its very foundation.

Quantz has some interesting remarks on this point:—

Chap. xi., § 10: " . . . . One must not slur the notes which should be detached, nor detach those which should be slurred. The notes must not seem to be *glued* together. The tongue must articulate on the wind instruments and the bow on the stringed instruments, always according to the intentions of the composer as indicated by dashes and slurs. The notes will thus obtain all their liveliness, and the expression will be distinguished from the bagpipe, which is played without articulation. However well ordered the fingers may be, they cannot alone produce musical speech; the tongue and the bow must help, and it is these latter which affect most the expression of a piece."

On keyboard instruments the articulation depends entirely upon the judicious introduction of rests. Those ingenious 18th century people whose ambition it was to reproduce mechanically the artistic and expressive interpretation of music, were constrained to study these details. We find in "La Tonotechnie" (quoted page 43) the following interesting pages:—

Page 6: "There are many things to observe in music, about which no author, as far as I know, has said anything, and without which one should feel hampered in the pricking [of cylinders]. I am compelled, therefore, to make a few observations, as a kind of supplement, to the principles of music. A musician acquiring by use and the habit of performing, the facility to render agreeably an infinity of things which are imperfectly indicated in the text, or even not at all, and upon which depend, however, the effects which give the character and expression, would have no need of my observations, which he can apply without thinking: but the Pricker of Cylinders being obliged to express everything in detail, could do nothing without some principles to guide him: therefore it is on those parts which I call *the effects*, always left out or badly indicated in the texts, that my observations will bear, to show the way to the Prickers; perhaps they may not be despised even by musicians, if they are desirous of transmitting to posterity the proofs of their genius without *any alteration*, by means of cylinders which could be adapted to harpsichords or organs, and which they would take pleasure in noting; and thus give the reason of the effects of their Art, in finding in my observations the principles of its details."

Page 18: "All the notes in execution, whether ornamented or not, are partly in *hold* and partly in *silence;* which means that they all have a certain length of *sound* and a certain length of *silence*, which united make the whole value of the note.

"These *silences* at the end of each note fix its articulation and are as necessary as the holds themselves, without which they could not be detached from one another; and a piece of music, however beautiful, would be no more agreeable without these *silences d'articulation* than these country songs of *Poitou*, performed upon insipid bagpipes which only give a noisy and inarticulate sound."

Page 23: "To be convinced of the necessity of these *silences* at the end of each note, let one play upon an organ, harpsichord, or any other keyboard instrument a piece of music, no matter which, and in the playing of it pay more attention to the execution than to the way it is written; it will be noticed that a finger which has just finished a note is often lifted long before it is placed on the next note, and this interval is necessarily a *silence*, and if one takes care, it will be seen that between all the notes there are intervals more or less long, without which the execution would be bad: even the notes of the most rapid shakes are separated by very small intervals. Those intervals, more or less long, I call *silences d'articulation* in music, from which no note is exempt, like the articulated pronunciation of consonants in speech, without which the syllables would have no other distinction than the inarticulate sounds of the vowels.

"A little attention in the pronunciation given to the articulation of the syllables will show that, to produce the effect of nearly all consonants, the sound of the vowel is stopped either by bringing the lips together or by pressing the tongue against the palate, the teeth, &c. All these stoppages of the vowel's sound are as many short silences which detach the syllables from one another to form the articulation of speech. It is the same in the articulation of music, with the only difference that the sound of an instrument being everywhere the same, and producing so to speak only one vowel, the *silences d'articulation* must be more varied than in speech, if a kind of intelligent and interesting articulation is to be produced."

Plenty of examples of these expressive rests will be found in the pieces from "La Tonotechnie," and the "Romance de Mr. Balbastre," from Dom Bedos, which are given in the Appendix of this book.

A word of warning, however, is necessary here. The staccato style of playing was fashionable *c.* 1770, and therefore exaggerated. It is unquestionable that these *silences d'articulation* are wanted; but they should be applied with moderation to the earlier music. The "insipid, noisy, and inarticulate" bagpipe gives pleasure to some; and even the bagpipe style of Bach playing of the present time has admirers.

SECTION XI.

Tempo Rubato (in English, "Stolen Time").

By *Tempo Rubato* are meant the alterations of time introduced by the performer for the sake of expression. This device is as old as music itself. It is obvious that emotional feeling, if there be any, will cause the player to linger on particularly expressive notes and to hurry exciting passages. If there are people who think that the old music does not require the *Tempo Rubato*, it is because they do not perceive its meaning; and are, moreover, ignorant of the fact that it was as common formerly as it is now.

In the chapter on "Expression," the general features of the *Tempo Rubato* have been brought out; a few special points only remain to be considered now.

The following examples from Caccini's "Nuove Musiche," 1601, are sufficiently clear. They should not, however, be taken too literally; they need a little additional *Tempo Rubato*, just to avoid stiffness :—

In Türk's "Klavierschule," 1789, there is a chapter on *Tempo Rubato*, of which the following gives the important points :—

"The so-called *Tempo Rubato* (*Gestohlnes Zeitmasz*) I have already mentioned as being the last means employed by the player for the expression of his emotion and feeling. It generally implies a shortening or lengthening, or a displacing of the notes. One note is robbed of some of its value, and as much is given to another. A certain passage (*a*) being given, we have at (*b*) the

Tempo Rubato through an anticipation, and at (*c*) through a retardation :—

"One can see from these examples that the length of the bar as a whole is not altered, consequently the common but ambiguous German expression, *Verrücktes Zeitmasz* (deranged time) is not appropriate, for the time of the bass has not been disturbed, the notes of the melody only having been displaced.

"Even in cases such as shown at (*e*) and (*f*), which are evolved from example (*d*) by the addition of notes, both parts come together again at the end of the bar, and there is no real disturbance of the time :—

"This *Tempo Rubato* must be applied cautiously, for it might easily render the harmony faulty. The example at (*f*) would only be tolerable in very slow time. Another kind of *Tempo Rubato* is produced by the displacing of the accent, when the emphasis which should be given to the *good* notes is transferred to the *bad* notes; for example, if one plays as at (*g*) instead of the usual way (*h*), or (*i*) instead of (*k*):—

"Undue licences with the text, or rather distortions of it, cannot possibly be allowed, unless the composer has given explicit instructions to that effect."

In the last edition of C. Ph. E. Bach's "Versuch, &c.," published in 1797, after the death of the author and eight years after Türk's book, there is a chapter on *Tempo Rubato* which agrees with the above, but from which the following additional indications can be gleaned:—

"The *Tempo Rubato* applies better to dissonant than to consonant harmony; it should be used in sad and tender phrases. A player with judgment and feeling will easily discover the degree of irregularity suitable to the occasion. When the keyboard instrument is played without accompaniment, the bass may be allowed occasionally to alter the time. There is no harm in this so long as the harmony remains undisturbed. One who has mastered the *Tempo Rubato* will find no difficulty in the playing of irregular numbers of notes, in groups of 5, 7, 11, &c.; he will know how to take a greater or smaller number according to his fancy."

SECTION XII.

ACCIACCATURA, PINCÉ ÉTOUFFÉ, ZUSAMMENSCHLAG, TATTO.

This is a very interesting ornament about which few of the old books contain any information. There is no true English name for it. The Italian verb *acciaccare* means to crush or scrunch. The word *acciaccatura*, besides its musical sense, means the pressure given to the pen in calligraphy to produce a thick stroke. It is therefore suggestive of emphasis and accent. The French *Pincé étouffé* literally means a "choked mordent," and the German *Zusammenschlag* means "striking together."

This ornament is related to the mordent and short appoggiatura, but in some of its aspects is different from both. It can only be used upon keyboard instruments, for it is performed by striking at the same time with a principal key another one a semitone below it, the sound of the latter being made as short as possible, whilst the principal note is held for its normal value. A sharp discord is thus produced which nothing could equal as a means of emphasis, and which if well used in combination with chords, enriches the harmony with strange and powerful discords, entirely independent of either preparation or resolution. It is very valuable on the harpsichord, clavichord, and organ.

Francesco Geminiani, in his "Rules for playing in a True Taste," &c., Op. viii., *c.* 1745, says: "With respect to the *Thorough-Bass* on the *Harpsichord*. . . . . In accompanying grave movements, he should make use of the *Acciachature*, for these rightly placed have a wonderful effect. . . ."

In "A Treatise of Good Taste in the Art of Musick," 1749 (the privilege being dated 1739), Geminiani has the following:—

"The *Acciaccatura* is a Composition of such Chords as are dissonant with respect to the fundamental Laws of Harmony; and yet when disposed in their proper place produce that very Effect which it might be expected they would destroy.

"No Performer therefore should flatter himself that he is able to accompany well until he is a Master of this delicate and admirable Secret which has been in use for above a hundred years; and of which many Examples may be found in the Book which I have compos'd for that Instrument (the Harpsichord).

"The Example which follows, has however something in it peculiar, as it serves to specify a signature called *Tatto*, which has a very great and singular Effect in Harmony, and which is perform'd by touching the key lightly, and quitting it with such a Spring as if it was Fire."

"**Examples of the Acciaccature as Passages of Melody, Appoggiature and Tatto for the Harpsichord: Observe, those notes with this mark ⁀ are to be play'd with one stroke of the fingers or by touching the chords successively from ye lowest Note upwards" :—**

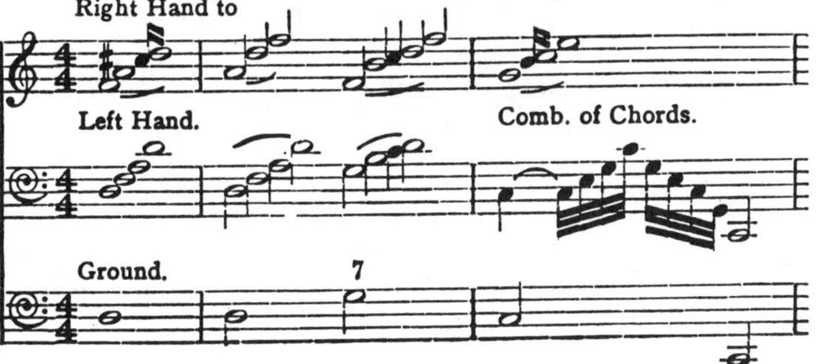

Acca.
#6

7
#
6
♮4

Appa.
7
#3
3
7
#3

5
♮6
6
♯4
6

7
7
♯3
♯3
♭3

Appa.
♯4
2
6
♯6
6
5
4
♯3

No author but Geminiani seems to have used the word *Tatto*. It means literally *touched*, and is equivalent to the French *Tactée* (see "*Silences d'Articulation*," page 318).

This *Tatto* is the true *acciaccatura*, whilst Geminiani's *acciaccatura* corresponds to the passing-notes of the figured arpeggio (see page 269). Some of his chords contain six notes for each hand, and others which only have five seem, nevertheless, unplayable in the ordinary way; but they can all be done, in some cases by playing two notes with the thumb, which does not prevent the release of the auxiliary note, or by sliding a finger from the acciaccatura to the next harmony note.

His quadruple appoggiatura appears rather formidable, but it sounds rich and effective if well done.

D'Anglebert, whose Table of Ornaments is so complete in other respects, does not mention the *acciaccatura;* yet he uses it frequently and in a masterly way, especially in those fascinating unmeasured free Preludes which are as yet inviolate from modern editors. In the excerpts given below, the resemblance of the notation to the example from Geminiani above cannot fail to be noticed. It points the way to their interpretation, which is nevertheless beset with difficulties.

Their realisation in ordinary notation being impossible, an opposite method is adopted here, which, by showing their bare harmonic structure, will enable a performer fairly conversant with interpretation to understand the ornamental clothing indicated by D'Anglebert's text.

The first two lines and the conclusion of the first Prelude are given. In the latter, a line between two notes respectively in the treble and bass will be seen. It indicates that these two notes must be played together; and inversely, that the others should not:—

&c.

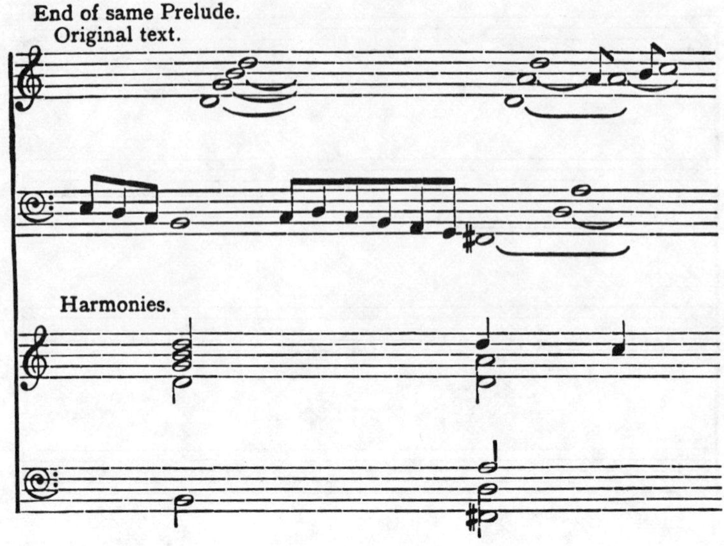
End of same Prelude.
Original text.
Harmonies.

Examples of acciaccature are not rare in late 17th and 18th century music. The auxiliary notes are often written like the harmony notes, the result to the uninitiated being chords comparable to the most venturesome of the present time. But in those days of figured basses everybody knew at least enough harmony to distinguish the acciaccatura from the principal notes. Even now many players would be able to do the same if they stopped to think, but this is a thing they do not often do.

Here follow a few examples in which arrows point to the acciaccature. It should be remembered that there is no need to break all the chords, even though they contain acciaccature; in some cases they may be slightly broken, but on short chords in a lively movement it is quite impossible. The chords, however, can never be so short that the acciaccature cannot be made a little shorter still; and the smallest difference is sufficient to render the intended effect :—

"Six Sonatas per il cembalo solo"

(Nuremberg). Sonata II. DOM. SCARLATTI.

Clementi's Edition, Sonata IV.

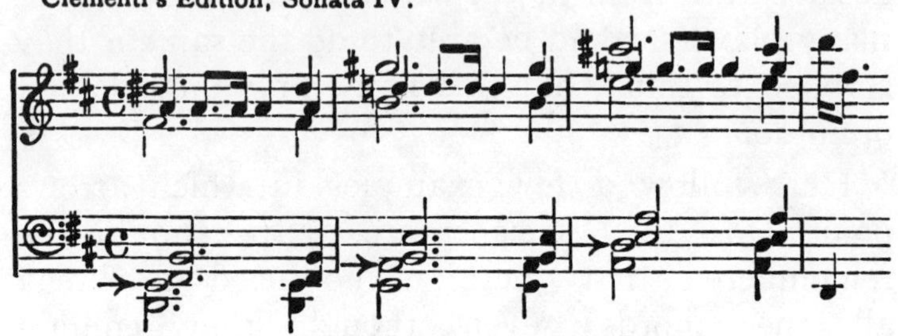

John Johnson's Edition, Vol. ii., page 18.

Sarabande from Partita VI. J. S. BACH.

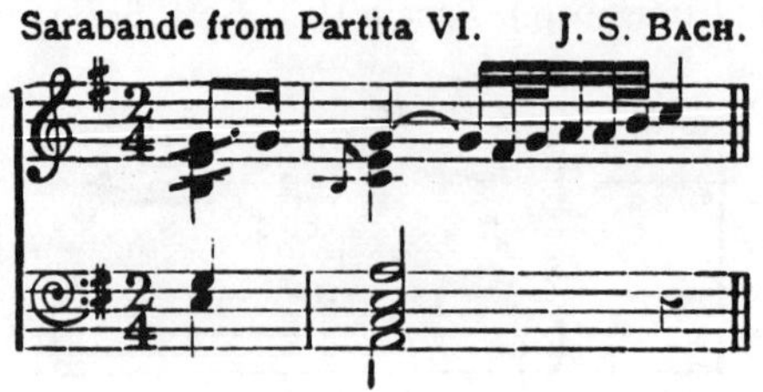

C. Ph. E. Bach, "Versuch, &c.," 1753, says :—

"Mordents. § 3. There is yet another way of playing a mordent when it must be made very short. The two notes of the following example being struck together, the higher only is held, the lower being instantly released :—

This manner of playing need not be avoided so long as it is used less frequently than other mordents. It can only be done *ex abrupto*, that is, unbound to the preceding note."

In Fr. Wilh. Marpurg's "Principes du Claveçin," 1755, Chap. xix., § 2, we find this : "Instead of playing the two keys alternately, they are often struck both at the same time ; but the auxiliary note is only held for half its value, so that the principal note may be heard alone afterwards. The manner of doing this is shown in the following example :—

This kind of mordent is called *Pincé étouffé*, in Italian *Acciaccatura*, and it is much used in the bass. When changing from *piano* to *forte*, it can be used successfully to reinforce the harmony."

SECTION XIII.

Compound Ornaments.

§ 1. Compound ornaments are frequently used; some of them are easily understood, others not. Among the former are the *Appoggiatura and Shake*, in which the appoggiatura consists of the first note of the shake made longer than the others. As this is the way most shakes should be made, and it has been explained before, there is no need to say much about it.

John Playford, 1654, Christopher Simpson and Dr. Ch. Coleman, 1659, and Th. Mace, 1676, call this grace *Back-fall shaked*, and use no other sign for it but that of the back-fall.

In Henry Purcell's "Lessons," 1696, the information given is as follows :—

" Plain note and shake thus :

Explain'd thus:

Jean Henri d'Anglebert, 1689, and Dandrieu, *c.* 1710, call this ornament *Tremblement appuyé.* J. Ph. Rameau, 1731, calls it *Cadence appuyée;* all three indicate it by this sign:

François Couperin, 1713, also uses the name *Tremblement appuyé*, but gives no other sign than that of the shake; in fact there is no need of a special sign, since according to his clear directions, every shake, excepting only the short ones, begins with the "appui."

Th. Muffat, ?1735, Marpurg, 1750, and J. S. Bach, 1720, use the sign given above, ; the last-named also uses this sign , and in the "Klavier-Büchlein vor Wilhelm Friedemann Bach," he mentions this ornament as follows:—

In the frequent cases, found in the works of most composers, when the sign for the appoggiatura is followed by that of the shake, the appoggiatura must be played as if it were alone; the shake takes place on what is left of the principal note.

§ 2. If a mordent is preceded by an ascending appoggiatura we have the appoggiatura and mordent. Many composers, including Th. Muffat and J. S. Bach, use this Grace, indicating it by their usual signs for the appoggiatura and the mordent. The treatment of such cases is simple. The appoggiatura must be given its full value, first, as usual, then the mordent is performed. It would be useless to give detailed examples. But in the following cases there are peculiarities of signs and names which have to be studied, although they bring no new effects.

John Playford, 1654, Christopher Simpson, and Dr. Ch. Coleman, 1659, give this :—

In Purcell's "Lessons," 1696, we find :—

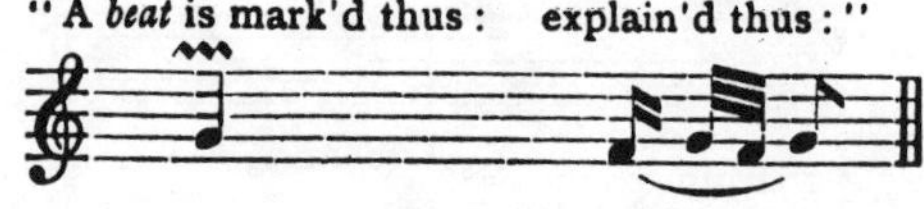

How troublesome that our usual sign for a shake ~~ should thus be misapplied!

D'Anglebert brings together his signs for the appoggiatura ((*cheute*) and the mordent ") " (*pincé*)) which, placed severally on each side of the note, produce the figure (‘♩’) so frequently seen not only in his works, but in those of Rameau, Mondonville, and others :—

Ch. Dieupart, 1731, also uses this sign, named *Port de voix et pincé*, and he gives it in English as "forefall beat."

Fr. Couperin seems to consider the mordent as indispensable to the appoggiatura, since he does not even mention the former in his examples:—

Dandrieu uses a special sign which is graphic enough, but restricted to himself:—

Rameau, 1731, uses the same sign as D'Anglebert (see above), but illogically calls the ornament *Pincé et port-de-voix*, although he would certainly have objected if the *pincé* had been played first.

J. J. Rousseau, in his "Dictionnaire de Musique," 1767, uses the names *Port de voix* and *Port de voix jetté*, and only indicates the appoggiature in the same manner as Couperin (see above) :—

J. J. ROUSSEAU, 1767.

§ 3. The Shake and Turn, or Turned Shake, is a common ornament. Its form :—

being already familiar to us, no technical explanations are required. It has been considered as a shake and turn :—

or as a shake and mordent :—

but the oldest and best way is to regard it as a shake with its natural termination, as it was in the earliest period covered by this book, when its name was "Groppo" (see p. 154).

This ornament is given in Th. Mace's "Musick's Monument," 1676, under the name of Single Relish. The author says (page 107) that it is generally done upon the *Ascension* and *Descension* of a third, thus:—

The appoggiatura should be short, according to the custom of that time, and a shake upon the dotted note is implied in both examples.

A most interesting and beautiful ornament which for want of a better place will be included in the present category, is the Double Relish. It seems to have been little known out of England, where it was very popular during the 17th century.

Christopher Simpson, in the "Division-Viol," second edition, 1665, gives the following foreign equivalents for it:—

English: *Double Rellishes.* Latin: *Teretismi.* French: *Des Cadences de nœuds et tremblemens.* Italian: *Cadenze di Groppo e Trillo.* And among the "Shaked graces," page 16: *Double Relish, Crispata Cadentia.*

The following explanations are taken from Playford's "Introduction to the Skill of Music," 1654, &c. The original long bars have been divided to facilitate the reading:—

Of these two versions the second was the more popular.

Similar examples are found in Ch. Simpson's "Division Violist," under the authority of Dr. Charles Coleman, with the only difference that the sign indicating the second version is given thus :—

In Th. Mace's "Musick's Monument," page 108, the following excellent explanation of the Double Relish is given. It is here translated from the Lute Tablature, and Mace's comments are appended verbatim :—

"All this, is but called the Double Relish expressing those 3 Plain Notes.

"In Encient Times, the Well, and True Performance of It, upon the several Keys, throughout the Instrument, (either Lute, or Viol) was accounted an Eminent piece of Excellency, though now, we use it not at all in our Compositions for the Lute.

"However, I shall commend the private use, and practice of it, to all Practitioners, as a very

Beneficial piece of Practice, for the command of the Hand. And although the very *Shape*, and *Fashion* of it, be not at this Day in General use; yet I will set down such allusions to it, or such kind of Dependences upon it, (when I come to give further directions for the Hand) as shall pass with very much *Grace*, and *Modish-Good-Applause*."

The further changes of names and signs of the Shake and Turn will be seen in the following synopsis :—

J. H. D'Anglebert, 1689: *Tremblement et Pincé.* Sign

Henry Purcell, 1696: *Turned shake.* Sign

François Couperin, 1713: No name. Sign .

Dandrieu, *c.* 1710: *Cadence fermée.* Sign

Rameau, 1731: *Double Cadence.* Sign

Th. Muffat, ?1735: No name. Sign

Dieupart, 1731. *Tremblement et pincé*; English: *A shaked beat.* Sign

Tosi, English translation by Galliard, 1723: *Trillo-Mordente*; English: *Shake with a beat.* No sign given.

J. S. Bach, Klavier-Büchlein vor W. F. Bach, 1720, *Trillo und Mordant.* Sign (In his works he also uses Couperin's double sign)

Fr. Wilh. Marpurg, "Die Kunst das Clavier zu spielen." Berlin, 1750: *Doppeltriller.* Sign

French edition, 1756: *Le tremblement double.* Signs ———

C. Ph. E. Bach, 1753, mentions the trill with a termination (*Nachschlag*), and gives the sign ⁓ for it; but he says that, the resemblance between this sign and that of the mordent being likely to bring confusion, he prefers to use the sign for the trill only, leaving it to the player to supply the termination. He frequently writes the termination in plain notes, and many composers do likewise. The figure:—

is common.

Whatever may be the sign to indicate the shake, or if there be no sign at all, the shake must be performed according to the usual rules; and whatever may be the value of the terminal notes, they must be played at the same rate as the shake itself.

The *Prallender Doppelschlag* of C. Ph. E. Bach should also be mentioned here. Its forbidding name need not scare anybody, for it is a pleasant Grace. Here is, in substance, what C. Ph. E. Bach has to say about it:—

"When the first two notes of a Turn (*Doppelschlag*) are repeated with the utmost rapidity, a sudden shake (*Prall-triller*) is combined with it. A *Prall-triller* ending with a *Doppelschlag* would come to the same thing. This ornament gives both grace and brightness to clavier playing. It might be likened to a shortened and enlivened turned shake. But the two must not be confused, for they differ as much from one another as a sudden shake, or a turn, differs from a regular shake. In the following example my sign for this ornament and its execution will be seen :—

"This *Prallender Doppelschlag* is used without or after an appoggiatura, but never otherwise than a *Prall-triller*, namely, after a descending second with which it must be connected *smoothly and softly* :—

"As this compound ornament entails more notes than the simple one, it will fill the time of a rather long note; and thus be preferable to a *Prall-triller* in some cases. The first three examples, *Adagio*, take the *Prallender Doppelschlag ;* the last, *Allegretto*, takes the *Prall-triller* :—

The sign given by C. Ph. E. Bach to his *Prallender Doppelschlag* had been used by Couperin and others to indicate an ordinary turned shake. "These ornaments must not be confused . . ." says C. Ph. E. Bach.

Why, then, does he make confusion almost inevitable by taking the sign of the former ornament for his new one ?

§ 4. Shakes with or without terminations were often combined with *slides* from below or above. An interesting series of compound ornaments was thus produced. In Playford's "Introduction" the following are given :—

Ch. Simpson gives the same names, signs, and explanations, but he adds on page 11 a Latin translation thus :—

Shaked Elevation.	Shaked Cadent.
Tremula Elevatio.	*Tremula Coalitio.*

M. Locke, in "Melothesia," 1673, gives this sign and name :—

"⩵ A Forefall and Shake."

No explanation is given, but the following is the only possible one :—

The trill may have a termination.

The subject of Locke's beautiful Fugue, or rather Fantasia, for the Organ ("Melothesia," No. 76), opens with a forefall and shake upon which a great part of the effect depends. The first eight bars are given here, with their execution, as being a most interesting example of ornamentation.

Of course, the beats of the long trill must not be divided mathematically, and the *tr* should be short and rapid, stopping on the dot when the note is dotted:—

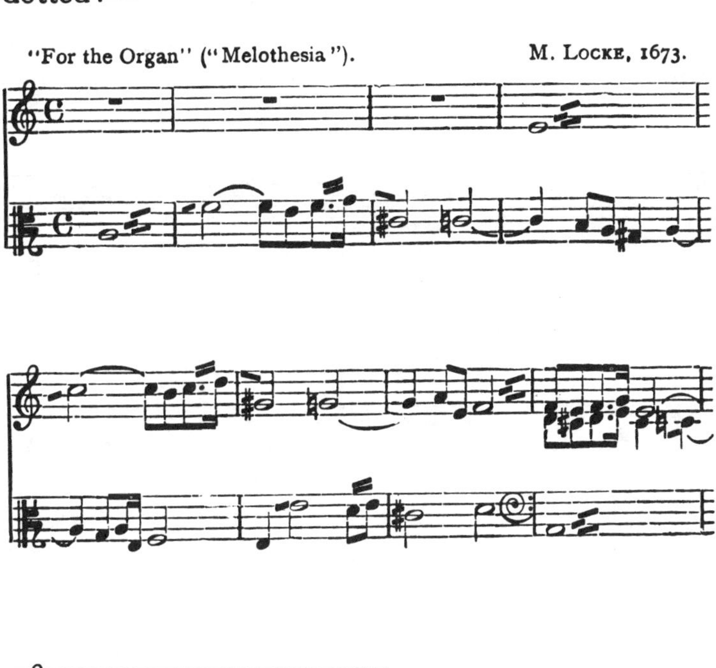

Execution.
6
tr
6
tr
tr
tr
tr
tr
tr

The various forms, signs, and names of these compound ornaments will be made clear in the following synopsis :—

J. H. D'ANGLEBERT, 1689.

Cadence. Autre.

The turns in these examples are unusual, comprising two notes below the principal instead of one above and one below. See the same thing in Dieupart on the following page :—

"Clavier Büchlein für W. F. Bach, 1720." J. S. BACH.

Doppelt-cadence
und Mordant.
TH. MUFFAT, ?1735.
CH. DIEUPART, 1731.
Double Cadence. A shake turn.

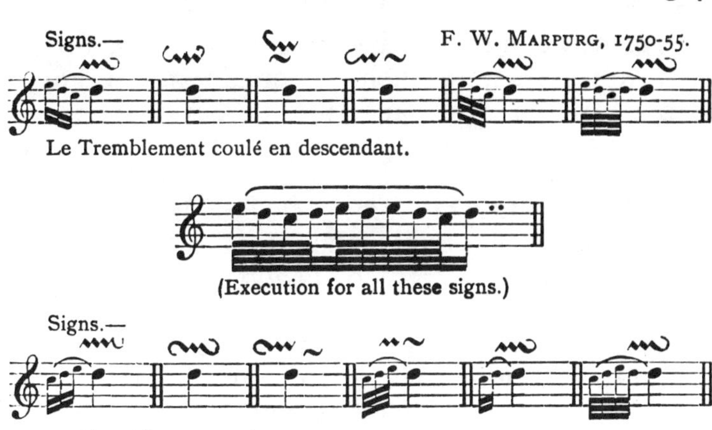

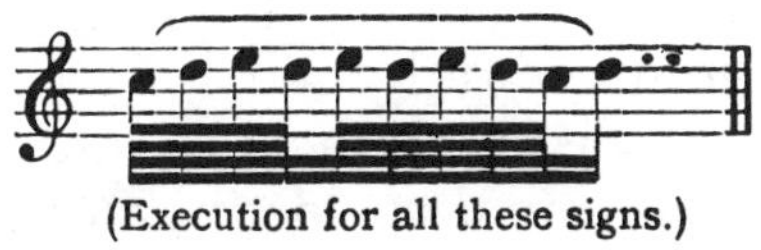
(Execution for all these signs.)

In Dom Bedos's "L'Art du Facteur d'Orgues" there is a series of plates containing diagrams of portions of the cylinder of a self-playing instrument which concern ornaments. The principle of the apparatus being understood, these diagrams can be translated into ordinary notation, and thus afford a mathematically accurate demonstration of the actual performance of these ornaments.

The names of the ornaments are given in every case, sometimes the signs also. Many are compound, and their execution is further complicated by alterations of rhythm and a profusion of "silences d'articulation." They could not conveniently have been classified, like the others, under several headings; besides, not only is their interest increased by their being grouped together, but the experience acquired in the previous study of ornamentation will help their understanding. They form a fitting conclusion to the present chapter.

It may be necessary to repeat that the book is rather late (1766), and therefore its examples should only be applied with caution to earlier music; moreover, the *silences d'articulation* were then at the height of fashion and therefore exaggerated.

Nothing could demonstrate more clearly the advantages of a simple text, the interpretation of which is understood, than its comparison with the fearful complexity resulting from the accurate notation of every detail. It is true that the simple text requires study and reflection; but the intelligence and taste of the student will benefit thereby, and the time thus spent can amount only to a fraction of that more or less cheerfully given nowadays to the thoughtless and profitless practice of scales and exercises.

In order that the notation of the tables may be kept as simple as possible, the following conventions have been used:—

1. A dash [ˈ] on any note denotes a "tactée"; in other words, it should be made as short as possible;
2. A dot [·] means that the note should be held one-half, or a very little more, of its value;
3. A line [–] means that the note should be held about three-quarters of its value;
4. Between all plain notes, a *very short* rest is implied;
5. Notes under a slur must be held to the full extent of their value.

1. Cadence Détachée Simple.
2. Cadence Détachée Double.
3. Cadence Liée Simple.
4. Cadence Liée Double.
5. Cadence Appuyée et Détachée.
6. Cadence Appuyée et Liée.
7. Cadence Ouverte et Détachée.
8. Cadence Ouverte et Liée.
9. Cadence Jettée.

10. Cadence Finalle.
11. Pincé Simple et Détaché.
12. Pincé Simple et Lié.
13. Pincé en Port de Voix.
14. Chutes de Pincés.
15. Chutes de Pincés.
16. Double.
17. Autre Double.
18. Port de Voix.
19. Port de Voix Pincé et Lié.

20. Port de Voix Pincé et Détaché.
21. Port de Voix Simple.
22. Port de Voix Simple avec Pincé.
23. Accord de Tierces Coulées en Montant.
24. Accord de Tierces Coulées en Descendant.
25. Secondes Coulées.
26. Coups Secs.
27. Liaison de Deux Nottes.
28. Liaison de Trois Nottes.

The first twenty-nine examples need no comment; but the last five are startling, for the interpretation practically destroys the original chords, and transforms them into mere successions of notes. The translation adopted in Exx. 30 and 31 would lend itself easily to some lengthening of the notes, if such were deemed advisable; but if applied to the example following, it would have resulted in a maze of complications on account of the chords being in three and four parts with acciaccature intermixed. At any rate, the notation employed represents faithfully the original diagrams.

In Exx. 23 and 24, the cases appear very similar to the above, but here the notes of the chords are fully sustained.

There is in Dom Bedos a diagram of the execution of the "Romance de Mr. Balbastre," which abounds in interesting cases of interpretation under its various aspects. It is a fairly long piece, and cannot be quoted here, but it is given in the Appendix.

SECTION XIV.

Divisions.

Some knowledge of divisions is necessary to the understanding of the old music. Much of the 16th and 17th century music is based upon divisions. The Italian music up to the latter part of the 18th century can hardly exist without them, and they contribute largely to the art of accompanying on a figured bass.

The admirable Treatise of Christopher Simpson, "The Division-Viol," second edition, 1665, resumes in a perfectly lucid and thorough manner all that preceded it; it will therefore greatly facilitate our study. We shall quote it verbatim, but we shall leave out the parts relating to *Descant*, these being outside our subject.

Page 28, §3. "*Breaking the Ground.* Breaking the Ground is dividing its Notes into more diminute notes. As for instance, a *Semibreve* may be broken into Two *minims*, foure *Crotchets*, eight *Quavers*, sixteen *Semiquavers*, &c.

"This Breaking or Dividing a Note admits divers ways of expression, according to the divers ordering and disposing the Minute parts thereof.

"*Five ways of Breaking a Note.* First, when there is no variation of Sound, by reason of the Minutes standing still in the same place, or removing in the Octave, which I accompt but the same Tone. Ex. 1.

"Secondly, when the Sound is varyed, and yet the Ayre retained, either by a quick return, or by keeping near to the place of the Note divided. Ex. 2.

"Thirdly, when the Minute Notes are employed in making a Transition to the next Note of the

Ground; as you see in the following Examples, where Notes are broken to all the several distances both ascending and descending:—

Division.
Ground.
Division.
Ground.
6
4
Division.
6
4
Ground.

Division.
Ground.

"I have set some part of the Example in a higher *Cliff*, because this Breaking a Note by way of Transition, holds good in higher Parts as well as in the Bass.

"*Fourthly*, when the *Minutes* are imployed in skipping into other *Concords*, as you see in breaking these four *Semibreves* :—

"*Fifthly*, when the said Minutes make a *Gradual* Transition into some of the Concords, passing from thence, either to end in the Sound of the Holding note,* or else, moving on to meet the next Note of the *Ground*. And though this moving into the Concords, be the very same as Descant, so long as it continues in that Motion; yet in regard of its returning either to its *own Note*, or to meet the *next following Note* in nature of a Bass, we must here rank it under the name and notion of Breaking the Ground. The manner of it you may see in these following Instances. Ex. 5.

[* *Holding-Note*, *Standing-Note*, *Ground-Note*, and *Note divided*, are the same.]

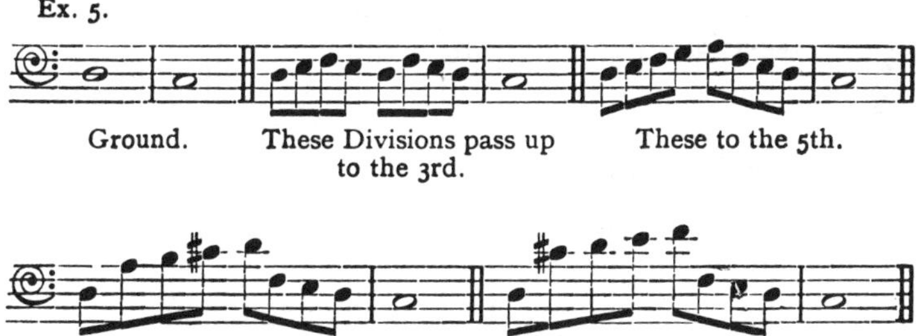

"The chief Mysterie of Division to a Ground may be referred to these three Heads. First, that it be harmonious to the holding Note. Secondly, that it come off so, as to meet the next Note of the *Ground* in a smooth and natural passage. Thirdly, Or if it pass into Discords, that they be such as are aptly used in Composition. As thus:—

Ex. 6.

"How Division is made harmonious to the Holding-Note, was shewed in the Fifth way of breaking a Note. And the Bringing it off to meet the next Note of the Ground, is much after the same way, viz., by making the last three, or more of the Minute Notes (at least Two of them) ascend or descend by degrees, unto the next succeeding Note, as you see here following, where the *Semibreve* in G is broken to all the distances in an Octave. Ex. 7. This holds good, be the Division quicker or slower; Onely that in quick Division more of the minutes will offer themselves in making this *Gradual* transition to the succeeding Note, as you see in the *Semi-quavers* of the following instances. Ex. 7:—

7th.
8ve.
Ground.
2nd.
2nd.
3rd.
3rd.
4th.
4th.
5th.
6th.
6th, &c.
Ground.
2nd.
2nd.
3rd.
3rd.

"By this which hath been shewed, you see (I suppose) what belongs to Breaking a note: but this requires not only a Notion but a Habit also, which must be got by practice. Wherefore I would have you prick down some easy *Ground;* and break each Note making a Transition still from Note to Note, according to what hath been delivered. To the better effecting whereof, I will set you an Example, with which take these Advertisements.

"First, That your Division be carried on smoothly, as we have formerly admonished; and that your *Flats* and *Sharps* have still relation to the Key and Ayre of your *Ground.*

"Secondly, you are to consider that a Seventh or Sixth falling is the same as a Second or Third rising, and so you may consider all other distances, with their opposite Octaves. And therefore you may choose whether you will meet any succeeding Note of the Ground, in the *Unison*, or in its *Octave* above or below it; for, concerning *Octaves*, the reason is still the same.

"Lastly, as your Division passes into the Third and Fifth, whilst it moveth above (by which it is made harmonious to the *Ground Note*) so, in moving beneath, it must pass into the under

Octaves of those Concords, viz., into the Sixth and Fourth below the Ground-Note. Thus:—

Ex. 8.

Ground. Divisions.

"These things being known, you may break your Ground in such manner as follows; where you have the Division placed over the Ground, that you may better observe the breaking of each note:—

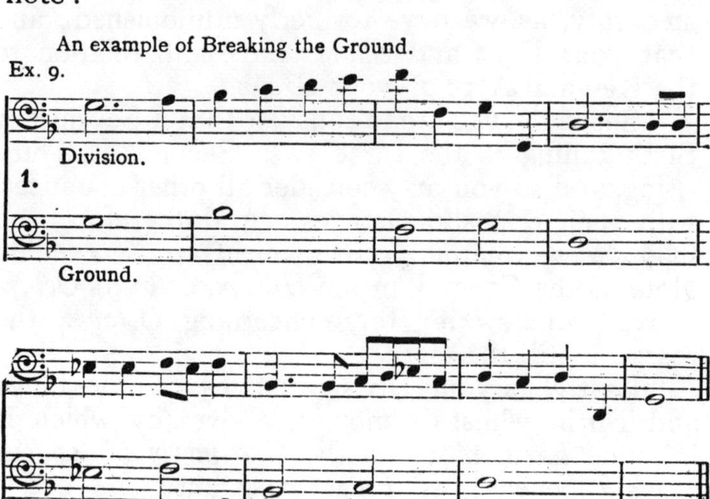

2.
3.
*
3d.

4.
5th.

"Here you see every Note of the Ground broken according to some One or Other of those five ways before-mentioned; only I have made the *Division*, in one place, to meet the Ground-Note in the Third, and in another place in the Fifth; both which are marked out for your imitation, when the Point, or any other convenience shall invite you thereunto.

"Here a doubt may arise, concerning the *Seventh* above and the *Second* below the *Divided-Note;* which, in the Division, is sometimes made Sharp, and suddenly Flat again, according to its own nature: in which doubts the Ear must always be chief umpire. Howbeit, in this particular, something (I think) may be deliver'd by way of Rule; which is, that if we descend to a Second and immediately ascend again, the Second must be made Sharp: The same is understood of the Seventh above, in reference to the Eighth, as you may see in breaking the two Semibreves in D:—

Ex. 10.

"Here your Ear will tell you that the note in C requires a Sharp: but, in the second Instance, where the next Note does not ascend, no Sharp is required.

"From this Rule we must except, that if the *Ground* do suddenly rise or fall to a Flat Second; or fall a Third, or make a Cadence: in these cases no Sharp is required, though the Note rise again, as you may see in these Instances:—

Ex. 11.

"Another observation is; that at a *Close*, I would always have the Division to end in the Sound of the Note next before the Close, and from thence leap off into the Sound of the Final note, as you see it does in the last strains of the last Example (Ex. 11, *a*—*b*). And here I cannot but take notice of an error which I have observed in some reputed excellent Violists; who in playing a Consort-Bass, would sometimes at the very Close, run down by degrees to the Concluding-Note; than which nothing is more improper: for if any *upper Part* do fall from a Fifth to an Eighth (a thing most frequent) the *Bass*, by such Running down by degrees, doth make two prohibited Eights to the said Part:—

"Though this Running down by degrees, be worse in playing a *Consort-Bass*, than in *Division to a Ground;* yet in this also it doth not want in bad consequence: the *Organist* commonly joyning such Parts to his Ground, as the Composer doth unto his Bass."

Simpson, though so complete, has, however, omitted one rule of some importance. It can, happily, be supplied from his own "Compendium of Musick," 1667, page 51:—

"Two, Three, or more Notes, standing together in the same Line or Space may be considered as one intire Note; and consequently capable of Transition":—

Ex. 13.

We shall now let Quantz carry on Ch. Simpson's teaching. He says:—

Chap. x., § 13: " . . . The pieces in the French style are for the most part characterized and composed with appoggiature and ornaments in such a manner that hardly anything can be added to the text; whilst in the Italian music much is left to the will and capability of the player. For this reason, the execution of the French music such as it is written, with its simple melody, and ornaments in preference to passages, is more binding and difficult to play than the Italian music, such as it is written nowadays. However, because it is not necessary for the execution of French music to know Thorough Bass or Composition, whilst on the contrary this knowledge is indispensable for the Italian music, on account of certain passages which are written in a very dry and simple manner, so that the player may vary them according to his ability and judgment, it is better to advise the student not to play soli in the Italian style prematurely and until he has some knowledge of Harmony, for otherwise his progress may be impeded thereby."

Chap. xiii., § 1: "I have explained the difference between a melody composed in the Italian style and one in the French style, with regard to Ornamentation. We have seen at chap. x. that the Italian music is not written with all its ornaments like the French, to which it is hardly possible to add any new ornament. There are, besides the essential ornaments already seen, other ornaments which are dependent upon the will and skill of the player."

Quantz thereupon proceeds to fill thirty-four large pages of text and fourteen plates of examples with an analysis of the various Divisions to be added to a simple text in the Italian style. We cannot follow him in this. Many of his Divisions are contained in Simpson, and the others follow the same principles. Three practical examples, each forming a complete piece, given in the Appendix, will suffice to give the student a good idea of what should be done in such cases. These examples consist of two slow movements from the sixth sonata of Corelli, with the ornamentation as played by the composer himself, from the edition published by Roger, of Amsterdam, and a solo for the flute by Quantz, from his "Versuch." In each case the variation is accompanied by the plain text, to facilitate comparison.

CHAPTER V.

THOROUGH BASS

Basso Continuo, Thorough-Bass, Basse Chiffrée, General-Bass.

NOTE.—The reader is supposed to have some knowledge of Practical Harmony.

THE practice of accompanying upon the Thorough Bass did not come into use much before 1600. In the 16th century, accompaniments were played to all kinds of vocal and instrumental music upon the organs, harps, lutes, chittaroni, viols of all kinds, and combinations of these. But the accompanist either played from a fully written out part, a method restricted almost entirely to instruments of the lute kind, or filled up by ear a plain bass part, or played from a full score when available.

About Thorough Bass proper, "General Bass" as he calls it, Prætorius gives detailed instructions covering some forty pages of the third volume of his "Syntagma Musicum," 1619. At page 144 he gives a noble example of the bass of the second part of his motet, "Wir glaubens," filled up by himself. It is reproduced below. The working out is free, not only with regard to the number of parts, but in the progression of the parts. It is just right for effect; but it would not get a high number of points in a musical examination:—

Many 17th and 18th century books treat of the Thorough Bass; but for the most part they only teach how to build the chords in four parts from the figures and how to connect them faultlessly together. They hardly say anything about the practical and artistic sides of the question, which depend upon a more or less conventional freedom of treatment, and which constitute the life and beauty of the accompaniment.

A fair amount of information can, however, be brought together on these points. Thomas Mace, to begin with, has some excellent advice to give, and good examples to show, as will be seen hereafter. His "Theorboe-Man" is one who can make an accompaniment on the Theorbo from the figured bass; all that is said about him applies to the organist or cembalist, only that on keyboard instruments the hands are much less restricted than on lutes, and therefore the task is easier.

"Musick's Monument," 1676, page 217:—

"Now you must know, that He who would be a *Compleat Theorboe-Man*, must be able to understand Composition; (at least) so much of it, as to be able to put *True Chorde*s together, and also *False*, in their proper Times, and Places; and likewise to know, how to make all kinds of *Closes*, amply and properly. And to assist you in that Particular, I shall only refer you to *Mr. Christopher Simpson's* late and very *Compleat Work;* where you may inform your self sufficiently in that matter, who hath sav'd me a Labour therein; for had it not been already so Excellently done by Him, I should have said something to it, though (it may be) not so much to the purpose; but my Drift is not to Clog the World with anything that is already done, especially so well.

" . . . But still you must further Know, that the Greatest Excellency in this Kind of Performance, lies beyond whatever Directions can be given by Rule.

"The Rule is an *Easie*, *Certain*, and *Safe Way* to walk by; but He that shall not Play beyond the *Rule*, had sometimes better be *Silent;* that is, He must be able, together with the Rule to lend his Ear, to the *Ayre* and *Matter* of the Composition so, as (upon very many Occasions) He must forsake His Rule; and instead of *Conchords*, pass through all manner of *Discords*, according to the Humour of the *Compositions* he shall meet with.

"The *Thing* will require a *quick Discerning Faculty* of the *Ear*, an *Able Hand;* and a *Good Judgment.* The 1st of which must be given in *Nature;* the 2 last will come with *Practice*, and *Care*:—

Ex. 2.

Ex. 3.

Ex. 4.

Ex. 5.

Ex. 6.

Ex. 7.

6 6 7 6 6

6 7 6 6

7 6 6 4 3

At the end of D'Anglebert's "Pièces de Clavecin," 1689, amongst the instructions for playing from a figured bass, which treat principally of elementary harmony, there are some useful things for us to learn. Thus, in the first example, concerning common chords, we can see how fully the chords were filled for accompaniment upon the harpsichord. The author is careful to state, however, that for the organ four-part harmony is better.

Ex. 2 also shows richly-filled chords. In Ex. 3 we have a "General Example with all the Ornaments," where the practical use of the arpeggio, plain and figured, and the acciaccatura are demonstrated. Ex. 4 shows an attempt by the author at writing out in full the preceding "General Example." Here the time values of the notes are only approximative; the arpeggios can be made more or less close; they might come down again after going up; in fact, be treated as we have seen before (page 271):—

Ex. 2.
3
6
4
6
5
3
6
4
5
4
3
Ex. 3.
" Exemple géneral avec les agréemens."
3
6
4
6
5
♯4
6
7
6
7
3
6
4
5
4
3

Ex. 4.

In 1747, Jean-Baptiste Antoine Forqueray, a famous French violist, published a collection of viola da gamba pieces composed for the most part by his father, Antoine Forqueray, who was a still greater master. They are printed in score, with figured bass, to be played by a second viol, or harpsichord, or both. The Preface says:—

"My intention in publishing these Pieces being to entertain three persons at the same time, and to form a concert of two viols and a harpsichord, I have thought proper to make the bass very simple so as to avoid the confusion which might arise with the bass of the harpsichord pieces, which I have ornamented as much as possible."

This passage is made clear by the recent discovery of a contemporary book containing the very same pieces, arranged for the harpsichord in such a way that they can be played with either or both of the viol parts. We thus actually possess a brilliant harpsichord part, fully written out. A few bars from one of the pieces given here below will show the style of these accompaniments":—

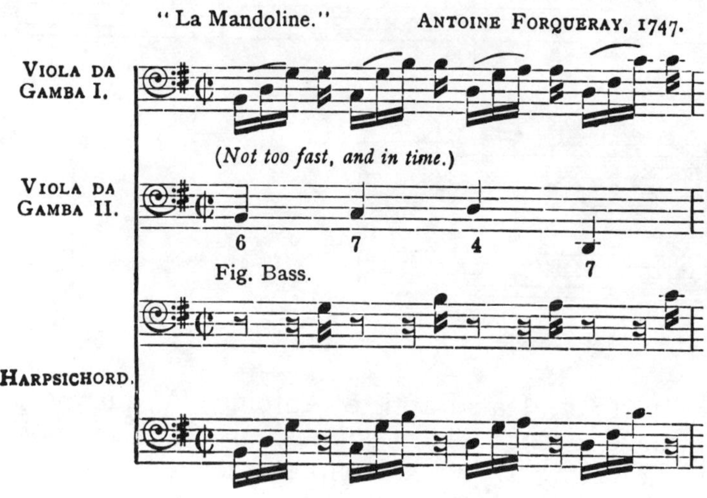

6
6

3
3
7

In 1755, Francesco Geminiani published: "The art of Accompaniment, or A new and well digested method to learn to perform the *Thorough Bass* on the *Harpsichord* with Propriety and Elegance." Op. 11. The work is in two books. From the first we need only quote one paragraph from the Preface, and one from the "Explanations to the Examples":—

Preface, par. 4:—"The Art of Accompagniament consists in displaying Harmony, disposing the Chords, in a Just Distribution of the Sounds whereof they consist, and in ordering them after a Manner, that may give the Ear the Pleasure of a continued and uninterrupted Melody. This Observation, or rather Principle, is the Ground of my Method, which teaches the Learner to draw from the Harmony, he holds under his Fingers, diversified and agreeable Singings. This Work will also be useful in leading the Learner into the Method of Composing, for the Rules ot Composition do not differ from those of Accompagniament: but the common Method of Accompagniament gives the Learner no Hint of the Course he is to take in Composing."

Page 2, Ex. 1: "I repeat here what I have said in my Preface, that the Art of Accompagniament chiefly consists in rendering the Sounds of the Harpsichord lasting, for frequent interruptions of the Sound are inconsistent with true melody. The Learner is therefore to observe not to exhaust the Harmony all at once, that is to say, never to lay down all his Fingers at once upon the Keys, but to touch the several notes whereof the chords consist in Succession."

From the second volume we quote the following:—

Introduction, par. 4: "It will perhaps be said, that the following Examples are arbitrary Compositions on the Bass; and it may be asked how this arbitrary manner of accompanying can agree with the Intention and Stile of all sorts of Compositions. Moreover, a fine Singer or Player, when he finds himself accompanied in this Manner, will perhaps complain that he is interrupted, and the Beauties of his Performance thereby obscured and deprived of their Effect. To this I answer that a good Accompanyer ought to possess the Faculty of playing all sorts of Basses in different Manner, so as to be able, on proper occasions, to enliven the Composition, and delight the Singer or Player. But he is to exercise this Faculty with Judgment, Taste, and Discretion, agreeable to the Stile of the Composition, and the Manner and Intention of the Performer. If an Accompanyer thinks of nothing else but the satisfying his own Whim and Caprice, he may perhaps be said to play well, but will certainly be said to accompany ill."

Sir John Hawkins, in his "History of Music," vol. v., p. 239, reports that when Geminiani was asked to play some of his violin sonatas before King George I., he intimated a wish that Handel might accompany him on the harpsichord, which was granted. This shows that he admired Handel's accompaniments, and therefore that their style cannot have been far removed from Geminiani's own.

The whole of Geminiani's second volume is filled with examples exhibiting many varieties on the same bass. They are generally linked with one another in order to show, presumably, how repeats can be joined together. The following excerpts will give some idea of his way of ornamenting the figured bass:—

Ex. 2.
Basso continuo.

&c.
Ex. 3.
6 ♯6 5 4 3 ♯6
Basso continuo.
6 ♯6 6 9 8 7 ♯3 4 ♯3

A magnificent example of a harpsichord part written by J. S. Bach exists in the second aria of the cantata, "Amore Traditore" ("Bachgesellschaft," 11th year, vol. ii., page 97). It is true that the fact of its being an "obbligato" part, the only one Bach thought worth his while to write out in full, proves that he considered it as something exceptional. However, many passages in it are pure accompaniment, and it seems that anyone thoroughly familiar with Bach's clavier technique could not help feeling that this is the very way the master himself would accompany an important work. The opening of the first part and the end of the second are reproduced here below. The whole work ought to be thoroughly studied; but care should be taken to play from the original "Bachgesellschaft" edition, and not from that of the "New Bachgesellschaft," which has been ruthlessly corrupted. Needless to say, the quavers must be uneven in the proper places, the big chords arpeggiated, trills added, especially in the penultimate note of the voice part, an appoggiatura from below placed before the last note of the song, &c. :—

Cantata, "Amore Traditore." J. S. BACH.

le cru - - - de . . ri - tor - - -
- - - te . . se . . non tro - va mer
- ce - de al pe - - - nar.

CHAPTER VI.

POSITION AND FINGERING.

Before the advent of pianoforte technique, phrasing and fingering on keyboard instruments were indissolubly connected. The only rules were to use "good fingers" for "good notes," and to order the fingers in such a way as to ensure easy and smooth connection between notes which required it. The phrasing suggested the fingering, and the right fingering made it almost impossible to phrase badly. With the ordinary modern system of pianoforte fingering the proper phrasing of the old music is always difficult—frequently impossible. It is therefore well worth trying to discover the fingering in use at the time a certain piece was composed, for it will help us to its right understanding and easy performance.

There is no lack of information about the old methods of fingering and the position of the body, arms, and wrists. About 1600 there were two different schools of fingering. They both agreed as to the necessity of using good fingers for the good notes, or in other words, of playing the accented notes with the strongest fingers; but whilst the

English considered the first (thumb), third, and fifth as the best fingers, the Germans and Italians gave the preference to the second and fourth. The English fingering had greater resources than the other; it eventually superseded it and became the foundation of the playing of Dandrieu, Couperin, Rameau, J. S. Bach, and C. Ph. E. Bach. The old German fingering is well exemplified in Nicolaus Ammerbach's "Orgel—oder Instrument—Tabulatur," 1571, from which the following examples are taken. Note that the various ways of numbering the fingers are translated in this chapter into the usual scheme in which the thumb is counted as "1," and the little finger "5," in both hands:—

Ex. 4.
Right hand.
&c.
&c.
Left hand.
Ex. 5.
Right hand.
&c.
&c.
Left hand.
Ex. 6.
Right hand.
Left hand.
Ex. 7.
Right hand.
Left hand.

Ex. 8.

Ex. 9.

Ex. 10.

Ex. 11.

The passing of the third finger over the second in the left hand, and the second over the third in the right, to be done smoothly and easily, requires the hands to be turned towards the right. When two consecutive notes are played with the same finger, as shown under the crosses in Exx. 3, 6, 7, 9 and 10, the first note must be made short. The different phrasings produced by the different fingerings indicated in Ex. 9 should be noticed. The first implies slightly detached notes of nearly even value. The second, groups of three, separated from one another. The same applies to all the examples.

Amerbach gives the following rules for the fingering of two simultaneous notes:—

"*Thirds* in both hands should be played with the second and fourth fingers. *Fourths*, *Fifths* and *Sixths* with the second and fifth fingers. *Sevenths*, *Octaves*, *Ninths* and *Tenths* with the Thumb and fifth finger."

The use of the thumb is thus clearly restricted by these rules, as well as by the examples given above, to exceptional cases.

We shall now study Italian fingering in Diruta's famous book. For the understanding of some of the author's sayings it is necessary to examine the conditions of virginal music in Italy in his time. Few people realise that whilst in England the art of virginal playing had reached such a perfection that it could not develop further on the same lines, it was in a backward state in Italy. The virginal players were called "Sonatori di Balli," that is, players of dances. "Music" was fit for the organ, but dance-tunes were the proper thing for virginals, and the difference between the two was clearly marked. A large amount of Italian organ music of that period is in existence; profound, learned canzone, toccatas, and ricercare, in which all the resources of scholarship are employed. The composers of such pieces were famous men such as Andrea and Giovanni Gabrieli, Florenzio Maschera, Luzzasco Luzzaschi, Diruta, and Claudio Merulo.

Of Italian music for the virginals there is very little. Frescobaldi (1615) was almost an innovator in that field. There are many dance-tunes; the roughness of their harmony, often a mere string of consecutive fifths and octaves, is not inconsistent with a rugged beauty and character, but was not considered music by the Gabrielis and Merulos. Two examples, given below, will show the style of these dance-tunes. The first is an anonymous Balletto, called "La Violetta," from a MS. in the Strozziani collection at Florence. The second is taken from the "Balli d'Arpicordo" (Vol. II) of Giovanni Picchi, 1618/19. It is worthy of remark that Picchi was "organist of the Cathedral in Venice," and not a mere "dance-player," and that the pieces were published seven years after Frescobaldi's first volume:—

(Despite the long notes in which these tunes are written, they should be played in a lively manner, with plenty of accent and an abundance of "Silences d'articulation.")

Another proof of the backward state of the Italian school of virginal playing can be adduced from the instruments themselves. It will be seen below that Diruta's first requisite for artistic playing upon the "quilled instruments" (Stromenti da Penna), as he calls them, is that they should be delicately and evenly quilled. It is evident that the ordinary instruments used by the "dance players" were provided with strong plectra, in order to obtain the sharp tone required for dance tunes. But these render the touch unpleasantly resistant and harsh; the snap of the quill is strongly felt by the finger. The keys can no longer be caressed; they must perforce be *struck*, and thus refined phrasing and elaborate ornamentation become impossible. Conversely, the delicately regulated virginals are not effective for dancing to, and for this reason the pipe and tabor, the treble violin, or other powerful instruments, were given the preference in England.

The first edition of G. Diruta's "Il Transilvano, Dialogo sopra il vero modo di sonar organi e stromenti da penna" was published at Venice in 1597. A second edition appeared in 1615, and a third in 1625. All three are very rare. We shall quote now from the first edition.

The book begins with a Preface in which the organ is extolled in eloquent words. Then follows a letter from Claudio Merulo to the author, his former pupil, commending and approving the teaching in the book. The elements of musical notation follow this, in the form of a dialogue, like most books of instruction of that period; and Diruta proceeds to give "Rules for playing the Organ with propriety and elegance." Here is a summary of these rules:—

"1°. The player should sit in the middle of the keyboard;

"2°. His body and head should be held upright and graceful, and there should be no movement of either in playing;

"3°. The arm should guide the hand; both should be held straight, neither being higher or lower than the other, which will happen when the wrist is kept at the proper height;

"4°. The fingers should rest upon the keys, slightly curved, not straight, and the hand should be light and relaxed, or else the fingers cannot move with agility and promptness;

"5°. And lastly, the keys should be gently depressed, never struck, and the fingers withdrawn in lifting the key.

"Although these precepts may appear of little or no moment, they are nevertheless of very great utility in rendering the harmony smooth and sweet, and freeing the organist from all impediments in his playing."

To this *Il Transilvano*, the pupil, says :—

"I allow that these rules may be useful; but what can that do to the Harmony, whether your head be straight or awry, or your fingers flat or curved ?

"*Diruta :* They do not affect directly the Harmony, but the gravity and elegance of the organist: they are the cause of that admirable combination of charm and grace so noticeable in Signor Claudio Merulo. He who twists and turns about shall be likened to the ridiculous actor in the Comedy. Besides, the work of such a man will not succeed as it might; he prefers his own caprice, and scorns true art, rendering difficult many things which would otherwise be easy.

"*Transilvano :* And will the endeavours of other good men who follow these rules succeed in the same way as Signor Claudio ?

"*Diruta :* Without any doubt . . ."

Then Transilvano questions again, and Diruta repeats in other words his previous explanations, ending thus :—"And how to hold the hands lightly, and loosely on the keys, I shall give you an example: When you want to give an angry slap, you use strength; but if you mean to caress, you use no strength, but on the contrary relax your hand as for fondling a babe."

The difference of effect produced by pressing or striking the keys is thus demonstrated by Diruta:—

and he adds:—"The bad organists who strike the keys and raise their hands lose half the harmony."

Now we shall learn from Diruta why the "Sonatori di Balli" do not succeed in playing the organ, and how it is possible to play musically upon the quilled instruments.

"*Diruta*: The Council of Trent wisely forbade the playing in churches of 'passemezzi' and other light dances, and all lascivious songs. The profane should not be mixed with the sacred, and such performances could not be tolerated on the organ. If by any chance some dance-player adventures to try something musical on the organ, he cannot refrain from striking the keys, whilst on the contrary an organist finds no difficulty in playing dance-tunes on the virginals.

"*Transilvano:* But I cannot see why dance-players could not succeed in playing music on the organ whilst organists can play dance-tunes well?

"*Diruta:* . . . Because the Sonatori who want to play music on the organ have to observe all the rules I have given about keeping the hands quiet and relaxed, holding the notes, &c., which are unfamiliar to them; whilst the organist who wishes to play dances can easily make an exception to the rules, especially that about the jumping of the hands and the striking of the keys; and in due reason he should do so, for the jacks and quills act better when struck, and this manner of playing is required by the particular style of the dances.

"*Transilvano:* But I wish to ask one more question. Why is it that most organ-players do not succeed in playing musically upon the virginals as they do on the organ?

"*Diruta:* There are many reasons for this, but I will only give you the principal; and I shall say, first, that the instrument must be quilled evenly and lightly, so as to speak easily. Its tone should be lively and long-sounding, and the playing adorned with shakes and all manner of graces. The effect of the wind, which in the organ sustains the tone, must be reproduced on the virginals; for example, a breve or a semibreve can be sustained on the organ, but on the virginals more than half the harmony is lost. You must therefore endeavour with vivacity and dexterity of hand to supply this defect by striking the key many times, rapidly and lightly; and, in short, he who would play with propriety and elegance should study the works of Signor Claudio [Merulo], in which he will find examples of all that can be done.

"Now it remains for me to say which are the good and the bad fingers, which will similarly play the good and the bad notes, for this is as necessary to the organist as to the virginal player. This knowledge is really the most important thing of all. There are five fingers in each hand, the thumb being accounted the first, and the little finger the fifth. The first plays a bad note (*noto cattivo*), the second a good note (*noto buono*), the third a bad note, the fourth a good note, and the fifth a bad note. The second, third and fourth fingers do most of the work; what I say about one hand applies equally to the other.

"Ex. 1. B C B C B C B C B C B C B C B [B stands for *Buono*, good, C for *Cattivo*, bad]. In the right hand the first note would be played with the 2nd finger, which is a good finger; the second with the 3rd finger, which is bad, like the note, and the third with the 4th finger, which is good again, like the note; then you follow on again with the 3rd and 4th until the end of the scale, the last note coming with the 4th finger. This is the way to play all ascending passages. In descending, begin with the 4th, follow on with 3rd, and 2nd, and so on, until you come to the last note with the 2nd, which terminates the passage naturally.

"*Transilvano:* Does thus the 3rd finger go with the 4th in ascending, and with the 2nd in descending in the right hand?

"*Diruta:* Yes, but whether ascending or descending, the 3rd finger must play all the bad notes, and again all the bad notes which skip; the 3rd finger thus is the hardest worked, since nothing usual is done without it, be it ascending or descending scales, skips, '*groppi*,' or '*tremoli*.' The same order of good and bad fingers applies to the left hand; the first ascending note in the same example (Ex. 1) would be played with the 4th finger, following with the 3rd and 2nd, ending always with the 2nd."

The above explanations in ordinary notation come to this:—

"*Transilvano:* But why should not the ascent be made with the 1st and 2nd fingers, and the descent with the 3rd and 4th (left-hand), since many worthy players do it so?

"*Diruta:* Your question is of the greatest importance, and with due reverence to the men you speak of I shall tell you which manner is the better. Know then that when you ascend with the thumb, it may turn well on the white keys, when you play in C major; but when you play in F, you have to pass the black keys which are shorter than the white, and if the thumb happen to fall on a black key it will prove very awkward, whilst the three fingers can do it with much more ease and agility. And you must never descend with the 4th finger, because the 4th finger of the left hand has less strength than that of the right hand, as you know.

"If it is one's caprice to ascend with the 2nd finger and thumb and descend with the 3rd and 4th, it can be done, but at a great disadvantage. Then observe the rule of the good notes for the good fingers if you want to succeed well."

So much for the rules; we have already seen Amerbach use the thumb in that way, and we shall see all the others, later, do most of these forbidden things! Below will be found the most important examples of Diruta. In the original, no figures are marked for fingering; the author uses the letters B and C for *Buono* and *Cattivo*, and describes some cases. The added figures make the examples clearer:—

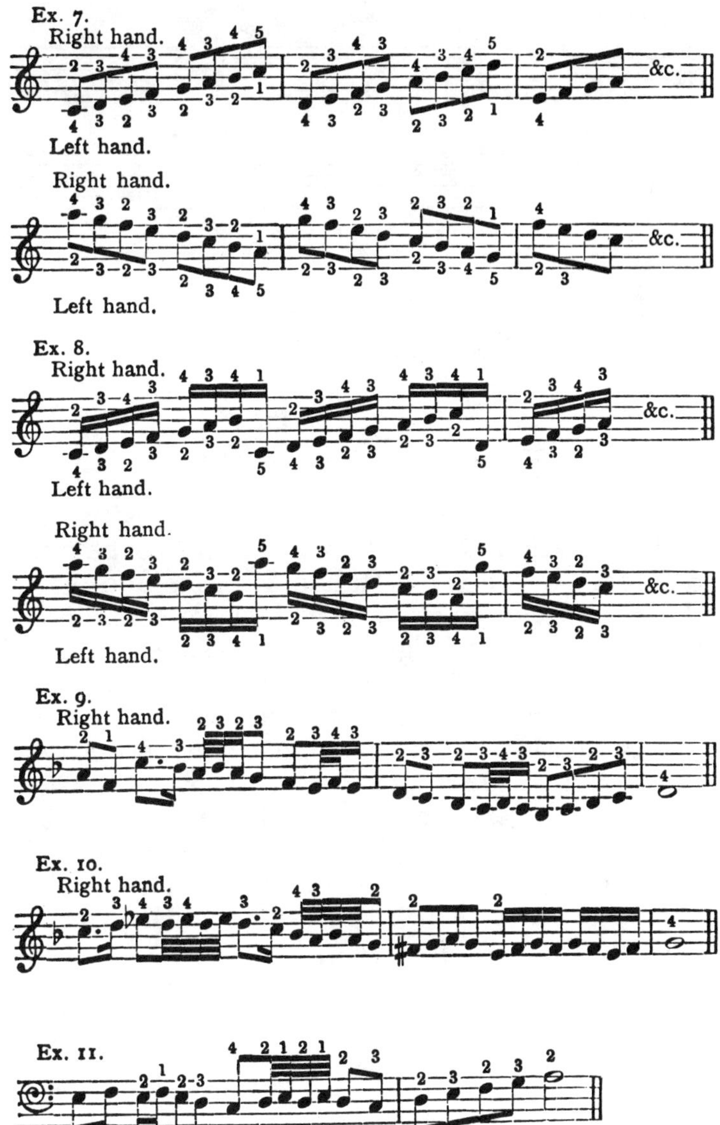
Ex. 7.
Right hand.
&c.
Left hand.
Right hand.
&c.
Left hand.
Ex. 8.
Right hand.
&c.
Left hand.
Right hand.
&c.
Left hand.
Ex. 9.
Right hand.
Ex. 10.
Right hand.
Ex. 11.
Left hand.

Ex. 12.

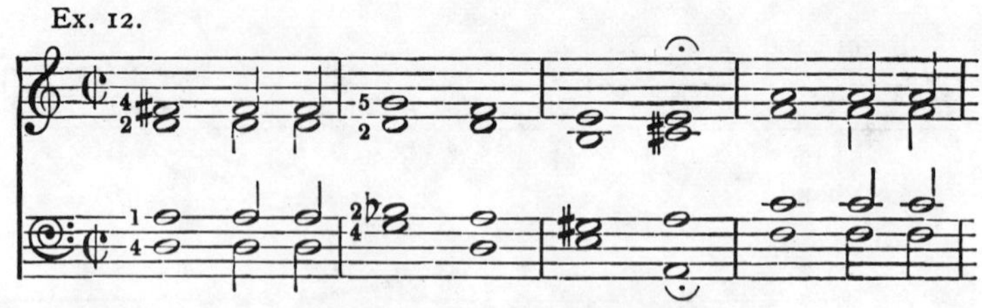

At first sight there does not seem to be much difference between the Italian fingering and that of the English virginalists, which we are now going to study. In the right hand we have the same crossing of the 3rd finger over the 4th in ascending, and of the 3rd over the 2nd in descending. But in reality there is a radical opposition between the two systems. It is possible, in theory at least, to cross the fingers smoothly and evenly, just as in theory the fingers of the modern pianist are supposed to be all equally strong and independent. But in practice there is a strong tendency for the effect to become thus:—

and to induce wrong accents by the instinctive

shortening of the 4th finger note, ascending, and the 2nd finger note, descending. No doubt it suited the music, or the music suited it. But play the same passage with the English fingering, and you get:—

It rings right and true, both for rhythm and phrasing, and naturally falls in with the "Harmonic System of Fingering," which we shall study presently.

An early source of information concerning the old English fingering is the "Fitzwilliam Virginal Book," where some of the pieces contain indicative figures which appear to be contemporary with the manuscript. They will seem strange enough to a modern player, but when the principles of 17th century English fingering are unfolded, much of that strangeness will disappear. Two points, however, are noticeable at first sight: the use of the thumb in the right hand, which is much more frequent with the English than with the old Germans and Italians, and the changes of fingers on the same note, which seem to have been used only by the English at that period.

Here are the examples:—

The first is the opening of a "Fantasia" by Jhon Munday, the second piece in the book. The sign stands here for a mordent. The complete fingering is given in the explanation, with the phrasing suggested by it:—

The second example is from the "Galiarda" by John Bull, No. 17 in the book, the 9th, 10th, and

11th bars, which are the beginning of a variation on the first strain :—

In the second group of bar 2, right hand, the given fingering implies the sliding of the fourth finger from G sharp to A, a common practice in the old fingering.

In the left hand the sign 𝅘𝅥 indicates mordents, except the second sign in the first bar on G♯, where a short shake is better. In this kind of music the same sign stands for either shake or mordent, the one or the other to be preferred, according to the context, as has been explained before.

The "Pavana" by John Bull, No. 34 in the book, contains many fingered passages, and among them the following :—

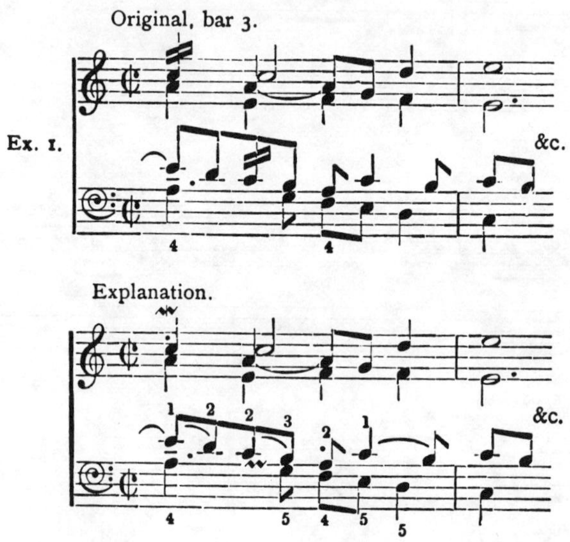

The two successive second fingers on D and C are not what they appear to be, for the shake on C begins on D, which must be played with the first finger to get the second on C; therefore a change of fingers on D, 2 to 1, is implied :—

Here the fingering helps to elucidate the ornamentation, for the short, sharp mordent indicated by the sign can hardly be played otherwise than with the first and second fingers in the left hand; and the same applies to the shakes :—

Explanation.

These bars, 14, 15, and 16, can be readily understood with the help of the explanation. The clear directions for changing fingers on the same key, marked xx, are worthy of notice as being the earliest on record. The sequential passages which follow take the same fingering.

In the two following bars (Ex. 4), which are the last of the variation on the first strain (the first form of which is given above), the changes of finger on the same key are so clear that no explanations could make them clearer:—

Ex. 4. Last bars of variation on 1st strain.

Ex. 5, below, is sufficiently elucidated by the fingerings which have been added to it in brackets. The phrasing is suggested by the fingering:—

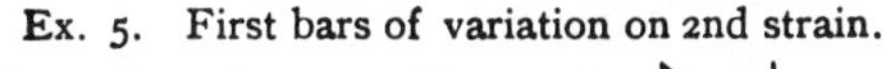
Ex. 5. First bars of variation on 2nd strain.

Interesting information concerning Old English Fingering is found in a manuscript collection of virginal music of the period *circa* 1600 which is preserved at the British Museum, Add. MS. 31403. On page 5 of this volume, in a blank space, the following bars of music have been written. The handwriting is of a later date than that of the pieces, but still has the character of 17th-century work, although no precise date can be ascribed to it, and nothing positive is known of the writer:—

(*See Note on p.* 418)

The arrangement of the bars in the explanation conforms to the original, and the queer English of the phrase is quoted verbatim.

It should be noted that only the first of these "Graces in play," the slide, occurs in the pieces of that collection; but the "dotted slides" are early in character, as well as the "double relish," which follows them. As to the fingering, it again suggests phrasing in an unmistakable manner. The free use of the little finger for shakes is startling to a pianist. It was commonly and most usefully practised until the increased heaviness of touch in pianofortes rendered it almost impossible.

A rich store of information concerning the old English fingering is in the possession of the writer. With a copy of Playford's "Select Musicall Ayres and Dialogues," the first edition, 1652, some thirty leaves of ruled paper were bound, and the first owner of the book began to transcribe on these some songs not included in the collection. He copied two: "O my Clarissa," by William Lawes, and "Come, Chloris, hie we to the bow'r," by Henry Lawes. The first was printed in the second edition of "Select Musicall Ayres and Dialogues," 1653, and the second in "Ayres and Dialogues," by Henry Lawes, 1653. Some slight differences between the printed and the MS. versions seem to indicate that the latter were copied from an earlier source. After the publication of these books, no more songs were copied, but the blank leaves were utilised for the musical education of a child. The "gamut" and some reading exercises with the sol-fa syllables attached were written in, and also a selection of virginal pieces, several of which are carefully fingered. No composers' names or dates are found in the MS., but one of the pieces is a Prelude by Orlando Gibbons, No. 21 in "Parthenia" (published 1611), also found in other MS. collections of the period. Another prelude, simple and short, and fully fingered, is evidently contemporary with the first. The dates of the other pieces vary between 1630 and 1675, approximately. The little prelude will be found below :—

The sign ═ indicates short shakes everywhere in the right-hand part; the same in the left hand, except the second, on C in the 6th bar, and the last also on C in the penultimate bar; these are mordents.

The fingering in bar 3, right hand, may be explained thus:—

Similar cases would be treated in the same way.

Excerpts from the other pieces will suffice for the present purpose, but the Gibbons Prelude, being most interesting, will be reproduced *in extenso* in the Appendix.

The following examples from the Gibbons Prelude and the left-hand part of a Sarabande confirm what we have seen already:—

The figures in brackets are explicative. In Ex. 2, left hand, the fourth finger is used on G on account of the necessary sequence : 3 2 1 2 1 2. In Ex. 3, right hand, the fingering 3 2 3 2 1 might seem more natural than 3 2 3 2 3; but it was a recognised principle that the thumb in both hands should not be held over the keys at the same time because it stiffened the muscles. As the chords and octaves in the left hand necessitate the use of the thumb, it is therefore avoided as much as possible in the right hand, which may be turned a little inwards, as a consequence.

In Purcell's "Lessons, &c." (1696), the following rules for fingering are given :—

"Right hand the Fingers to ascend are the 3d and 4th, to descend yᵉ 3d and 2d.

"Left hand the Fingers to ascend are the 3d and 4th, to descend yᵉ 3d and 2d.

"Observe in yᵉ fingering of your right hand your Thumb is yᵉ First so on to yᵉ fifth.

"In yᵉ fingering of your left hand your little finger is yᵉ first soe on to the fifth."

A valuable source of information concerning fingering is the rare "Pièces de Clavecin courtes et faciles," &c., by Jean François Dandrieu. The book bears no date of publication, but it is earlier than two other books of harpsichord pieces of the same size and engraving which, like the first, are in the possession of the writer. All three appear to be earlier than the other less rare books of pieces by this composer. The date of the first book can be assigned to the period 1705-10. All the pieces in it are fingered. No fingering is given when the fingers run naturally in their regular order. One of the suites will be found in the Appendix. A few excerpts are given here to show the principle of the fingering.

In the Prelude the semibreves do not indicate a slow movement, but free Rhythm and Tempo. The slurs mean the prolongation of the notes from which they start until their end. The dotted lines between the Treble and Bass show the notes to be played together. A finger mark on an ornamented note applies to the *principal note;* if the ornament begins with the note above, the next finger must be used. This often brings about a change of fingers on the same note. The ornaments are: , Shake; , Prepared Shake; , Slurred Shake; , Shake and Turn; , Mordent; , Appoggiatura, or Slur; , Arpeggio:—

&c.
Sarabande, Id.
&c.
Rondeau, Suite IV.

A number of passages from François Couperin's "L'Art de toucher le Clavecin," 1716, which concern the present subject have already been given at pages 18 to 21. We shall now supplement them with further information and examples:—

Page 3: "To be seated at the proper height, the underneath part of the elbow, wrist, and fingers should be level; a chair should be selected in accordance with this rule. Something more or less high should be placed under the feet of children, so that their feet, not being in the air, may support the body in right balance.

"The distance at which a grown-up person should be from the keyboard is about nine inches from the waist, and less in proportion for children.

"The middle of the body and that of the keyboard must correspond.

"The body should be turned slightly to the right, the knees not pressed together, the feet on a line, and the right foot well turned outwards.

"With regard to grimaces, they can easily be corrected by placing a looking glass on the desk of the spinet or harpsichord."

Page 7: "It is better and more proper not to beat time with your head, body or feet. Your attitude at the harpsichord should be easy, without looking too fixedly at anything, nor seeming vacant; in short, look at the company, if there is any, as you would if you were not otherwise occupied. This advice is for those who play without book."

Page 19: "Manner of connecting several mordents following one another by degrees, by changing fingers on the same note":—

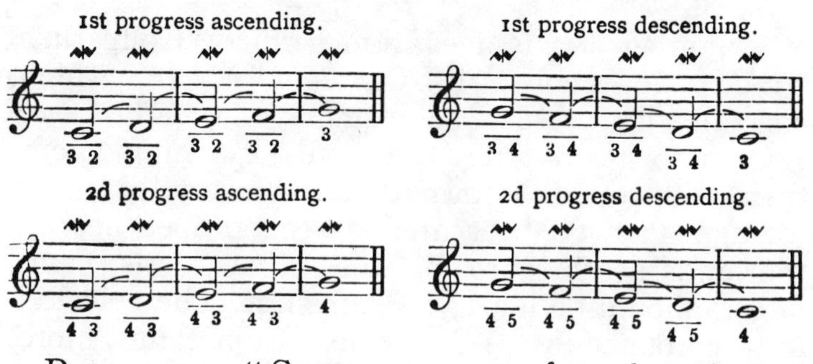

Page 20: "Same manner for the slurred mordents in the left hand:—

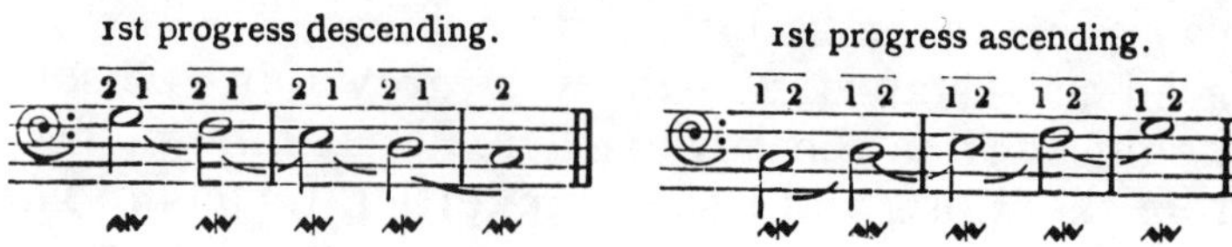

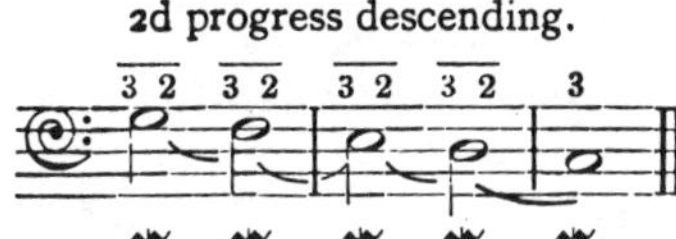

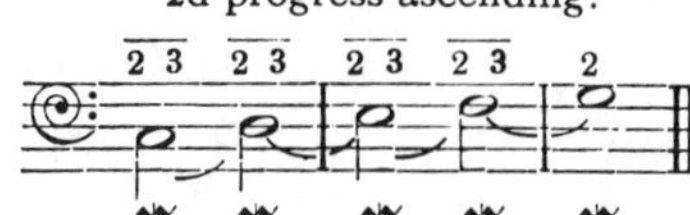

"I have found that there are two ways to finger the appoggiatura; for me one is preferable to the other:—

"I only allow the ancient manner on the occasions where the hand has two parts to play, for then it is too uncomfortable, especially if the parts are far from one another."

"*Reasons for preferring the new manner of the Appoggiature.* The finger marked 3 in the third progress and the finger marked 4 in the fourth, being obliged to quit the last quaver to restrike the appoggiatura, allow less connection than at the first progress, where the finger marked 3 is more promptly replaced by the second finger, and at the second progress, where the finger 4 is also sooner replaced by the finger marked 3.

"I have proved that without seeing the hands of the person who plays, I can distinguish whether the two notes in question have been struck by the same finger or by two different fingers. My pupils feel it like myself, from which I conclude that there is some truth in it."

Couperin seems to imply that he invented, or at least was the first to introduce, this system of fingering. But Dandrieu, at least, used it just like Couperin. An example can be seen at p. 395, in the Allemande from Suite IV.

Page 22: "It would be very useful if pupils could be exercised to shake with every finger; but, as this depends partly on natural talent, and some have more or less freedom and strength with certain fingers, the choice must be left with the teacher."

Page 23: "The most frequent shakes are those of the 3rd with the 2nd finger and of the 4th with the 3rd, in the right hand; in the left, those of the 1st with the 2nd and of the 2nd with the 3rd."

Page 29: Ex. 1 shows Couperin's fingering for scales, the same as that used in England over a century before.

Ex. 2, "An easier fingering for Keys with sharps and flats."

Ex. 3, "Ancient ways of playing thirds in succession."

Ex. 4, "New fingering for binding these thirds."

Ex. 5, "Another way of connecting thirds."

Page 30: "A propos of these slurred thirds, I must state briefly that, one day, teaching them to a young pupil, I tried to make her beat two shakes together with the same hand. Her happy dispositions, her excellent hands, and the great habit she had already acquired of it brought her to the point of beating them very evenly. I have lost sight of this young lady since.

"Indeed, if this practice could be acquired, it would add great lustre to the play. I have heard, since, a man make them (otherwise much skilled); he, perhaps had begun too late, but his example did not encourage me to torture myself in order to succeed in doing them as I think they should be done. I confine myself to encouraging young people to begin at the proper time. Should this practice become established, it would bring no inconvenience with pieces already written; it would only be a question of adding a shake, in thirds, to the one already written."

Ex. 6: "Progress of shakes linked by the method of changing fingers on the same note":—

Ex. 6.

Page 46: "Passages from my First Book of Harpsichord Pieces, difficult to finger." (Exx. 7 to 17.)

Exx. 7 and 8. Note how the phrasing, indicated by the fingering, is based upon the harmony. More will be said on this point, especially in connection with J. S. Bach's fingering. Here is the harmony of Ex. 7; Ex. 8 can be analysed in the same way:—

Ex. 7. "La Milordine."

Ex. 9, Couperin's original note: "As the second and fourth of these slurred notes are those which bear the harmony with the bass, it is necessary that they should be played with the same fingers as if the melody were simple, and without passing-notes." (See Ex. 10):—

Harmony notes of the same.

Ex. 10.

Ex. 11. Note the break in the fingering between bars 2 and 3 (x), which indicates the phrasing, based on the harmony:—

Same Piece.

Ex. 13.

Ex. 14. Courante, 5me Ordre.

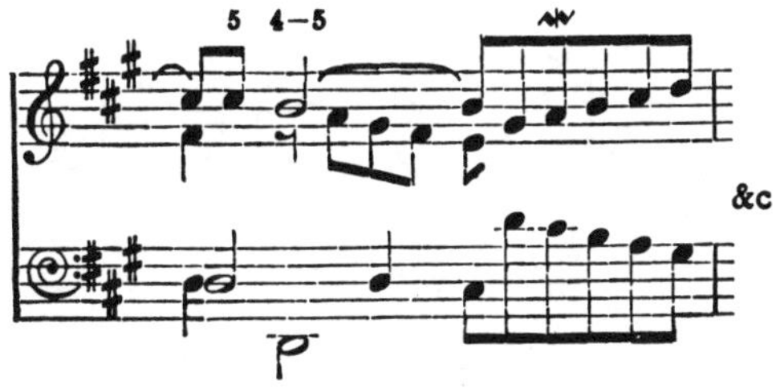

Ex. 15. "Les Ondes."
Right hand.

Ex. 16. Same Piece.

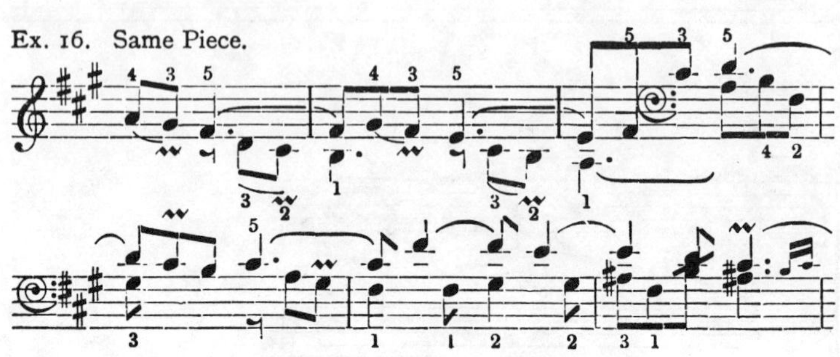

Ex. 17, Couperin's note: "It will be seen in Ex. 17 that two consecutive notes by degrees may be played by the same finger, when the first is detached, or when the second is in the last part of a beat":—

Ex. 17. Same Piece.

In Ex. 18, in the place marked by a cross, the same finger plays G♯ and A by sliding from the first to the second, as we have seen before :—

Ex. 18. Same Piece.
Right Hand.

Exx. 19 to 28: "Passages from my Second Book of Pieces, difficult to finger."

In Ex. 20, see how the fingering suggests the phrasing. In the last bar of this example, the first finger on B♭ is an obvious misprint; the second finger is intended. Nobody could question this who has followed Couperin's fingering so far. Yet this very passage has been selected for reproduction in "Grove's Dictionary," art. "Fingering," where it forms the ground for such appreciations as "very uncomfortable," "very unpractical," "a chaos of unpractical rules," &c., &c. Another misprint occurs at bar 5 [N.B.] where 4 5 4 should be read 5 4 5:—

"Les Bergeries."

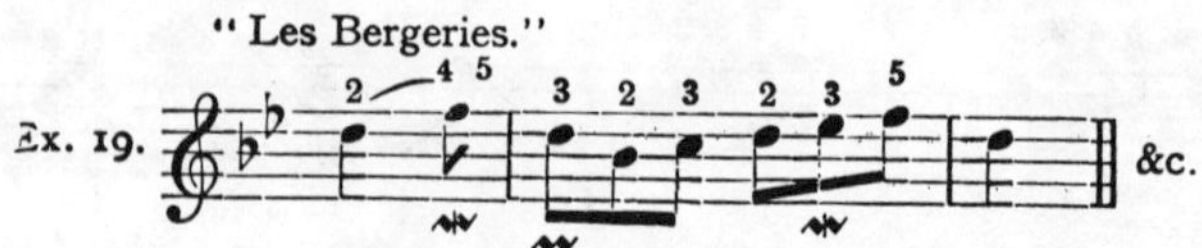

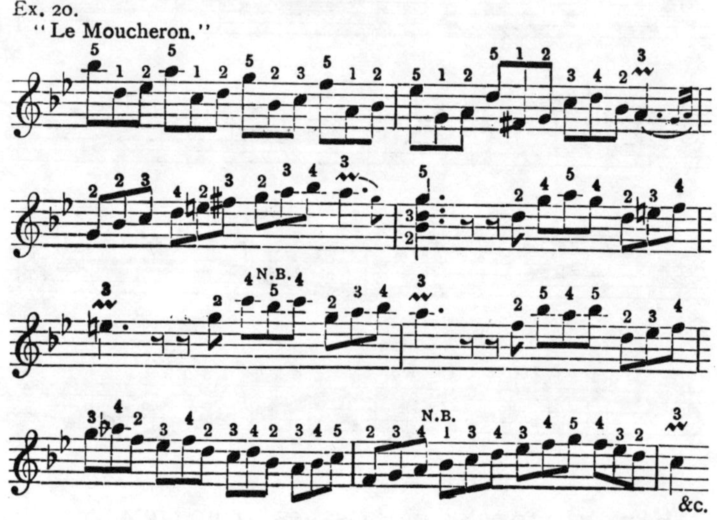

Ex. 21. Passacaille.

Ex. 22. Same Piece.

Ex. 23. Same Piece.

Ex. 24. "La Triomphante."

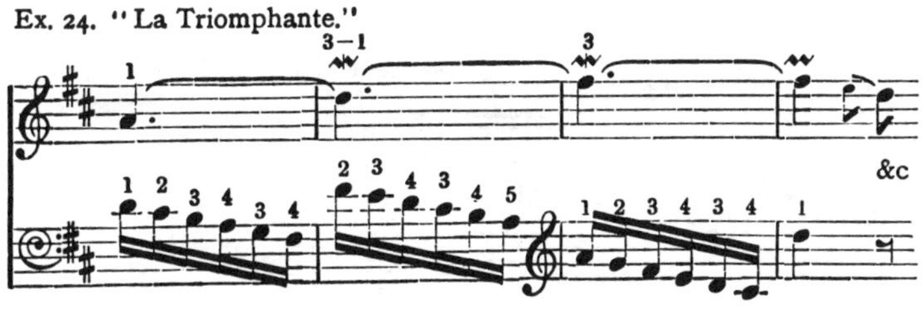

Ex. 25. "L'Amazône."

J. Ph. Rameau, in the Introduction to his "Pièces de Clavecin," 1731, gives some examples of fingering and a charming little "Menuet en Rondeau," fully fingered, which are reproduced below.

Note the curious misprint in Ex. 3, where 1 stands for 5, and 5 for 1. Another misprint occurs in the Menuet, where a 3 is marked instead of a 2, as in similar passages :—

J. PH. RAMEAU, 1731.

" The thumb (1) must be used in the middle of this Battery :

First Lesson, Right hand.

Left hand.

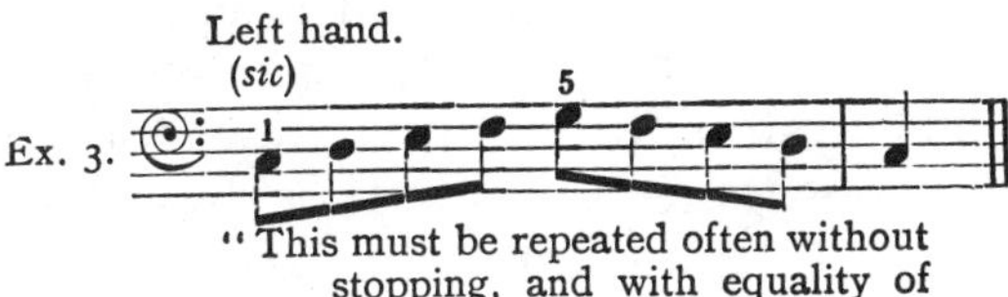

" This must be repeated often without stopping, and with equality of movement."

Ex. 4.

Menuet en Rondeau.

In the "Code de Musique Pratique," published in 1760, one of his last works, Rameau describes an ingenious system of his invention for accompanying on the figured bass. It is based mainly on fingering. Certain intervals are assigned to certain fingers in such a manner that the resolution of discords and the sequence of chords without consecutive fifths and octaves are obtained, to a certain extent, mechanically. The chords are restricted to the right hand, and the thumb is hardly ever used. But the harmony thus produced is coarse and thick; the system was rejected by the best contemporary musicians.

In Quantz's "Versuch, &c.," from which so much valuable information has been already derived, there is a most interesting passage on harpsichord touch and tone-production, which is here given *in extenso* :—

Chap. XVII., Sect. VI., § 18: "On every instrument the tone can be produced in different manners, and the same thing is true of the harpsichord, although, judging from appearances, we might believe that everything there depends upon the instrument, and not upon the player. Experience proves that if two musicians of unequal skill perform on the same harpsichord, the tone will be much better with the better player. There can be no other cause for this than the difference in the touch, and on this account it is necessary that all the fingers should act not only with the same strength, but with the right strength; that the strings be allowed sufficient time to vibrate without impediment, and that the keys be not depressed too slowly, but, on the contrary, with a certain snap which sets the strings vibrating for a long time; thus it may become possible to counteract, to a certain extent, the natural defect of this instrument, which is the impossibility of slurring notes together as on some other instruments. It is important to see whether one finger presses stronger than another, which can come from the habit of curving some fingers more than others. This not only causes unevenness in the tone, but it prevents the passages from being round, distinct, and agreeable; in this manner, should a rapid scale occur, the fingers will do no more than tumble upon the keys. If, on the contrary, the habit has been acquired of curving the fingers equally, we shall not fall so easily into this fault. Moreover, in the performance of such rapid passages, the fingers should not be suddenly raised; their tips should rather be slid up to the forward end of the key, and thus withdrawn, for this will ensure the clearest possible execution of the runs. My opinion in this is based on the example of one of the most highly skilled harpsichord players, who followed this method, and taught it."

In the index of his book, Quantz explains that the eminent harpsichord player in question was J. S. Bach.

Concerning Bach's fingering, the following study is based upon those pieces which he marked with his own hand, rather than upon what he may have said about it, which we have only at second hand at best, and is often not consistent with the facts. These pieces are: a short Prelude, called "Applicatio," and a "Præambulum," both in the "Clavier Büchlein für W. Fr. Bach," and a Prelude and Fugue which present a shorter and simpler version of the Prelude and Fugue in C major from the second volume of "Das wohltemperirte Klavier." They are all very fully fingered. The first two are given below; the Prelude and Fugue will be found in the Appendix.

A curious resemblance exists between the "Applicatio," the old English Prelude on p. 389, and the Dandrieu Prelude on p. 393, especially between the last two, where the first nine notes and their harmonies are identical.

In the "Applicatio," Ex. 1, the "Trillo und Mordent" on F, bar 2, and B, bar 6, should be played thus:—

Here again we have a daring use of the little finger), all the more remarkable if we remember that this piece was intended for a beginner:—

Ex. 1. Applicatio. J. S. BACH.

An analysis of the fingering of the "Præambulum," Ex. 2, shows that it is based upon its harmonic foundation, or, in other words, that, as far as possible, the same fingers are used on consecutive notes as if they were to be played together as chords:—

Ex. 2. Præambulum. J. S. Bach.

Ex. 3.
"Præambulum" (Analysed.)
J. S. BACH.
&c.

Ex. 3 shows a reduction of this Præambulum into plain chords, to which the original fingering has been transferred, and which will demonstrate this important principle at a glance. It has already been alluded to in connection with Couperin (page 400).

The melodic phrases in the music of that period being almost entirely evolved from the harmony (the reverse is quite exceptional), it happens frequently that the same fingering is suggested both by the harmony and the phrase; nevertheless, the practical value of this harmonic principle is very great. It applies to a large portion of the music not only of Bach but of his contemporaries and 17th-century predecessors. It is the fingering that would naturally suggest itself to people accustomed, as they were, to play on a Figured Bass.

Several interesting examples will be found in the Prelude in the Appendix. Specially in bar 6, 2nd beat to first beat of bar 7, right hand, bar 7, 3rd and 4th beats, and 1st of bar 8, right hand, and both hands in bars 12 and 13.

C. Ph. E. Bach has written so extensively about fingering that the reproduction of his precepts and examples would fill a book, and exceed the limits of the present work. Besides, being the pioneer of a new school, his system does not apply unreservedly to the earlier music, about which our store of information is already fairly complete. We shall therefore content ourselves with reproducing, in the Appendix, the first movement of his beautiful and characteristic Sonata in F minor, fully fingered, which will give some idea of his system.

Elway Bevin was organist of Bristol Cathedral from 1589 to 1637. In 1605 he was made Gentleman Extraordinary of the Chapel Royal.

CHAPTER VII.

THE MUSICAL INSTRUMENTS OF THE PERIOD.

Some knowledge of the principal musical instruments of the 16th, 17th, and 18th centuries would be a help to the understanding of the music of that period. A thorough study of each type of instrument would fill volumes, and could not be attempted here; but the principal facts about technical capabilities, individual colours of tone and their combinations, and, above all, an account of the practical differences between the old instruments and their modern representatives, can be given in a concise form and may prove very useful, considering the scanty amount of reliable information available on these subjects.

SECTION I.

The Virginals.

The term "a pair of virginalls" was often used, meaning one instrument. Under that name are comprised all the keyed instruments with strings, the tone of which is produced by the action of a plectrum. There are many types of virginals, varying in size, form, and complexity; but all have in common the same mechanical means of tone-production, which is the jack.

The earliest known jacks, which date from the 15th century, do not differ from those of the 18th, or even the 20th century, except in unimportant details. When well made and well regulated they answer to the touch with the utmost precision and rapidity, and instantly stop the vibrations of the string when the key is released by the finger. The dynamic varieties resulting from a heavier or lighter touch are not great, if compared with the hammer action of a pianoforte; but they are perceptible, and sufficient to give rhythmic accents.

A variety of materials have been used for the plectra, the principal being quills and leather. The latter was much used in the 16th century; but for a century or so from about 1650 it was almost entirely superseded by quills. Leather was reintroduced in the 18th century, at times replacing the quills altogether. There is a marked difference between the tone-colour produced by these two materials, especially when *buff* leather is used. The quills give a sharp and brilliant tone, but one not so pure and sweet as that of leather. For wearing qualities, leather is much superior to quills.

Raven quills, well cut and taken from the backbone of the feather, last for a reasonable time; but they break eventually, and must be replaced, whilst leather of the proper quality, thickness, and cut seems to be practically everlasting.

The ordinary virginals, the most common, had one string and one jack for each note, and consequently no variety in tone-colour. Their form was rectangular in England and Northern Europe. In Italy, in the 16th century, they often affected the beautiful and convenient form of an elongated pentagon, which was rendered possible by the general habit, in Italy, of keeping instruments in cases, whilst in other countries they were self-contained, a plain lid, with a hinged front, fixed to the rim of the instrument, closing it. This simple arrangement was not adaptable to the Italian shape.

Some very small virginals were made, hardly any longer than the four-octave keyboard with which they were provided. They were called in Italy "Ottavina" or "Spinetta," in England Octave Virginals, on account of their pitch being an octave higher than that of the regular instruments, and thus corresponding with the 4-ft. stops of the organ. Others were somewhat larger, being tuned a fourth or fifth lower. The common full-size instruments were of 8-ft. tone, their compass extending from the C with two additional lines below the bass stave, to the C with two additional lines above the treble stave, and sometimes to the D, E, and F above. In the bass also three or four more notes were often added, carrying the scale to the G or F of the 16-ft. octave. This made a total of five octaves, F to F, which was sufficient for all music until the beginning of the 19th century.

In Italy, before the 18th century, all the keyboard instruments had an incomplete scale in the bass; the keyboard started apparently on E, but this note was tuned to C, the next F♯ to D, and the G♯ to E;

this arrangement was called "Short Octave." As the Italian music of that period is written mostly in the keys of F and C major, D and G minor, and anyway the music was adapted to that shortened scale, the absence of the low C♯, D♯, and F♯ was not much felt. But if English music be played on such instruments many passages are crippled, for the English virginalists used a wider range of tonalities than the Italians, even going through the complete cycle of 12 keys, as witness the "Ut, ré, mi, fa, sol, la" of John Bull in the "Fitzwilliam Virginal Book."

The French name for these instruments was "Epinette" or "Espinette"; the German, "Instrument" or "Symphonia," the latter two being very misleading. An *upright* variety was the "Clavicytherium," and another about which very little definite information is available was called "Arpicordo."

In all these simple instruments, excepting the last two kinds, the strings were stretched parallel with the keyboard. Virginals made on this principle could be small and their price low. But when there was no need to economise either space or money, the instruments were allowed to take their natural form, which is that of a harp, placed horizontally and with its strings perpendicular to the keyboard.

The advantages of this construction were that the strings could be given their full length and consequent richness of tone, and that more space being available between the strings a most important series of developments and improvements became possible. Thus a second set of strings was added side by side with the first, and a second row of jacks to play upon them. The *guides* which keep the jacks in position being movable, a very small displacement from left to right, commanded by a stop, would cause the plectrum either to catch the string or pass it silently at will. Two strings in unison were thus available for each note, either severally or together, making three varieties of strength and tone-colour usable. A third set of shorter strings, tuned in the higher octave, being placed under the two unisons, further enriched the instrument with a four-foot register and made seven combinations of tone available.

By the addition of a second row of keys, two different sets of strings of contrasted tone could be made to dialogue together, by placing each hand on a different keyboard, and an instantaneous change from soft to loud became possible, one of the keyboards sounding one string only, and the other all the three strings.

That such instruments were in use in the early part of the 16th century is proved by the following entry in the "Privy Purse Expenses of King Henry VIII.":—

"1530. (April). Item, the vi daye paied to William Lewes for ii payer of virginalls in one coffer with iiii stoppes brought to Greenwiche iii li. And for ii payer of virginalls in one coffer brought to the More other iii li. And for a little payer of virginals to the More. xxs. . . . . vii li."

They were called Claricymbel, Clavicymbel, Clavicembalo, Gravicembalo, Cembalo, Clavecin, Clavessin, Harpsicon, Harpsichord, Flugel.

The harp or theorbo stop found in many harpsichords had no special strings or jacks. Its peculiar pizzicato effect was produced by the contact of a row of little pieces of soft leather or cloth with the strings near to their nut, which modified their tone so as to make it resemble that of a harp or lute.

Some harpsichords possessed an additional fourth row of strings, placed above the unisons and double their length or thereabouts, giving 16-ft tone. These instruments were necessarily very large, and never became common; but they had a wonderful depth and grandeur of tone. J. S. Bach had one, and this explains why some passages in his music demand 16-ft. tone to produce their full effect.

In the early harpsichords all changes of tone were controlled by hand stops, and therefore could only be used when a rest allowed a hand to be withdrawn from the keys. An English maker, about 1660, found a way to effect these changes by the action of the feet. A description of this invention is given by Th. Mace in "Musick's Monument." The author, after describing the effect of voices and viols with organ or theorbo accompaniment in certain pieces of music, "wonderfully Rare, Sublime, and Divine beyond all Expression," says:—

Page 235: "But when we would be most *Ayrey*, *Jocond*, *Lively*, and *Spruce;* Then we had Choice and Singular *Consorts*, either for 2, 3, or 4 parts, but not to the *Organ*, as many now a days Improperly and Unadvisedly perform such Consorts with, but to the *Harpsicon;* yet, more properly and much better to the *Pedal*, an

Instrument of a late invention, contriv'd as I have been inform'd by one Mr. *John Hayward* of London, a most Excellent kind of Instrument for a Consort, and far beyond all Harpsicons or Organs that I have yet heard of, (I mean for *Consort*, or *single Use;*) but the organ far beyond it, for Those other *Performances* before mentioned.

"Concerning This Instrument, (call'd the *Pedal* because it is contriv'd to give *Varieties* with the *Foot*) I shall bestow a few lines in making mention of, in regard it is not very commonly used, or known; because few make of them well, and fewer will go to the price of them: Twenty Pounds being the ordinary price of one; but the Great Patron of Musick in his time, Sir *Robert Bolles*, who in this University I had the happiness to Initiate in *This High Art* had two of them, the one I remember at 30*l*. and the other at 50*l*. Very admirable Instruments.

"This Instrument is in *Shape* and *Bulk* just like a Harpsicon; only it differs in the order of it, thus, viz.

"There is made right underneath the keys, near the ground, a kind of *Cubbord*, or Box, which opens with a little pair of doors, in which box the Performer sets both his feet, resting them upon his *Heels*, his *Toes* a little turning up, touching nothing, till such a time he has a pleasure to employ them; which is after this manner, viz. There being right underneath his Toes 4 *little Pummels of Wood*, under each foot 2, any one of those 4 he may Tread upon at his pleasure: which by the weight of his foot drives a *Spring*, and so causeth the whole instrument to *Sound*, either *Soft* or *Loud*, according as he shall chuse to Tread any of them down; for without the foot nothing speaks.

"The out-side of the *Right Foot* drives one, and the in-side of the same foot drives another; so that by treading his foot a little awry, either outward or inward, he causeth a *Various Stop* to be heard, at his pleasure; and if he clap down his foot flat, then he takes them both, at the same time, which is a 3d. variety, and *Louder*.

"Then has he ready, under his *Left Foot*, 2 other *Various Stops*, and by the like Order and Motion of the Foot, he can immediately give you 3 other *Varieties*, either Softer or Louder, as with the right foot before mentioned he did.

"So that you may perceive he has several Various Stops at pleasure; and all *Quick* and *Nimble*, by the ready turn of the foot.

"And by this *Pritty Device*, is this instrument made wonderfully rare, and excellent: So that doubtless it Excels all Harpsicons and Organs in the world, for *admirable sweetness and Humour*, either for a private, or a consort use.

"I caus'd one of them to be made in my House, that has 9 several other varieties, (24 in all), by reason of a stop to be slip'd in with the hand, which my workman calls a *Theorboe-Stop;* and indeed it is not much unlike it; but what it wants of a *Lute*, it has in its own *Singular Prittiness*.

"We had in those days choice consorts, fitted on purpose to suit with the nature of this instrument.

"The truth is, the great grace which Musick receives by the Right ordering of this instrument, to compositions and performances suitable thereunto, is such, that it far exceeds any Expressions that can be made of it."

Hayward's invention did not make much headway at the time, but seventy or eighty years later most harpsichords were provided with pedals, or knee levers which produced the same effects.

Mention should be made of the Spinet, which on account of its graceful wing-shape and pretty tone became so popular in England in the 18th century, that it entirely superseded the oblong virginal. It is, in fact, a small harpsichord with single strings disposed obliquely and forming an angle of about 45° with the row of jacks, the latter being parallel, or nearly so, with the keyboard.

The first spinet was perhaps made by a relative of the same Hayward, or Haward, who invented the Pedal; at any rate, one Haward was early in the field making some, for there is no spinet known which can be safely ascribed to a date earlier than the following entries in Pepys' Diary:—

"April 4, 1668. To White Hall. Took Aldgate Street in my way and there called upon one Haward that makes Virginalls, and there did like of a little espinette, and will have him finish it for me: for I had a mind to a small harpsichon, but this takes up less room."

"July 10, 1668. To Haward's to look upon an Espinette, and I did come near to buying one, but broke off. I have a mind to have one."

"July 13, 1668. I to buy my espinette, which I did now agree for, and did at Haward's meet with Mr. Thacker, and heard him play on the harpsicon, so as I never heard man before, I think."

"July 15, 1668. At noon is brought home the espinette I bought the other day of Haward: cost me £5."

When Pepys says "I had a mind to a small harpsicon, but this takes up less room," he points out one of the chief causes of the great popularity of the spinet. It takes very little room, and its triangular shape makes it fit in nooks and corners where an oblong virginal could not be placed. It was not expensive: £5, compared with the £20 to £50 for a Pedal! But it never was but a makeshift for a harpsichord, for it possessed none of those wonderfully varied colours of tone and combinations of registers which are the glory of the latter.

Now comes the question: How were the various stops and combinations of the harpsichord employed practically? Scanty information is available on that point. Composers' indications concerning harpsichord stops are as rare as those relating to organ stops, and probably for the same reason, that harpsichords were as variable as organs in their stops and combinations. Only a few general indications can be obtained.

François Dandrieu explains in the Preface to his "Livre de Pièces de Clavecin, etc.," 1724, that the "Concert des Oiseaux" (Birds' concert) must be played with both hands upon the first keyboard, but after withdrawing the two unisons and leaving the *petite octave* (4-ft. stop) only.

"Le Timpanon" (The dulcimer) also requires the *petite octave* alone, but the right hand should play upon the *second* keyboard and the left hand upon the *first*. (This raises the bass part one octave, and makes it cross through the treble.)

"Les Fifres" (The fifes), on the contrary, should be played with the same arrangement of stops, but with the right hand upon the *first* keyboard and the left hand upon the *second*. (This raises the melody one octave.)

In "Les Caractères de la Guerre," the piece called "La Charge" has several places marked *Coups de Cannon*, which show only the four notes of a common chord; but in order better to express the cannons' roar, instead of these four notes, you may strike as many times with the full length of the flat hand all the lowest notes of the harpsichord.

François Couperin, in his "Third Book of Harpsichord Pieces," 1722, gives several *Pièces Croisées* in which the parts for the two hands lie in the same section of the scale. Couperin explains that such pieces should be played on two keyboards, with unison stops.

Many works of J. S. Bach are specially composed for a harpsichord with two keyboards, in which various combinations are implied by the context; as, for example, some of the "Goldberg Variations," which demand two keyboards of equal strength, but with tones of contrasted colour, or the "Italian Concerto," where soli passages marked *piano* occur in both hands, the tutti being marked *forte*. The *forte* parts must be played with 8-, 4-, and occasionally 16-ft. tone, on the first keyboard, the *piano* parts on the second keyboard with one 8-ft. stop.

A comparison between the harpsichord and the pianoforte presents difficulties on account of the great differences which exist between these two types of instruments. It is, indeed, not easy to understand why the former was discarded in favour of the latter, seeing that the pianoforte can no more replace the harpsichord than the harpsichord can replace the pianoforte.

The most beautiful and characteristic pianoforte effects, which cannot possibly be realised on the harpsichord, are those of a melody and a bass, widely separated, the intervening space being filled with arpeggios or other more or less indistinct figures, the whole combination of tones being sustained by the action of the damper pedal until the next change of harmony. It might even be said a little *beyond* the next change, for in modern pianofortes the vibrations of the strings are too powerful for any dampers to stop them dead; the sound continues for some time after the finger has been lifted from the key. This inadequate damping, and the presence of those enormously thick felt coverings on the hammers, necessitated by the prevailing fashion for vague, luscious effects, account for the lack of clearness and definition in pianoforte tone, which qualities are indispensable for the performance of the old music. The great pianists are well aware of this; they make unceasing efforts to obtain hard hammers from the makers. Paderewski will not play upon a pianoforte the hammers of which have not been specially hardened for him. His skilled fingers can be trusted to soften and sweeten the tone when he wants it; but nothing can put life into that blurred dullness consequent upon soft hammers, which helps to cover so many of the sins of the ordinary player.

Another serious point is the enormous emphasis given by the blow of the hammers to the beginning of each note, which continually attracts the attention of the listener to every note as it comes, making it difficult to follow the movements of individual parts. For this reason contrapuntal music is much more difficult to understand on the pianoforte than on the organ or harpsichord; although the latter does not really sustain the tone nearly so long as a good pianoforte, yet it seems to do so in carrying on the inner parts.

In fact the pianoforte, despite its wonderful development, has remained true to its origin. It is a keyed dulcimer. The writer had the good fortune recently to be allowed to examine a very early pianoforte, dated 1610, unquestionably genuine, which anticipates by over one hundred years the first instruments of Cristofori, hitherto reputed inventor of the pianoforte. It is apparently of Dutch origin, and was made for a French nobleman. It has very small hammers, attached to the keys, showing a simple form of the Viennese action. It has *no dampers*, and never had any. No doubt the player occasionally stopped the vibrations of the strings with his hands, as dulcimer players do, when confusion became objectionable. The instrument altogether looks much like a large dulcimer. The most attractive part of its decoration is a painting which fills the inside of the lid, representing an outdoor scene, with gaily dressed ladies and gentlemen dancing in a park to the music of a little band of musicians grouped round the very pianoforte which it embellishes, and which is there carefully and delicately painted. The fortunate owner of this charming instrument is M. René Savoye, whose collection in the Avenue de l'Opéra, in Paris, contains many other rare and exquisite musical treasures.

The absence of dampers in this instrument is not very surprising. There are plenty of people who practically do away with them by putting their foot on the pedal before beginning to play, and leaving it there until they have finished; but it is not considered good taste. And, indeed, with the long-sustained tone of modern pianofortes, it is well-nigh intolerable. But it does not seem to have been objected to in the time of Mozart, and even Beethoven, for in the little square pianofortes of the period 1760-1800 there is no other means of controlling the dampers but by a hand-stop placed in a box on the left side of the keyboard. In the original edition of Beethoven's so-called "Moonlight Sonata," the indication *senza sordini* at the beginning of the first movement means that the dampers are to be lifted, and thus remain until the end of the piece.

For accompaniments or concerted music the harpsichord cannot be replaced by the modern pianoforte. The tone of the latter does not easily blend with the voice, or with string or wind instruments. Nothing is more difficult for a pianist than to play concerted music with a violin or violoncello. If he employs his usual strength the string instrument is drowned; if he spares his partner and plays delicately, the softened pianoforte tone becomes still more woolly, and the contrast proves too great, with the sharpness of the string instrument, for blending to be possible.

The harpsichord, on the contrary, is at its best in chamber music; it harmonizes beautifully with most other instruments, for colour as well as power. The blending is so perfect, in fact, that it becomes difficult at times for unaccustomed ears to distinguish the tones of the various instruments. When allied to a string quartet—as, for example,

Jesus' recitatives in Bach's "St. Matthew" Passion —no separate part can distinctly be traced, but the whole effect is one of indescribable richness and beauty.

Until the harpsichord lost favour there were two in each orchestra. At the first sat the concert-master, who accompanied the soli; at the second the accompanist, who played the tutti. The first pianofortes which replaced them did not effect a marked change: they had not yet lost their string-tone. But both pianofortes and orchestra very soon began to grow, and the more they grew the less they agreed. And what could a harpsichord do now against a hundred players or so? Whilst for power the modern pianoforte can nearly match an orchestra.

SECTION II.

The Clavichord.

The clavichord is an instrument of very great simplicity. It has no jacks, no hammers, no stops, no pedals: in fact, no mechanical aid to variety of tone; and of tone so little that it compares better for colour and power, to the humming of bees than to the most delicate among instruments. But it possesses a soul, or rather seems to have one, for under the fingers of some gifted player it reflects every shade of the player's feelings as a faithful mirror. Its tone is alive, its notes can be swelled or made to quiver just like a voice swayed by emotion. It can even command those slight variations of pitch which in all sensitive instruments are so helpful to expression.

The clavichord has strings of brass, very slender, two for each note. If you pluck one it gives no sound, for unlike those of other instruments, the length proper for each note has not been measured off yet. But if you look through the gold web of which the close strings give an illusion, you will see on each key-end an upright blade of brass ready to come and touch the strings, like the fingers of the violin-player, when that note is required. This blade of brass is the tangent; its contact alone makes the tone. When the finger releases a key the strings at once become dead, for beyond the striking point their unused length is interlaced with strips of woollen cloth. The player, through the keys, keeps in touch with the strings, and thus can impel them with every motion of his mind. But he is debarred from the one thing people prize most nowadays, and that is making a big noise. As, however, infinite softness is possible on the clavichord, the range of gradations is equal to the demands of expression. The smallness of its tone is no drawback in itself. It can be heard by large audiences when occasion arises, for it fascinates them into a keen receptivity. But it cannot consort with any other instrument; in its efforts to equal even the meekest opponent its delicate beauty is lost. The clavichord is, above all, an intimate instrument.

In early clavichords the tangents played several notes on the same strings, like the violinist's fingers; and only one of these notes could be heard at the same time. This does not hamper melodies nor chords which do not include two notes from the same strings. But discords of a second are destroyed, for only the higher note sounds.

Some people use this point as an argument that J. S. Bach made little use of the clavichord. The evidence of his music disproves this, for much of it can only make its proper effect upon this instrument. The fact is that clavichords with special strings for each note (*Bundfrei*) were known in Bach's time; and who would have had one if not he?

Moreover, the best *gebunden* clavichords (fret-bound) are so cleverly disposed that in none but extreme keys could the two notes of the same string be wanted together. A search through the Forty-eight Preludes and Fugues of "Das wohltemperirte Klavier" (*Klavier, i.e., Clavichord*) will show that the passages that would suffer in that way are rare.

Jakob Adlung, 1699-1762, a contemporary of Bach, treats at length of the clavichord in "Musica Mechanica Organoedi." A few extracts from his book will confirm these statements:—

§ 571: "A good clavichord, well played, is sweeter and more heart-stirring than any other instrument."

§ 572: "It is indispensable for study. Whoever has learned it can easily play the organ and the harpsichord . . . . Some people despise it because its tone is faint, and, in truth, some are too weak; but others sound like the music of violins; and although they be fainter than other instruments, their 'delicatesse' remains, and none can express the graces so well. Herr Mattheson's remark is very true when he says (*Orch.* i., P. III., cap. iii., § 4) 'The beloved clavichord, from all others, takes the prize.' Men's natures vary; some like *douce* music; others prefer the strong. Some cannot endure the scratching of a harp, others revel in it. Everyone to his taste."

§ 579: "It is a great accomplishment when a clavichord is *Bundfrei*. Some are made so that 3 or 4 tangents strike the same strings; when playing syncopations, and a major or minor second is formed, the upper note only is heard, and the harmony spoilt. . . . Therefore I do not recommend clavichords that are not *Bundfrei*. These clavichords (*Bundfrei*) are often made nowadays, and the trouble and cost they entail are disregarded; for it has been discovered long ago that they have great advantages over the others."

SECTION III.

THE ORGAN.

The organ remained faithful to the old ideals longer than other instruments. The makers of 1815 worked much on the same principles as those of 1615. In most houses there was a little organ, soft and sweet, easy to play, ready to warble like a bird, or with two stops to make you feel the ecstasies of God's worship. The church organs in addition had that power based on sweetness which constitutes majesty. The change came on, and for the sake of louder tone, pressure of wind was doubled and trebled. The same pressure acting on the valves which let the wind into the pipes made them too heavy for the fingers to move through the keys. A machine was then invented which did the work at second hand. Instead of shutting your own door, if you call a servant to do so, the door may get shut, but not so quickly. So the music of the organ dragged on after the player's fingers as best it could. Personal touch, which did so much for phrasing and expression, was destroyed.

Then fashion decreed that the organ should be an imitation of the orchestra, and it got stops which sound like horns, flutes, and violins; but without the life that players instil into their instruments. The organist, if he is clever, can give a chromo-lithograph of the "Meistersingers" Prelude; but he has not the right tone with which to play a chorale, if his organ is up-to-date. Modern compositions are intended for this machine, and all is well with them; but it is a revelation to hear Handel's or Bach's music on a well-preserved old organ.

SECTION IV.

The Lute.

The lute is known to everybody by name; not, perhaps, because it was popular once upon a time as the best of instruments, for that was four hundred years ago, but because its sweet-sounding name has been persistently used in romance and in poetry, even to this day, to evoke vaguely the pleasant image of some fascinating instrument.

The fact is that the lute has become one of the rarest and most precious amongst old instruments. This book has already given a good deal of information about it, incidentally with other matters. We shall not repeat it. Our endeavour will be to complete and co-ordinate the whole as far as possible within the limits of this study.

The lute in use towards the beginning of the 16th century had five sets of double strings (two unisons for each note), and one single string, which is the highest.

The tuning was as follows:—

In the 17th century other tunings were introduced under the name of *French tunings;* but this remained the classical one, and it was always used for accompaniments.

The body of the lute is pear-shaped; the sound-board flat, with a rose (or sound-hole) most skilfully cut out of the board itself in some Gothic design, often of surpassing beauty. The bridge, very low, is glued to the sound-board, and the strings are attached to it. The neck, broad and thin, is of sufficient length to accommodate seven frets. The frets, made of a piece of gut string, must be tied round the neck and adjusted by the player himself, who is thus given the chance of having an instrument as delicately tuned as his ear and experience allow.

By the middle of the century, lutes were being provided with an additional pair of strings in the bass, which increased the compass down to the D with one ledger line below the bass stave. This is the lute of Dowland, and other players of the Elizabethan period.

Then special lutes were made for accompaniments with as many as seven pairs of long bass strings, tuned in octaves instead of unisons, reaching to the F two octaves below the F of the bass clef, and supported by an additional neck. The body of these lutes is so large that the treble string, and sometimes the second and even the third pairs of strings, cannot be pulled up to their proper pitch, and must be tuned an octave lower.

It brings hopeless confusion in the movements of inner parts; the instrument is thus reduced to a formless filling up of chords, which no doubt originated the idea of harmony, as a vertical combination of sounds in opposition to counterpoint, the art of weaving independent parts. These large lutes were called *arcileuto* in Italy, *theorbo* in England.

With the exception of the bass parts, figured or not, used by the theorbo players to construct their accompaniments, all the lute music was written in a special notation called *Tablature*, which was also used for guitars, cithrens, and other instruments of a like nature, and in some cases for viols and even violins.

The tablature does not directly represent musical sounds. Its signs show how notes are to be produced on the particular instrument intended. You cannot sing from it or play the music on any instrument, as with the ordinary notation. Let us imagine a series of six horizontal lines, stave-like and corresponding to the six strings or pairs of strings of the old lute; the uppermost line pertains to the treble string, the second line to the second string, and so on to the sixth or last, which is for the bass strings. If a letter *a* is marked upon the first line, the first string is to be played open; if it is marked on the second line, the second string is to be played open, and it is the same with all the other strings. A letter *b* marked upon any line means that the corresponding string must be stopped at the first fret; if it is a *c*, at the second fret, and so on. If two or more notes are to be played together, their several letters are placed over one another, chord-like.*

* In these explanations the two strings tuned in unison, and which are always played together, are counted as one.

The time-values of the notes are indicated by signs analogous to those in the ordinary notation :—

𝅝 𝅗𝅥 ♩ ♪ 𝅘𝅥𝅯

or in the older music :—

| ⌈ F F F

These signs are placed above the stave, over the letters. They are affected by dots in the usual way. If a time-sign is found without a letter under it, a rest of corresponding value is intended. When several notes of equal value follow one another, the trouble of repeating the time-sign is saved by placing it over the first note of the series only, it being understood that no change takes place unless indicated by a new sign. If a note or chord is to be held whilst other parts are moving, a line is drawn under the letter, which shows by its length the duration of the hold. These lines are only useful in special cases, for it is a rule that all notes must be held until their vibrations naturally die, whenever possible, or until their prolongation becomes undesirable for melodic or harmonic reasons.

Whatever may be the number of strings of the lute, no more than six lines are used in the tablature; for a seventh string the letters are marked below the sixth line. If there are more bass strings, ledger lines are used, the number of which indicates the order of the strings; above three ledger lines, the figures 3, 4, 5, &c., are employed for clearness' sake.

An example of tablature, with its translation, is given here below. It is a fragment from a Fantasie for the lute by John Dowland, which exists in a MS. in the British Museum, *c.* 1590 :—

"Fantasie for the Lute" (fragment). JOHN DOWLAND.

The advantage of tablature for certain instruments can be seen at bars 5 and 6 of the above example. If written in ordinary notation, the player would probably be puzzled to find how the passage could be done, but in the tablature all is clear.

The tablature is also advantageous for instruments with variable tunings, as whatever the tuning, the reading and finger-work remain the same. With ordinary notation the difficulty of finding the places of the notes on a French lute of twenty-one strings in some unfamiliar tuning would be appalling.

The tablature as explained above was used in England, France, and Germany. In Italian and Spanish tablatures the principle is the same, but the order of the lines is reversed, the uppermost representing the bass string and the lowest the treble string. Furthermore, figures are used instead of letters: 0 for the open string; 1, 2, 3, &c., for the frets.

The lute has a beautiful tone—sweet, clear, full of character. It is charming for solo pieces, and incomparable for accompanying the voice. It resembles the guitar more than any other instrument, but Thomas Mace is right when he calls the guitar "a bit of the old lute," for it is inferior to it. As, moreover, the literature of the lute is very extensive and important, there is good reason why the revival of the instrument should spread. Quite apart from actual playing, earnest students should render themselves familiar with the tablature, for it can help them to the solution of troublesome problems in the old music. Those barbarous passages in Elizabethan virginal and other music which occur in contemporary texts, and are often rendered worse by the emendations and suggestions of modern editors, are for the most part caused by the lax use of the signs for accidentals so general at the time. In tablature there are no accidentals; each sign means a definite sound, and no such blemishes occur. There are, of course, passages where the logical progress of the parts brings together, for example, a B natural and a B flat, or an F natural and an F sharp, which scare an untrained ear; but these harshnesses are logical. They are quite different from the barbarities mentioned before, which can often be authoritatively amended from tablature versions of the same pieces.

The Quinterna is a small lute, with four or five pairs of strings tuned like the higher strings of the lute, but an octave above. The Pandurina is a still smaller lute, with only four pairs of strings, generally tuned G D G D, played with a quill and used, like the quinterna, for dances and popular pieces.

The Chittarone, on the contrary, is a kind of large theorbo, 6½ ft. long and more, with twenty-two or twenty-six wire strings, of which six or eight pairs are open basses. It was played with the fingers and used for accompaniments.

Other instruments of the lute kind, but with wire strings, are the Orpharion, an English instrument tuned and played exactly like the lute and using the same music, the Bandora, and the Penorcon, which did not differ much from the orpharion.

The Cithren (cittern or citharen) is a delightful instrument with four pairs of wire strings (sometimes more) tuned in this strange manner :—

and played with a quill or with the fingers, according to the desired effect. It was extremely popular in England in the 16th and 17th centuries, and with a modified tuning until the end of the 18th, under the name of "English guittar." There is a fair amount of fine music written for it. Its tone is like that of the mandoline, but more delicate.

SECTION V.

The Viols.

Until the "single soul'd ayres" of the violins sounded the final overthrow of English music, it was the privilege of the viols to play this incomparable concerted music in contrapuntal style, of which the English masters had the secret, and which in the near future will undoubtedly be understood and appreciated even as are other 16th century works of art at the present time. Thomas Mace, our faithful mentor, deploring in his old age "the Fashion has Cry'd these Things down, and set up others in their Room," describes these Consorts of Viols in the following words:—

"Musick's Monument," page 234: "We had for our *Grave Musick*, *Fancies* of 3, 4, 5, and 6 *Parts*, to the *Organ;* interpos'd (now and then) with some *Pavins*, *Allmaines*, *Solemn* and *Sweet Delightful Ayres;* all which were, as it were, so many Pathettical Stories, Rhetorical and Sublime Discourses; Subtil, and Accute Argumentations; so Suitable, and Agreeing to the *Inward*, *Secret* and Intellectual Faculties of the *Soul* and *Mind;* that to set Them forth according to their

True Praise, there are no Words sufficient in Language . . . . .

"The authors of such like compositions have been divers Famous English Men, and Italians; some of which, for their very great Eminency, and worth, in that *Particular Faculty*, I will here name, viz., *Mr. Alfonso Ferabosco, Mr. John Ward, Mr. Lupo, Mr. White, Mr. Richard Deering, Mr. William Lawes, Mr. John Jenkins, Mr. Christopher Simpson, Mr. Coperario*, and one *Monteverde*, a Famous Italian author; besides divers and very many others, who in their *Late Time*, were all Substantial, Able, and Profound Composing Masters in this Art, and have left their works behind them, as fit *Monuments* and *Patterns* for Sober and Wise Posterity, worthy to be *Imitated*, and Practiced. . . .

"And these things were performed, upon so many Equal, and *Truly-Sciz'd Viols;* and so exactly *Strung, Tun'd* and *Play'd upon*, as no one *Part* was any *Impediment* to the Other; but still (as the composition required) by Intervals, each *Part amplified*, and *Heightened the Other;* the organ evenly, softly and sweetly Acchording to All."

Notwithstanding appearances, the only Italian's name included in the above list of composers is that of Monteverde. Alfonso Ferrabosco was born at Greenwich. Thomas Lupo was one of the musicians of King James I., a composer of anthems, songs, and maskes, and an Englishman. As to Giovanni Coperario, his real name was John Cooper.

The viols differ outwardly from the violins. Their back is flat, their sound-holes are C-shaped, their ribs higher, especially in the small viols, their shoulders meet the neck at a tangent, instead of squarely as in the violins, their corners are turned inwards instead of outwards. But none of these features are of serious import; viols are often at variance with one or more of them. The vital points, those which affect the musical results, are:—

1°. The number of strings, which in English viols is always six.

2°. The thickness of the strings, which, being less in proportion than it is in violins, renders them less tense and causes the tone to be sweeter and more easily yielded.

3°. The thinness of the wood in all parts of the viol body, consequent upon the low tension of the strings, and which helps the tone to be sweet and pure.

4°. The tuning, in fourths, with a third between the two middle strings, which brings an interval of two octaves between the treble and bass strings, and affects the method of fingering and playing the instrument.

5°. The frets, of gut-string, and movable like those of the lute, which give to the stopped notes the same clear ring as the open strings.

6° and lastly, the manner of holding the bow and ordering its strokes, which being the reverse of what is done on the violin, prevents the strong accents characteristic of the latter, facilitating an even and sustained tone.

This latter clause requires elucidation. The bow of the violin or violoncello being held under the hand, the wrist and arm are higher than the bow, and their weight is upon it. The accented note being played with a down bow, which begins right under the hand or very near it, feels the full strength of the arm and wrist in addition to their weight; the up-bow note, which begins at the point of the bow, receives no benefit from this weight, and only a very small fraction of their strength. Thus in the violin everything concurs in giving preponderance to the down stroke. Skilled players endeavour, and succeed after long practice, in equalising the strokes and gaining a full command of the tone; but they are working against nature, and cannot do it with the ease and repose of the viol player, who has everything in his favour and does these things without effort.

We shall now let Christopher Simpson teach us the elements of viol-bowing:—

"Division Viol," Part I, § 3: "A Viol-Bow for Division, should be stiff, but not heavy. Its length (betwixt the two places where the Hairs are fastened at each end) about seven and twenty inches. The nut, short. The height of it about a finger's breadth, or little more."

§ 5. "Hold the Bow betwixt the ends of your Thumb and two foremost fingers, near to the Nut. The Thumb and first finger fastned on the stalk; and the second finger's end turned *in* shorter; against the Hairs thereof; by which you may poize and keep up the point of the Bow. . . . Holding the Bow in this posture, stretch out your Arm, and draw it first over one String, then another; crossing them in right angle, at the distance of two or three Inches from the Bridge. Make each several string yeild a full and clear sound; and order your knees so, that they be no impediment to the motion of your Bow."

§ 10: "When you see an even number of Quavers or Semiquavers, as 2, 4, 6, 8, you must begin with your Bow forward; yea, though the Bow were imployed forward in the next note before them. But if the number be odd, as 3, 5, 7: (which always happens by reason of some Prick-Note or odd Rest,) the first of that odd number must be played with the Bow backward. This is the most proper motion of the Bow, though not absolutely without some exception. . . ."

§ 12. "I told you before that you must stretch out your arm streight, in which posture, (playing long Notes) you will necessarily move your shoulder joint; but if you stir that joint in quick notes; it will cause the whole body to shake; which (by all means) must be avoyded; as also any other indecent Gesture. Quick notes therefore must be express'd by moving some joint nearer the Hand; which is generally agreed upon to be the Wrist. . . . . To gain this motion of the wrist, the ordinary direction is, to draw the Hand (in moving the Bow to and fro) a little after the Arm. . . . This motion or looseness of the wrist we mention is chiefly in *Demisemiquavers*, for, in *Quavers*, and *Semiquavers* too, we must allow so much stiffness to the wrist as may command the Bow *on*, and *off* the String, at every Note, if occasion so require."

To resume. The arm and wrist are under the bow, in an easy and natural position, in no way weighing upon it. The accented stroke being naturally *forward*, begins at the point of the bow, where the pressure of the fingers is least strong. These conditions being reversed with the unaccented backward stroke, it follows that everything concurs to promote evenness of tone.

This bowing is easy to learn; far more so than violin-bowing. As, furthermore, the presence of the frets upon the viol insures correct intonation, and as the individual parts of even the most intricate consort are generally easy to play, we can understand how performers without great proficiency could give good performances of this admirable music; provided always that the viols be strung, fretted, and tuned by a master.

A full consort of viols consists of two trebles, two tenors, and two basses. All the instruments are similar in form and stringing. The bass viol, or viola da gamba, is about the size of a violoncello, but with a longer neck, and strings measuring about 30 inches from the nut to the bridge. Its tuning is:—

being the same intervals as in the old lute. The lowest string is tuned down to C whenever the key of the composition requires it.

The tenor viol is tuned a fourth higher, from G to G, its size being proportionate, and its length of strings, therefore, about 22½ inches.

The treble viol is tuned an octave above the bass, and is in consequence half its size.

All these viols were played alike, for position as well as bowing; they were held downwards, and never over arm, in the violin way, however small they might be. Their tone is well balanced; they blend much better with one another than a quartet of violins, and they express the complications of counterpoint with wonderful clearness.

The resources of the bass viol as a solo instrument had been developed to the highest degree of perfection in England by the end of the 16th century. The English players were famous all over the world. Foreign princes were willing to pay handsome salaries for the privilege of having them at their courts. Foreign musicians came to England to study not only the viols, but the lute and other instruments. The conditions were in fact the reverse of what they are to-day.

The viola da gamba lends itself admirably to rich chords and music in parts, as well as to rapid and brilliant divisions. In the high register, beyond the frets, it can do all the tricks of expression of the violin, and with as free a tone, owing to its thin strings. Furthermore, a continual variety of effects was derived from varied tunings, of which there were many. The music for these fancy tunings was always written in tablature, and the instrument called "lero" or lyra-viol. Pizzicati for both hands are frequent with it; they were called a "Thump," and prove most effective, being harp-like in tone. There is a large amount of music for one, two, and three lyra-viols, in tablature, by eminent English composers, Alfonso Ferabosco and Giovanni Coperario being the most famous among them. A French violist, André Maugars, came to England about 1620 to study the style and technique of these masters. He obtained admittance to the private band of King James I. for some time, and returned to France in 1624. He entered the service of the famous Cardinal de Richelieu, and became the founder of that great school of French viol-players, which through Ste. Colombes,

Hottman, Marais, de Caix d'Hervelois, and the Forquerays, achieved such admirable results in their own way at a time when the English, driven from the viol by fashion, were compelled for their living to imitate the Italian violin music, in which uncongenial task they gained but moderate successes.

The tenor viol did not attain to independence as a solo instrument, and the treble viol fared no better in England than the tenor; but in France, under the name of "Dessus de Viole," the latter became fashionable as an exponent of simple, expressive music. A fair number of good compositions were published for it, and also for the "Pardessus de Viole," a small kind of treble viol tuned a fourth higher than the Dessus.

An "alto viol, or Haute contre," tuned a tone lower than the treble, C to C, existed, but was rarely used, as its part could be played with good result upon either treble or tenor.

The Double-bass viol, or violone, does not seem to have been much used in England or in France until late; but it was common in Italy and Germany. In its original and perfect form it had six strings tuned an octave below the bass viol, thus reaching to 16-ft. C by the lowering of the bass string from D to C, which was done as on the bass viol. The tone of the violone, notwithstanding its depth, is clear, pure, and free. The instrument, being fretted, plays in tune. Its effect with a quartet and harpsichord, as it doubles the violoncello part an octave lower, is quite indescribable in its mellow, velvety richness.

The present double-bass is a violone which, through the strengthening of its body and the thickening of its strings, has become powerful, but coarse and impure in tone. At one time it had been reduced to three strings. It eventually regained another, and is now on its way to acquire a fifth. It may in due course get back to the original six.

Another feature which the double-bass has lost, and that it is most desirable it should regain, is the frets. Double-bass players, with few exceptions, play out of tune, and thus spoil the orchestra. It can be explained by the difficulty of tuning low notes, and by the fact that players on the double-bass have few opportunities of hearing themselves play alone, and are thus deprived of a check which is helpful to other string-players.

Nobody would consider it advisable to fret the violoncello, as it would thus lose those slides and vibratos which are necessary in modern music. But the double-bass has no need of these means of expression. The frets, besides, would give clearness to many rapid passages which at present only make a rumbling noise. A conductor with enough power and determination to force his double-bass players to fret their instruments would deserve the thanks of all; but he would have a hard fight with his men, whose principal ambition is to emulate the violoncellists, just as the latter imitate the violinists.

SECTION VI.

THE VIOLA D'AMORE.

The Viola d'amore stands on the borderland between the viols and the violins. By its many strings, six or seven in number, and its varied tunings, mostly in thirds and fourths, it is akin to the viols; but it has no frets, and it is held and bowed like a violin. Its name means the love-viol, a pretty name, but probably a corruption of "viol da more," the viol of the Moor, an opinion which we need not discuss here, but that is rendered probable by the fact that the sympathetic strings, the characteristic feature of the viola d'amore, exist in many Eastern instruments. These sympathetic strings are made of fine brass or steel wire, stretched under the ordinary strings, out of reach of either bow or finger, and therefore not intended to be played upon directly, but to vibrate sympathetically when a note played in the ordinary way is in tune with them or with some of their harmonics. These sympathetic vibrations obscure the tone somewhat; but they give it a fascinating silvery ring and a curious ethereal quality which is effective for some kinds of music. Vivaldi, Handel, Bach, and others have used it in special works, and a few—very few—solo pieces exist for it. On account of the various tunings to which the viola d'amore is subject, its music was written in a kind of tablature, derived from the ordinary notation, which first appeared in the sonatas published about 1721 by Attilio Ariosti, one of the early players on this instrument.

SECTION VII.

The Violins.

Concerning Violins, the conditions are peculiar. Those who can afford it play upon instruments which were made two centuries ago. For the last hundred years violin makers have continued to announce their discoveries of the great masters' secrets. As their instruments can be bought for a small sum, whilst a Guarnerius or Stradivarius is worth a fortune, it would be idle to discuss whether the moderns rival the ancients or not. But these old violins must be altered before they are considered fit for modern requirements. The original bass bar is replaced by one longer and stronger. The neck is lengthened, broadened, and thrown more backward. The fingerboard is prolonged to reach extreme high notes. The bridge is raised, and its curve increased so that the bow may press harder on one string without fear of touching the next.

Whether these changes increase the amount of pure tone available is doubtful, but the violin thus treated has become more gritty, more assertive, more capable of holding its own against its aggressive neighbours.

The radical changes undergone by the bow in the last quarter of the 18th century had even more important results, musically, than the alterations of the violin.

The old violin bow was only about 20 inches long. Its stick was curved outwards, like a shooting bow. It was thick at the base, and finished in a delicate point, and had in consequence great firmness, lightness, and very little momentum. With it, detached notes could be performed extremely rapidly and distinctly. Staccato effects attained a crispness quite unapproachable with a modern bow. A sharpness of accent and clearness of phrasing were obtainable for which the "staccato leggiero" of the Tourte bow affords no compensation. The writer, after considerable experience in playing with the old bow, has no hesitation in pronouncing it preferable to the modern bow for playing the old violin music.

The violins form a complete family of six different sizes, including the treble, our ordinary violin; the alto or haute-contre, our viola; the tenor, which has disappeared; the bass, our violoncello; the double-bass, which was never much used, being inferior to the violone; and, lastly, the violino piccolo, the smallest of all, tuned a fourth higher than the treble. The violino piccolo has been effectively used by Bach. Its tone is quite distinct; it should not be replaced by an ordinary violin playing in the higher positions, as the effect is not at all the same. It is given to children to learn the violin with, and being tuned like an ordinary violin, sounds wretched. As it is perfectly delightful when tuned at the pitch proper to its length, it is difficult to understand why this should not be generally done. But accompaniments would have to be transposed, and modern teachers like the beaten track.

How the tenor violin ever came to be discarded is incomprehensible. Any orchestral score, be it Haydn's or Wagner's, shows the crying need of it. The instrumental tenor part, like the tenor part in the vocal quartet, is indispensable in music. There being no proper string instrument for it, composers are obliged to distribute it as best they can among the others. Sometimes it is given to the alto-viola and played upon its lowest strings, which are not effective for that purpose on ordinary instruments; or, worse still, the violoncello may have to play it upon its highest string, which is too strident. Moreover, in the first case, whilst the viola plays the tenor part, the alto part falls to the second violin, which has not the right timbre for it, and might be better occupied in playing a second treble part. In the second case, whilst the violoncello plays the tenor part, the real, true string-bass is unavailable. It has to be given to the bassoon or some other wind instrument, for the double-bass alone is no good for it; or, again, the violoncellos or the violas are divided, or the violins subdivided, &c., the which makeshifts cannot replace a normal tenor part played on the normal notes of a tenor violin.

The tenor violin, being tuned an octave below the treble, would quite naturally double the melody of the violins in octaves, and enrich the orchestra in many various ways, which none of the latest noise machines can do.

The tenor violin is not a rare instrument. Like the violino piccolo, it is used nowadays for children, and being tuned much too low for its length of string, sounds still more wretched than the violino piccolo tuned as a treble. There is no difficulty whatever for a violoncellist to learn to play the tenor.

SECTION VIII.

The Wood-Wind Instruments.

In the great order of wood-wind instruments profound changes have happened. There were complete families of each type of instrument in four, five, or six different sizes, ranging from the lowest to the highest registers. Many of these have wholly disappeared—for example, the shawms, the cromornes, the cornets, and the recorders; in other cases, like the bassoons, oboes, clarinets, and flutes, one or two members have survived, though much altered by modern improvements. Only two amongst these lost instruments have yet been revived: the recorder and the 18th century one-keyed flute. The writer having no authority to speak of the others, can only say that he regrets not to know them, but feels confident, from contemporary evidence, that their revival, if it comes, would be well repaid by the results.

At the first sound the recorder ingratiates itself into the hearer's affection. It is sweet, full, profound, yet clear, with just a touch of reediness, lest it should cloy. People often say: "How much more beautiful it is than the flute! How can it have been superseded?" Even professional flautists have said this. Did time and space allow, it might be of interest to philosophise upon the causes of our loss; but we must restrict ourselves to effects, and thus see in the recorder one of those delicate shades among the wonderfully varied colours from which the fortunate musician of past times could select the decoration of his works.

The intonation of the recorder right through the chromatic compass of two octaves and one note is perfect, if you know how to manage the instrument; but its fingering is complicated, and requires study. To the ignorant person who just blows into it, and lifts one finger after another to try the scale, it seems horribly out of tune; but that is not the fault of the instrument.

This brings about the whole question of the alleged imperfections of the old wood-wind instruments. The 18th century one-keyed flute, for example, has been tried more than once in recent years, and in every case the same verdict was returned: that its tone, whilst it is inferior in power to the modern flute, especially in the low notes, is much more beautiful and characteristic, but that its intonation is defective.

This last sentence is not true. The one-keyed flute has been thoroughly and patiently studied recently by a flautist who followed the instructions contained in the "Principes de la Flûte Traversière," by the famous Hotteterre le Romain, Ordinaire de la Musique du Roy, Paris, 1707, with the result that he can now play on the old flute more perfectly in tune than he ever did before upon a highly improved and most expensive modern instrument. And the reason is not far to seek. On the old flute, almost every note has to be qualified by the breath, or some trick of fingering, or the turning of the flute inward or outward, to cover more or less of the *embouchure*, by which means the pitch of the notes can be affected to a great extent. This requires the constant watchfulness of the ear, which thus becomes more and more sensitive to faults of intonation.

On the modern flute, a most ingenious and complicated system of keys has been devised, which is supposed, at the expense of beauty of tone, to correct automatically all the imperfections. Under ideal conditions it might come near doing this. But in practice the instrument may be flat from being cold, or sharp from being warm, or be affected by the variations of wind-pressure necessary for the lights and shades, and the player whose ear is not only untrained but hardened by the instruction he has received, goes on playing out of tune, often to a most painful extent, without feeling in the least distressed, for the simple reason that trusting to his instrument, he does not even listen to what is going on around him, which is the absolute condition to obtain such effects as can satisfy a discriminating auditor.

There are in the old books innumerable instructions, rules and warnings, intended to foster pure intonation in all instruments. Quantz's "Versuch" is full of such; everything concurs to prove that the old musicians were extremely sensitive on that point.

The Cornets (Italian: Cornetto; German: Zinke) formed an extremely important family of instruments, equally admirable to support and brighten the voices in a chorus as for playing in consorts, if we may judge from old descriptions. The picturesque "Serpent," the bass of the family, was still common in French churches about the middle of the 19th century; and although, as a rule, the players had no great skill, those who have heard its tone combined with deep men's voices in Plain-song melodies know that no other wind or string instrument has efficiently replaced it.

The cornets are akin to the wood-wind instruments, because they are generally made of wood, and their notes are produced by the opening of holes controlled by the fingers. They resemble brass instruments by the principle of their tone-production, which is similar to that of the Trumpet, that is, the vibration of the lips in a cupped mouthpiece.

In Bach's works, cornets are frequently introduced, and even in Gluck's operas they are to be found. They ought to be revived, but unfortunately they are very rare, and difficult to play. Once a genial professor, lecturing on old musical instruments, blew into a cornet to demonstrate its tone to the students ; it sounded like the bleating of a calf; great laughter. The superiority of modern instruments was proved. It may, however, have occurred to some, that had he tried to demonstrate the tone of a violin he might have obtained an equal success; for the mewing of a cat is as risible as the bleating of a calf. But this happened a generation ago, and the thick fog of ignorance surrounding these things has begun to disperse.

SECTION IX.

The Brass Instruments.

Amongst the brass instruments we need only consider the Trumpets, the Trombones, and the Horns. The plain French horn, without valves, can still be met with, although it is becoming very rare.

The trombones are with us, still unspoiled, although the majestic bass trombone has been practically replaced by the coarse, thick tuba.

A trumpet we have also, but modified by valves, and quite incapable of playing those extremely high, brilliant, and florid parts which are often found in the music of Purcell,

Handel, and Bach. Some thirty years ago a so-called Bach trumpet was introduced which reaches the high notes, if not the highest, and when tempered by a large orchestra and chorus does not sound ill; but it is not in the least fit to consort on equal terms with a flute and a violin, nor to execute *piano* the florid passages reaching F *in altissimo* of the famous Bach Concerto.

The modern substitute has little in common with the original instrument, and the picturesque straightness of its tube, possible with a 4-ft. length, would hardly be possible with the 8-ft. length of the real trumpet. It is a short soprano cornet (the ordinary kind), using mostly the second and third octaves of its harmonics, the gaps of which are filled by the valves, whilst the old trumpet, being double the length, uses the third and fourth octaves of its harmonics, rendered possible by a slender tube and a small mouthpiece.

The writer's unsuccessful attempt at reviving the old trumpet may be related here, as it may help to the eventual accomplishment of this desirable object.

Two trumpets were made by an excellent maker. The writer produced some of the high notes on them, but could not himself undertake the study of this difficult instrument. A few other people tried it: one succeeded in obtaining the highest notes with great beauty and purity, but was not otherwise musical enough to justify the hope that he could eventually play a concerto of Bach. A skilled player of the modern trumpet was persuaded to take the instrument away and practise it. He returned after a few weeks, having succeeded in playing some difficult passages perfectly well; but he declared that the small mouthpiece spoiled his lips for the ordinary trumpet, and he could not be prevailed upon to continue the experiment. There is no doubt that the lip difficulty would have disappeared in time, for the solo-players of Bach's time were often ordinary trumpeters as well. It is like the temporary trouble of a violinist playing the viola—it can be got over with a little patience.

SECTION X.

Combinations of Instruments.

As we have seen before, the old instruments formed complete families of one kind: music in from three to six parts was framed for such, and much appreciated.

The oft-recurring stage directions in Elizabethan plays: *Enter Cornets, enter Recorders, enter Hoboys*, are meant for a full consort of each kind of instrument. The old English expression, "whole consort," was applied to this kind of music. However, though single colours in music were esteemed, combinations of these were also in frequent use. They formed the "broken consorts," or "broken music," often mentioned in the literature of the 16th and 17th centuries. The third volume of the "Syntagma" of Prætorius explains at length how the families of instruments, as well as the single members, can be associated with one another, or with choruses or single voices. We might dream of the effects of tone-colour thus produced when under the spell of those legions of adorable angels, playing and singing, evoked by Gaudenzio Ferrari's genius under the cupola of the Saronno Church in Italy; but modern music cannot realise them for us.

There is an English painting in the National Portrait Gallery in London which could give us no such heavenly visions, but touches this subject in a modest and practical manner. It represents the chief episodes of the life of Sir Henry Unton, who was English ambassador in France in 1591. One of these shows a consort of five viols—two trebles, one tenor, and two basses. The players look sedate, and are gentlemen playing serious music. Sir Henry plays the tenor part, and seems proud of doing so. The other represents a festive scene. The family and guests are sitting at the dinner table. A company of dancers dressed for a "Morris" or some such jollity are dancing to the merry tunes of a little band consisting of a bass-viol, a tenor viol, a violin or rebec, a lute, a cithren, and a flute, the latter being a transverse flute, not a recorder, which shows fine discrimination, for the recorder's tone might be too grave for the occasion. This combination of instruments is well contrived; it must have sounded gay and brilliant. Needless to say, the ambassador does not take part in it; he is presiding at the banquet. The musicians are professionals.

In 1599 Thomas Morley published "The first booke of Consort Lessons, made by divers exquisite authors, for six Instruments to play together, the Treble Lute, the Pandora, the Cittern, the Base-Violl, the Flute and Treble-Violl, newly set forth at the coast and charges of a Gentle-man, for his private pleasure, and for divers others his frendes which delight in Musick."

This is also a jolly combination. The "flute" here is a tenor recorder that plays a middle part instead of a tenor viol.

These "Consort Lessons" are intended for "private pleasure." On great occasions we find more elaborate schemes. Here is a list of the instruments which took part in a Maske arranged by Cesare Negri, at Milan, on June 26th, 1574, in honour of Don Giovanni of Austria: Cornetto, trombone, bagpipe, fife, dolcain (soft bassoon), flute, spinet, viola da gamba, violino, lute, cithren, hoboy, dulcimer, tenor viol, triangle, pipe and tabor, harp, kit, theorbo, a quartet of viole da braccio (violins). They probably did not play much all together, but were combined in a sort of kaleidoscopic scheme in the manner described later by André Maugars.

Another galaxy of instruments was assembled at Munich under the direction of Orlandus Lassus, on the occasion of the marriage of Duke William V., in 1568. They formed separate bands, which do not seem to have joined together:—

1. Five cornets and two trombones.
2. Six trombones and one contra-bass trombone.
3. Six viols.
4. Six viols, five trombones, one cornet, one regal.
5. Six large viols, six flutes, six voices, and one harpsichord.
6. One harpsichord, one trombone, one flute.
7. One lute, one bagpipe, one cornet, one viola da gamba, one oboe.

8. Three choirs of instruments which were heard separately and together:
   a. Four viols; *b.* Four recorders;
   c. One dolcain, one bagpipe, one fife, and one cornet.
9. A piece for six recorders and six voices.

André Maugars, the French musician who came to England to study the viol, as we have seen at page 450, went to Rome in 1639. His skill on the gamba excited great admiration there. He states that there were no Italian players of any importance on that instrument at the time; but he heard some good music in Rome, and sent an admirable description of it to some friends in Paris. Here is a translation of some parts of his letter:—

"I will describe to you the most celebrated and the most excellent concert which I have heard in Rome, on the eve and the day of the Fête of St. Dominic, in the Church of the Minerva. This church is fairly long and spacious; in it were two large organs elevated on each side of the altar, where two choirs of music had been placed. Along the Nave there were eight more choirs, four on one side and four on the other, elevated on stages eight or nine feet high, separated from one another by the same distance and facing one another. In each choir there was a portable organ, as is customary: this should not astonish you, for there are over two hundred of them in Rome, whilst in Paris it might be difficult to find two of the same pitch. The Master composer beat time in the first choir, which comprised the most beautiful voices. With every one of the others there was a man who did nothing else but keep his eyes upon that original time in order to follow it, so that all the choirs sang in perfect time, without dragging.

"The counterpoint of the music was florid, filled with beautiful melodies and many agreeable recitatives. Now a treble of the first choir recited; then that of the third, fourth and tenth answered. Sometimes they sang two, three, four and five voices together, from several choirs, and at other times all the parts of all the choirs recited in turn, vying with one another. Now two choirs would compete with one another, then two others responded. Another time they sang three, four, five choirs together, then one, two, three, four and five voices alone: and at the *Gloria Patri* all the ten choirs would go together.

"I must avow that I never before had such ravishment; but above all in the Hymn and in the Prose, where usually the Master endeavours to do his best, and where I truly heard perfectly beautiful melodies, most elaborate divisions, very excellent inventions and a most agreeable variety of movements. In the Antienne, they had very good symphonies of one, two or three violins to the organ, and some archlutes playing certain dance-tunes [!] and answering one another."

Further, Maugars speaks of the "Oratorios" which were given at the Chapel of St. Marcel by a congregation composed of the greatest noblemen in Rome, and which attracted the élite of Society:—

"This admirable and ravishing music is only given on Fridays in Lent, from three till six o'clock. The church is not quite so large as the Ste Chapelle in Paris (*i.e.*, very small). At the end of it there is a spacious loft with an organ of medium size, very soft and suitable for the voices. On both sides of the church there are again two other small stages where stood the most excellent instrumental players. The voices began with a Psalm in Motet form; then all the instruments played a very good symphony. Afterwards, the voices sang some story from the Bible, in the form of a sacred play, like that of Suzanna, of Judith and Holofernes, of David and Goliath. Each singer represented one of the characters of the story and expressed perfectly the energy of the words. Afterwards, a celebrated preacher gave an address, which being finished, the music recited the gospel of the day, as the story of the Good Samaritan, of the Canaanitish Woman, of Lazarus, of Mary Magdalene, or the Passion of Our Lord. The singers imitated perfectly well the divers characters mentioned by the Evangelist. I could not praise sufficiently this recitative music; it must be heard on the spot to be appreciated according to its merits.

"As to the instrumental music, it was composed of an organ, a large harpsichord, two or three archlutes, an 'Archiviole-da-Lyra,' and two or three violins. Now a violin played alone to the organ, then another answered; another time all three played different parts together, then all the instruments went together. Now an archlute made a thousand divisions on ten or twelve notes, each of five or six bars length, then the others did the same in a different way. I remember that a violin played in the true chromatic mode, and although it seemed harsh to my ear at first, I nevertheless got used to this novelty and took extreme pleasure in it. But above all, the great Frescobaldi exhibited thousands of inventions on his harpsichord, the organ always playing the ground. It is not without cause that the famous organist of St. Peter has acquired such a reputation in Europe, for although his published compositions are witnesses to his genius, yet to judge of his profound learning, you must hear him improvise. . . ."

Will this music ever be heard again? Will music, like the sister arts, ever retake possession of its past, its heirlooms, its rightful inheritance? Yes, it must; and by patiently working backwards, mastering each step, the now dim past of music will be brought to life, and will take its place side by side with the other arts, to which it never was inferior. But it is not through the deadly kind of research in which the Germans have led the way that any advance will be made. Is it worth while to devote years of labour to compile an exhaustive list of all the operas and other compositions that were performed at some German Court during two or three centuries, with the names and particulars of all the composers, singers, musicians, dancers, copyists, &c., engaged there, and the dates of their entering and leaving the service, and their salaries, &c., when not a single phrase of any of that music can be correctly heard? What avails it to know when the grandfather's uncle of a certain lutenist was baptized, or how many wives he had, if neither the lutenist's music nor a lute is procurable?

We crave to hear the music itself in its original form, and this is what the "musicologue" hardly ever thinks about. And so little progress has yet been made! Only the 18th century can be considered as conquered; a fair amount is known about the 17th century, although the unknown begins to make itself felt as we recede into it. But how little we know practically about the 16th century, which tantalises us so cruelly! How many years will it take before we shall have revived and mastered all these unknown instruments, and learned the unrecorded secrets of their music?

Researches and experiments are long and costly. Music, it is true, has rich and powerful patrons; but would there be one among them far-seeing enough and so disinterested as to support an undertaking yielding no immediate tangible, brilliant results? He would render a service of paramount importance to the art of music, for the future of all arts must be grafted upon the past, and music does not know its past.

English music, even more than any other, is in need of it, for the French, the Germans, the Italians, the Slavs, have at any rate preserved their nationalism, without which no music, however good, is of real value; whilst the English so thoroughly destroyed their own art two centuries ago that the memory of it hardly remains.

It is not by pressing a few old English tunes into a work that might be French or German, or by disguising popular tunes with incongruous harmonies, that the English school will be revived. The works of its masters must live again, and become the daily bread of the younger generation, who in studying them, performing them, and assimilating them, may recover the lost thread of

English art, which will never be found in the schools of Leipzig or Berlin.

But these are dreams of the future. Amongst our present needs the most pressing is the publication of correct texts in a convenient form and at reasonable prices, for without them we are hampered at every turn.

The modern editions available exhibit an extraordinary variety of faults. In some, bars have been added; in others, whole passages suppressed. The fugues of Bach can be had printed in four colours, to help dull pupils' understanding. The performing editions of the new Bachgesellschaft have levelled the music by thinning some places and filling up others. Some editors have smothered the text under ornaments most elaborately, though incorrectly, written out—slurs, dots, dashes, accents, crescendos, fingerings, &c. Another one, reacting, has come down to bare notes, sweeping everything away, even those original marks of expression which are so rare and so precious. In some editions, figured basses reduced to bare notes without figures compensate the "Bach So-and-so's" thundering pianoforte versions. We cannot trust even those cumbersome, expensive monumental publications which were not even intended for performance, but to serve as hunting grounds for editors. The French edition of Rameau's complete works is full of grave inaccuracies; in the Bachgesellschaft text, signs for ornaments have been removed or replaced by others.

Should not modern musicians treat the works of their masters as they wish their own may be treated in future centuries? Yes, but the unreasoned conviction of their own superiority obscures their mind.

They are like those *littérateurs* who, during a dark period in the 18th century, "re-wrote" Shakespeare and "made it into plays." These times are past for literature; correct texts are now plentiful. Difficult passages may be annotated, but that is all; the original remains untouched. It should be the same with music. We can no longer allow anyone to stand between us and the composer.

BIBLIOGRAPHY

Aldrich, P. C. *Ornamentation in J. S. Bach's Organ Works.* New York: Coleman-Ross, 1950.

———. "The Principal *agréments* of the Seventeenth and Eighteenth Centuries: A Study in Musical Ornamentation." Unpublished Ph.D. dissertation, Harvard University, 1942.

Arnold, F. T. *The Art of Accompaniment from a Thorough-Bass as Practised in the XVIIth and XVIIIth Centuries.* New York: Dover Publications, [1965]; reprint of 1931 edition.

Bach, C. P. E. *Essay on the True Art of Playing Keyboard Instruments.* Translated and edited by W. J. Mitchell. New York: W. W. Norton, 1949.

Baines, A. (ed.). *Musical Instruments through the Ages.* Harmondsworth, Middlesex, Eng.: Penguin Books, 1961.

Bukofzer, M. F. *Music in the Baroque Era.* New York: W. W. Norton, 1947.

Couperin, F. *L'Art de toucher le clavecin.* Edited and translated into German by A. Linde and into English by M. Roberts. Leipzig: Breitkopf & Härtel, 1933.

Dart, R. T. *The Interpretation of Music.* 4th ed. London: Hutchinson, 1964.

Donington, R. *The Interpretation of Early Music.* London: Faber & Faber, 1963.

Emery, W. *Bach's Ornaments.* London: Novello, [1953].

Geminiani, F. *The Art of Playing on the Violin.* Facsimile, edited by D. Boyden. London: Oxford University Press, [1952].

Mozart, J. G. L. *A Treatise on the Fundamental Principles of Violin Playing.* Translated by E. Knocker. London: Oxford University Press, 1948.

Newman, W. S. *The Sonata in the Baroque Era.* Rev. ed. Chapel Hill: University of North Carolina Press, 1966.

Praetorius, M. *Syntagma musicum.* Vol. III. Translated by H. Lampl. Unpublished Ph.D. dissertation, University of Southern California, 1953.

Quantz, J. J. *Versuch einer Anweisung die Flöte traversiere zu spielen.* Translation and comments by E. R. Reilly. Unpublished Ph.D. dissertation, University of Michigan, 1958.

INDEX OF SIGNS

GENERAL INDEX